The Way to Christianity

THE WAY TO CHRISTIANITY

THE HISTORICAL ORIGINS OF CHRISTIANITY

JOHN LARKE

AuthorHouse™ UK Ltd.
1663 Liberty Drive
Bloomington, IN 47403 USA
www.authorhouse.co.uk
Phone: 0800.197.4150

© 2014 John Larke. All rights reserved.

No part of this book may be reproduced, stored in a retrieval system, or transmitted by any means without the written permission of the author.

Published by AuthorHouse   05/14/2014

ISBN: 978-1-4969-7825-7 (sc)
ISBN: 978-1-4969-7804-2 (hc)
ISBN: 978-1-4969-7826-4 (e)

Library of Congress Control Number: 2014907738

Any people depicted in stock imagery provided by Thinkstock are models, and such images are being used for illustrative purposes only.
Certain stock imagery © Thinkstock.

This book is printed on acid-free paper.

Because of the dynamic nature of the Internet, any web addresses or links contained in this book may have changed since publication and may no longer be valid. The views expressed in this work are solely those of the author and do not necessarily reflect the views of the publisher, and the publisher hereby disclaims any responsibility for them.

Dedication

For Ben, Toby, Suzi and Jake

With all possible love

And in memory of

Gillian Luke 1944-2013

Contents

DEDICATION v

FOREWORD xv

Chapter 1   INTRODUCTION

Chapter 2   THE PEOPLE OF YHWH AND THE 'LAST DAYS' OF JUDAISM

    The People of YHWH 10
    Early Leadership 17
    Early Prophets 19
    The Northern Tribes 20
    Babylonian Conquest 25
    Second Temple Judaism 26
    Persian Rule 27
    Loss of Independence 31

Chapter 3   JEWISH HOPE AND MESSIANIC EXPECTATION

    Isaiah 34
    Maccabeans 36
    Daniel 37
    Wisdom of Solomon 40
    Enoch 40
    Sibylline Oracles 41
    Psalms of Solomon 43
    The Assumption of Moses 44
    Philo 45
    Josephus 46
    The Essenes 47
    Apocalypse of Baruch 52
    Ezra 53

	Shemoneh Esreh	54
	Hadrian and the Second Jewish Uprising	56
Chapter 4	THE FOLLOWERS OF THE WAY	
	Zealots and Sicarii	59
	The Way—Hasidic Traditions	59
	The Way—Sources	60
	John Ben Zechariah	62
	Hereditary Leadership of the Way	69
	Jesus Ben Joseph	70
	Faith Healing	71
	Folk Medicine	72
	Exorcism	73
	Jesus' Teachings	74
	Parables	76
	The Last Week	77
	Leadership After Jesus' Death	81
	Simon Peter or James?	83
	The Family of Jesus and James	83
	Trial Before the Sanhedrin	84
	Simeon Ben Clopas	87
	The Decline of the Way	92
Chapter 5	PAUL OF TARSUS	
	Conversion and Aftermath	96
	The Risen Messiah	98
	Missionary Travels	100
	An Apostle to the Gentiles	101
	House Assemblies	102
	Constituency	103
	The Weekly Meal	103
	Appearing Before James and Peter	104
	An Argument with Peter and Barnabas	106
	Further Travels	106
	Paul and Misogynism	107
	Problems with Converts	108
	The Letter to the Romans	110
	The Last Journey to Jerusalem	112
	Trial and House Arrest	113

	The Journey to Rome	115
	Paul's Death and Legacy	117
Chapter 6	CHRISTIAN GENESIS	
	Judaism	122
	The Way	124
	The Prayer	124
	From Jesus to Christ	126
	Early Converts	137
	The Didache	138
	Clement of Rome	141
	Ignatius	143
	Church Rituals	145
	Church Structure	146
	Differing Emphases	148
	Christian Anti-Semitism	149
Chapter 7	THE LITERATURE OF THE WAY AND EARLY CHRISTIANITY	
	The Letters of James and Jude	151
	The Letters of James	153
	The Letter of Jude	155
	'Jewish Christian' Literature	156
	Paul and the Law	158
	The Synoptic Gospels	159
	The Gospel of John	164
	The Acts of the Apostles	165
	Letters of the Christian Bible	166
	The Revelation of John	167
	Apocryphal Literature	169
	The Homilies and Recognitions of Clement	169
	Gnostic Literature	170
	Unacceptable Works	171
	Letters Falsely Attributed to Paul	172
	Jesus' Early Life	173
	Apocryphal Acts	174
	Apocryphal Apocalypses	175
	The Shepherd of Hermas	176
	Conclusion	177

Chapter 8   EARLY PERSECUTION AND MARTYRDOM

    Ignatius 180
    The Arena... 181
    Polycarp 182
    Ptolemy and Lucius 183
    Justin Martyr... 184
    Speratus and His Companions 185
    Vienne and Lyons 185
    Third Century Rome 186
    Decius and State Persecution... 187
    Valerian 188
    Diocletian... 189
    Numbers and Attitudes to Martyrdom 192
    Martyrdom and Suicide 193
    Perpetua 194
    Roman Attitudes to Martyrdom 194
    The Decline of Martyrdom 195
    Christian Persecution 197

Chapter 9   GNOSTICISM

    Simon Magnus.. 202
    Valentinius 203
    Carpocrates 204
    Basileides... 205
    Marcion 207
    Manichaeanism 209
    Gnosticism and Christianity 212
    The Persistence of Gnosticism... 214

Chapter 10 THE GROWTH OF THE WAY AND
              EARLY CHRISTIANITY

    The Way 217
    Early Christianity... 220
    The Social Backround of Early Christians 221
    Slaves.. 222
    Women 223
    The Roman Church... 225
    The Alexandrian Church.. 226

	The Church of Carthage	226
	The Second Century	227
	Rome and Its Army in the Second Century	228
	Roman Emperors	230
	Persecution and Paganism	232
	Expansion and Difficulties	233
	The Ascetic Life	235
	Eusebius	236
Chapter 11	MAN AND GOD	
	Jesus	241
	Paul of Tarsus	241
	God and Jesus	242
	Son of God	243
	Justin Martyr	245
	Irenaeus	245
	Tertullian	246
	Origen	248
	Early Bishops	250
	Hippolytus	252
	Fabian and Novation	253
	The Empire in Crisis	254
	Confessors	254
	Novation and Cornelius	255
	Cyprian	256
	The Great Persecution	258
	Arian	258
	The Nicaean Creed	262
Chapter 12	CONSTANTINE	
	Parents	264
	The Court of Diocletian	265
	Constantius Chlorus	265
	Civil Wars	266
	Battle of the Milvian Bridge	267
	Emperor of the West	267
	Undisputed Emperor	270
	Taxation Under Constantine	272
	Foreign Wars	273

Constantine the First Christian Emperor 275
Constantine's Faith 276
Church Matters 279
Buildings 280
St. Peters 281
Family Murders 281
Helena 282
Byzantium 284

CONCLUSION 289

List of Illustrations

Figure 2.1 Approximate boundaries of Israel two thousand years ago indicated by broken line 11

Figure 2.2 The "Promised Land" showing the approximate distribution of the twelve tribes of Judaism 12

Figure 2.3 Egyptian location of Avaris and shallow reed covered lakes in the Nile Delta 14

Figure 2.4 The traditional and northern routes of the Exodus 14

Figure 2.5 The land of Judah following the conquest of the ten northern tribes 22

Figure 4.1 Present day shrines and Churches associated with 'John the Baptist' based on an original drawing by Gibson S. Century (2004) 219 65

Figure 4.2 Locations of Pella and Jerusalem 88

Figure 4.3 The Way: Leaders and probable disciples/ missionaries 91

Figure 5.1 Paul's trade routes and House Assemblies 101

Figure 5.2 Paul's last journey to Rome 116

Figure 10.1 Probable early centres of The Way outside Jewish Palestine 218

Figure 10.2 The calculated and actual rate of Christian conversion compared.(From data originally published by Roger Bagnall) 221

Figure 10.3 The distribution of Christian sites to 325CE. Reproduced by kind permission of Rodney Mullin. 239

Foreword

To a greater extent than many would be prepared to admit, we are all the products of our cultures and the prisoners of our personalities. This creates particular problems when it comes to writing religious history as we are also strongly influenced by our beliefs, or lack of them. There seems no satisfactory answer to this conundrum. Perhaps the best that an author can do is to constantly bear in mind the subjectivity of their efforts. It may also be incumbent to give some indication of personal experience and a statement of attitudes of religion may be appropriate. At the very least this gives the reader an indication of the writers views, which can be taken into account when assessing his work.

I was raised in a Christian household and as a teenager and young man I read voraciously and indiscriminately for a period of about ten years, sometimes reading two or three books a week. Perhaps because I read so much I slowly lost my faith. The worlds created by Steinbeck, Pasternak and Sartre seemed so much more vivid and alive than the repetitious Church services that my brother and I were expected to attend. I never became an atheist, at least not in the declamatory mould of Richard Dawkins, but I was, and am, sceptical of at least some of Christianity's claims.

My career was spent in one of the clinical sciences, where for thirty years I led the conventional life of an academic. I taught and supervised post-graduate research sat on Government Regulatory committees and acted as an industrial consultant.

By the time I was in my early fifties, the work that I had begun as a Doctorate student was completed, and I was looking for a new area of research.

At about this time the University, in which I had so happily worked, initiated a never to be repeated early retirement scheme and my time became largely my own, but my brain nagged me. Having read around a number of subjects, the history of early Christianity appealed, primarily because I felt that the traditional accounts seemed largely untenable as history. Fifteen years later this book is the result.

As I was not trained as an historian, I was unfamiliar with historical techniques, so I resorted to the scientific method. Somewhat to my surprise this seemed to work. Of course the details are different; in science the most important factor is to ask the right questions. Predictions are tested experimentally and, however unexpected, it is always crucial to be led by results. In history ideas cannot be tested in this way, but they can be tested against the historical sources. Initially most of my ideas were either contradicted by the sources or simply not supported by them. Slowly, and it was often very slowly, ideas that found support began to take shape. This gave some of the pieces of the jigsaw and the task became to fit them together. It was immediately apparent that there were some significant gaps, but what surprised me most were not the gaps, but how much information was available.

In some cases the historian's requirement for two independent but supportive accounts of the same event can be met. For example the life and death of John Ben Zechariah, known to Christians as John the Baptist, is recorded in both the Christian gospels and the writings of the Jewish historian Flavius Josephus. In other areas the sources are silent: after the death of Paul of Tarsus some of his followers continued his work and began, for the first time, to see Jesus in ways that were recognisably Christian, however, who they were and how they achieved this is entirely unknown. In between these two positions are various shades of grey, with some areas better supported than others.

I have followed the principle that everything should have at least one documented source. I have also tried to link separate episodes together using hypothetical scenarios based on an approach of 'best fit', even if this involves some degree of conjecture. For example, when Paul of Tarsus was a persecutor of Jesus' followers, it was on the road to Damascus that he experienced his famous conversion. But we lack any documented rationale as to why he made this difficult and potentially dangerous journey. Looking more widely to other concurrent events may give an answer: After Jesus' crucifixion the new leader of his followers was his brother James. When James was attacked on the steps of the Jerusalem Temple, his legs were broken and he was taken to Jericho to recover. Jericho is on the ancient trade route to Damascus. Was the reason for Paul's journey in pursuit of the new leader of Jesus'

The Way to Christianity

followers? There is no source that states this. Where I link episodes in this manner I have tried to say so in the text.

There are some technical matters that are customary to cover: I have tried to write in an accessible way for the reader who has an interest in, but no specialist knowledge of the subject, and have avoided abbreviation and acronyms as much as possible. I have also tried to avoid jargon. For example, phrases such as high or low Christology clearly have meaning to the cognoscenti but are often puzzling for the rest of us.

Reading all the literature on early Christianity would take a lifetime, which, in the nature of things, I no longer have, but I have tried to read as much as I can. I am indebted to the Humanities Library of the University of Wales, which gives lifetime admittance to former faculty members. This allowed my initial background reading to take place free of charge. Over time I began to acquire books and so my trips to the Library became less frequent. But two things irritated, and continue to irritate me.

Firstly, overly long footnotes, and secondly endnotes placed at the back of a book. Overly long footnotes often disturb comprehension and sometimes seem designed to dazzle rather than to illuminate. Endnotes necessitate almost constant page turning. This is immensely annoying when trying to read a large body of literature. I have opted for placing references at the bottom of the relevant page, and have kept footnotes to a minimum. This is not the convention in historical books, but it seems to me to be a better scheme.

Christians refer to Jesus as 'Christ' and to most of his followers, and many others, as 'Saints.' These are later religious appellations; during his lifetime Jesus would have been known as Jesus, the son of Joseph or in Aramaic, the language he spoke, Yeshu Bar Yoseph. In English, Jesus son of Joseph reads rather awkwardly, whilst the Aramaic will be unfamiliar to most. I have opted for a combination of the two languages, so that Jesus becomes Jesus Ben Joseph. This may cause some criticism, but this is a book about the history, rather than the religion of early Christianity and part of my purpose is to delineate this distinction.

In writing in an area of understandable religious sensibilities I have tried to avoid giving gratuitous offence, whilst at the same time, writing somewhat below a position of reverence.

Unless otherwise stated, the bible cited in this book is the New Revised Standard version, published by Oxford University Press, which comes with Apocrypha, for the 'Old' and 'New' Testaments. I prefer the terms the Hebrew and Christian bibles, as this more accurately reflects the religious adherence of both the compilers and their intended audience.

The size and shape of the Jewish homeland varied greatly over the centuries. Up until the final Assyrian conquest of the ten northern tribes in 732BCE (see Chapter 2), the northern kingdom was called Israel. After the conquest the name Israel began to be applied to the whole of the Jewish nation, as indeed it has been since the establishment of the Jewish State in 1948. As an alternative, some writers have used the term Jewish Palestine. I have followed this practice and used Israel to refer to the northern kingdom prior to the Assyrian conquest, after which the names Israel and Jewish Palestine are used interchangeably.

When entering a new area of research, help is always appreciated and everyone whom I have approached has been unfailingly kind. Dr. Rod Mullin, sometime research fellow at Birmingham University helped me obtain a copy of his heroic gazetteer of early Christian Churches, from a publisher whose purpose seemed to be to prevent rather than disseminate his work. Kath Davies, an independent editor, provided useful support on an early draft of part of this book, and my oldest son, Ben, subsequently edited and proof-read the manuscript prior to submission for publication. My daughter, Suzie, prepared the art work, Marc Heatly produced a front cover which is a great improvement on our own initial efforts, my second son, Toby, gave enthusiastic and unfailing encouragement and practical advice on dealing with literary editors and publishers, whilst my youngest son Jake provided help with computer graphics. I am enormously indebted to them all.

I am particularly grateful to my late partner, Gill Luke. She acted as administrative assistant, typist and general sounding board. Faultless in keeping track of the numerous drafts of individual chapters, she had a quiet habit of saying, 'I don't think this quite works,' which I learned to ignore at my peril. The title of this book, with its intended pun, was entirely her idea.

> John Larke
> Kashi's
> Fort Cochin,
> Kerala,
> Southern India.

CHAPTER 1

INTRODUCTION

People who believe in God usually have personal reasons for doing so. Often such rationales relate to their upbringing, their friends and their families, although, just occasionally, charismatic individuals are also involved. However, whilst faith is personal and uniquely experienced, the way in which it is organised is not.

Christian churches are hierarchical, with a single individual at the top and layers of individuals of lesser influence further down. For the majority of adherents this does not seem to matter very much; they are content to believe, and leave the administration of their faith to others, but this is not true for all. Some individuals—and they often are the most devout—are ready to criticise the hierarchy, particularly if it does not meet their own high standards. However, the response of the established churches to such criticism—albeit often heartfelt and well-intended—has been in many cases to dismiss or ridicule those raising the issues. In some cases the criticism made by the dissenter appears as so manifestly just, that it appeals to others and a new revivalist movement is born.

Two well-known examples of movements borne of reactions to an established Church are Martin Luther's protest against the Roman Catholic Church, which led, in time, to the protestant Reformation, and John Wesley's attempt to change the Anglican Church from within, which eventually brought about the formation of the (Wesleyan) Methodist Church. Martin Luther was appalled by the venal practices of medieval Rome, and sought a return to the imagined purity of the early Church. John Wesley objected to the way in which the Church of England had become a gentleman's club, providing a parish living supported by a compulsory levy, to: *'Men who knew something of Greek and Latin, but who knew no more of saving souls than of catching whales.'* [1]

Both of these movements sought a vigorous faith, which intruded more righteously between individuals and their God. Both survived the death of their charismatic leaders, and were successful, although not necessarily in the way that their leaders had originally envisaged. As such, they are anomalous to a historical reading of the establishment of sects, which are seemingly continuously being created only to lapse when their leader dies. Very, very few go on to become world movements. The best example of a revivalist sect that not only survived, but went on to become a separate world religion is Christianity.

The origins of early Christianity, from about 25 to 150CE are far from straightforward and, lie within Judaism, and in my view specifically within a small, historically unimportant, revivalist sect which became known as 'The Way.' Followers of The Way believed that they were living in the 'last days', when the kingdom of the Jewish God YHWH, would be established in Jerusalem. The movement's leadership rested with the male members of an extended family of Holy men/Prophets, which included Jesus

Within The Way, itself a relatively small and potentially inconsequential movement, was a further sub-division—a Gentile offshoot—which grew steadily and eventually rejected the parent movement. It did this as a result of developing its own radically different view of Jesus' life and death, which from a Jewish viewpoint, was deeply heretical. As far as is known, the seeds of this Gentile offshoot were sown by a small unprepossessing Jewish tent-dealer, Paul of Tarsus.

Paul established a small number of House Assemblies, which, after his death, became the seminal churches of Christianity. One central message to his Gentile followers was that they should: *'Put on the Lord Jesus Christ,'* [2] as a replacement for the Jewish Law. Advocating abandoning the Law was deeply blasphemous; Jews believed that the law was a central requirement of their religion and was given to them by God.

---

[1] Hattersley Roy. John Wesley a Brand for the Burning. Little Brown (2002) 1, 13

[2] Rom.13:14

Paul died probably in the mid-sixties CE, almost certainly in an early persecution of Christians by the Emperor Nero. Even before his death, some of his followers were known to be lapsing, but new leaders emerged who kept the faith and the movement slowly grew. For Christians this is one of the great miracles of their religion, and even for non-Christians this seems an extraordinary sequence of events.

Paul's death allowed a radical change in his message to take place as Jesus began to be seen not only as a divinely appointed Messiah, but also as the 'Son of God.' This was intended literally, rather than in a Jewish sense, where a deeply religious man who sought to do the will of God could be regarded as a true "Son of God.'[3] Jesus' birth was also increasingly thought to be the result of an immaculate conception, whilst Jesus' mother Mary began to be described as a "perpetual virgin," beliefs which had clear parallels in Pagan religious mythology. These changes in the emerging Christian view of Jesus after Paul's death are poorly chronicled, and can only be deduced from later beliefs.

During the period between the two Jewish wars against Rome, 66-74 and 132-135CE, the first elements of the Christian bible were compiled. Prior to the first war, the writing of a proselytising account of Jesus' life and death was unnecessary, given that Paul, as a follower of The Way, would have been expecting God's imminent arrival with its implicit 'last judgement' rendering all literature redundant. Two factors probably altered expectations around an imminent judgement: Paul's death and the destruction of the 'Holy of Holies,' in the Jerusalem Temple. Paul did not anticipate death prior to God's arrival and was apparently unprepared, even for the demise of his own followers. Likewise, the destruction of Jerusalem Temple in the latter stages of the Roman assault, seems to have been an important catalyst in the initiation of Christian belief. The 'last days' now became much less important than the inspirational details of Jesus' life, and more particularly his death.

Interestingly, the Christian bible does not initially seem to have been held in high regard. Justin Martyr, by no means the first Christian martyr, regarded the Gospels as 'memoirs,' which probably reflected a widely held view. In the very early days, accounts that were passed by

---

[3] Vermes G. The Changing Face of Jesus. Allan Lane. Penguin Press (2000) 32-34

word of mouth were as highly valued as those that were written down. This was true, even for a literate man like Justin.[4]

However, within one hundred and fifty years of Jesus' death, the Christian bible was increasingly seen as the bedrock of Christianity, representing all Christian truth. In a way that is inconceivable to many of us today, it provided answers to all life's questions and established its origins: the world had been created in six days—using biblical information it was even possible to calculate the day and time of creation. The world created by God was at the centre of the universe, and humankind was at the centre of the world. As such, to make a distinction between spiritual and historical 'truth' was meaningless.

As centres of Christendom were established, students of religion studied and interpreted the bible. However, any questioning of the basic tenets of Christian faith was heresy; if the heretic was lucky and had powerful protectors, they might only be required to renounce their beliefs in a degrading and humiliating ceremony—those less fortunate were burnt to death. As a result, Christianity remained basically unquestioned for hundreds of years, and it was not until the sixteenth century that changes slowly began with the Reformation.

The freedom that the Reformation offered for religious thought coincided with the beginnings of the European enlightenment. This movement substituted a critical and questioned approach for the mere acceptance of ideas.

However, it was not until the 18th and 19th centuries that significant progress in the historical criticism of Christianity was made. Hermann Reimarus, a Professor at Hamburg, wrote a seminal work questioning the historical veracity of the bible. Perhaps wisely, he forbade publication until after his death and it was not until the early 1800's that parts of his work saw the light of day.[5]

The 19th century saw great activity in biblical scholarship, particularly in Germany, where over twenty university theological departments existed. German scholars were required to produce critical works of religious study for their Doctorates, and academic progress

---

[4] Chadwick H. The Early Church. Penguin Press (1993) 74-79

[5] Schweitzer A. The Quest of the Historical Jesus. (1998) Reprinted by the John Hopkins University Press. 3-4

was rapid. Amongst numerous scholars of real repute, two stand out in the early part of the century: W.M.L. De Wette argued that there was a lack of historical basis to much of the Hebrew Bible, and D.F. Strauss demonstrated that the Christian gospels were not eye witness accounts, but later compositions drawing on a number of sources.[6] A reactionary backlash was perhaps inevitable and Professor Strauss was prevented from teaching theology for the rest of his life.

The opposition to historical criticism in England was largely centred in the 'Oxford Movement', particularly in the person of E.B.Pusey, who as Regis Professor of Hebrew in Oxford, vigorously opposed the development of critical historical studies. It was not until his retirement in 1882, that progress again became possible.

The beginning of the 20th century saw radical changes in the way that Jesus' mission was understood. The remarkable Franco-German polymath Albert Schweitzer published a series of books, two of which are of particular relevance; The Quest of the Historical Jesus (1901)[7] and The Mystery of the Kingdom of God (1914).[8] Using the gospels as his source, Schweitzer demonstrated that Jesus' exclusive concern was the imminence of the approaching Jewish apocalypse and the arrival of YHWH in Jerusalem. This world-changing event would be followed by the 'Final Judgement,' in which Jews and *possibly* righteous Gentiles would be judged for entry into the newly arrived Kingdom of Heaven on Earth. Since many Christians felt that Jesus was the founder of their religion they objected to Schweitzer's analysis. Nevertheless the view was increasingly accepted and despite recent criticisms remains the basis for much current thinking.

The remainder of the twentieth century saw somewhat variable progress. In tune with the times, specialisation grew and: 'more and more became known about less and less'.

Some time ago, a post-graduate student presented a Doctoral Thesis on Pontius Pilate. Since relatively little is reliably known of Pilate, the

---

[6] Rogerson J. (Ed). Beginning Old Testament Study. (1998) SPCK 19-20

[7] Schweitzer A. The Quest for the Historical Jesus (1998) Reprinted by John Hopkins University press.

[8] Schweitzer A. The Mystery of the Kingdom of God. English Translation (1985) Prometheus Books.

submission may seem unduly optimistic. Nevertheless, the thesis was coherently argued, and one more PhD joined the ranks of academia.[9] Alongside those undertaking their academic apprenticeship are established scholars who have devoted a lifetime's work to a particular topic. Amongst the very best is Ed Saunders, who has undertaken a particularly thorough textural analysis of the Synoptic Gospels (Matthew, Mark and Luke). Whilst the renowned Jewish scholar Geza Vermes has published a corpus of work placing Jesus within his Jewish context. It is worth noting, that these two scholars, utilising different techniques, have reached a similar view of Jesus the man. Indeed, Geza Vermes has made what I consider to be a critical contribution to the debate in asserting that the study of early Christianity cannot be separated from the study of contemporary Judaism.

Alongside scholarly effort, the remarkable preservative qualities of the desert sands have given up unexpected treasures. In 1948, a young Arab shepherd investigating the caves around Qumran discovered what has become known as the 'Dead Sea Scrolls'. This library, almost certainly Essene, gives a unique insight into a Jewish religious movement which, in its last days, was contemporary with the revivalist movement of The Way. In 1945 farmers seeking fertiliser outside the village of Nag Hammadi in Egypt uncovered a Gnostic library contained within earthenware jars. Amongst the scrolls was an unknown Gospel, the Gospel of Thomas.

Taken together, the combination of scholarly effort and the fortuitous discovery of lost documents have radically changed the view of many contemporary biblical scholars.

Up until the early 19th century, the conception of the historical origins of Christianity was largely based on Christian belief, which in my view is clearly an inversion of the relationship between the faith and its historical antecedents. Christianity is a religious interpretation based, rather loosely in places, on the history of what occurred, and thus this book is an attempt to recover that underlying history with a view to engendering a better understanding of the evolution of the religion. To an extent history and religious interpretation can have an almost

---

[9] Bond H.K. Pontius Pilate in History and Interpretation. Cambridge University Press (1998)

independent existence. A very recent example may help to illustrate this point:

The recent Boxing Day Tsunami has a modern history. On the 26th December 2004, a sudden subduction of approximately 400 kilometres of the Indo-Australian tectonic plate displaced 30 cubic kilometres of sea water which generated the second largest tsunami in seismographic history. The wave travelled across the Indian Ocean, coming ashore first of all on the Sumatran coastline at Banda Ache. Later in the day it impacted on the coasts of countries as far apart as India and Thailand. In all almost a quarter of a million people perished.

A number of Islamic religious leaders have interpreted the Tsunami in a religious way, notably Shaykh Salid Al Fawzan. The Saudi Professor saw the Tsunami as a chastising punishment from God:

> *'It happened at Christmas when fornicators and corrupt people from all over the world come to commit fornication and sexual perversion . . . I say this is a great sign and punishment on which Muslims should reflect.'* [10]

In case it should be thought that this was an exclusively Muslim sentiment, similar views were published by a number of American Christians following the destruction of New Orleans by hurricane Katrina.

These two views, one historical and the other religious, are almost independent, although they relate to the same event. This probably does not matter where both the history and religious interpretation are known. However, in some aspects of early Christianity, the religious interpretation is all that is available, making the recovery of the underlying history difficult at best. Christian copyists and editors have also, on occasion, changed the historical record. Today this would be regarded as unacceptable, but sometimes it has preserved documents that would otherwise have been lost.[11]

---

[10] Schwartz S. Allah and the Tsunami. FrontPage Magazine.com (2005) 1

[11] Schurer.E.The history of the Jewish people in the age of Jesus Christ (1874) Revised English text Vermes.G. Millar. F. Goodman M. Black M. (Eds) T&T Clark (1987) 1 432

A well-known example of religious documentation establishing a widespread and commonly held account of a historical event is the trial of Jesus. The biblical account of these events is held by many to be definitive, despite its lack of conformity to both contemporary Roman or Jewish legal custom and practice.

Overall, however, what seems remarkable is not what has been lost, but what has survived. The events described in the following chapters took place two thousand years ago, at a time when history in the modern sense of the word, did not exist. Yet the outline of what occurred is accessible to all and the majority of the important documents are available in translation, usually in English, as are critiques of many of the contentious points.

Many of the scholars working in this field are academics in Divinity Schools. It is a tribute to the ultimate success of the enlightenment that many Christians can critically examine the origins of their religion and contribute to our understanding of its history.

Almost universally, writers in this area refer to the family and early followers of Jesus as 'Jewish Christians'. This seems to me to be an attempt by later Christians to claim these individuals for their own. There is no historical, or indeed biblical, support for this view. In the few instances where the early followers of Jesus are questioned about their beliefs, they refer to themselves as members of a Jewish sect called 'The Way.' Substituting 'The Way' for the commonly used phrase 'Jewish Christians' may appear only a small change, but it is one that carries significant implications. In particular, it makes a clear distinction between an exclusively Jewish revivalist sect and a later Gentile Christian movement, which is the key to understanding what really happened two thousand years ago.

Although the view of Jesus belonging to a Jewish sect is not new, it is one that has not always gained wide acceptance, particularly amongst the clergy. It therefore remains the opinion of a small minority, of whom I am one.

CHAPTER 2

THE PEOPLE OF YHWH AND THE 'LAST DAYS' OF JUDAISM

The Hebrew Bible is a narrative work of epic proportions written for the guidance and inspiration of the Jewish people. It is a saga of the Jewish race from God's creation of the world, to the time of the Book of Daniel. The Hebrew Bible provides Judaism with both its history and its constitution, setting out in considerable detail God's requirements for his chosen people and, as such, Jews see themselves as the 'People of the Book'. It lists the kings and occasional female leaders of Israel, giving opinions on their religious observance and also includes works of the prophets, along with the psalms and other inspirational writings.

Many people now doubt the veracity of much of this information; whilst there are those who believe that God did indeed create the world and all that is in it in a little under a week, this view is now held by only a small minority. For the great majority, the Garden of Eden, Noah's flood and Abraham's potential sacrifice of his only son are allegorical, which does not of course detract from their religious relevance.

The lives of Adam, Noah and Abraham give Judaism some of its most distinctive features: Adam's eating of 'forbidden fruit' in the Garden of Eden explains sin entering God's perfect world; Noah's building of the Ark preserved the world's animals and demonstrated his obedience to his God, in return for which, God undertook never again to destroy the Jewish people. God also required Noah's descendants not to kill each other and to refrain from eating meat containing blood. Abraham's willingness to sacrifice his much-loved son showed the depths of his faith. As a symbol of that faith, all his male descendants were to be circumcised.

These and other beliefs are the earliest documented expressions of Judaism. Since they relate to individuals, they may be the remembered mythology of a single family, or perhaps a small group of related families, where the heroic deeds of long-dead ancestors were passed by word of mouth from one generation to the next.

Initially, the God worshipped by Adam, Noah and Abraham was only one deity amongst many. Claims for an exclusive, single God, were not to be made until much later and it is not entirely clear what God was called at this time. The name that persisted is YHWH, hence the expression 'the people of YHWH' for his followers. In later Christian times, vowels were added to give the name 'Jehovah'—a practice that is now considered to be rather spurious, hence the original vowel-less Hebrew term has come to be more commonly used.

The People of YHWH

Over time, the influence of the people of YHWH spread and their tribal areas increased. It is in the land that they occupied that many scholars see the beginnings of recoverable history. Two thousand years ago, the land of Israel stretched from the verdant humidity of the headwaters of the River Jordan, to beyond the summer aridity of the vertiginous Masada outcrop. (Figure 2.1)

The Way to Christianity

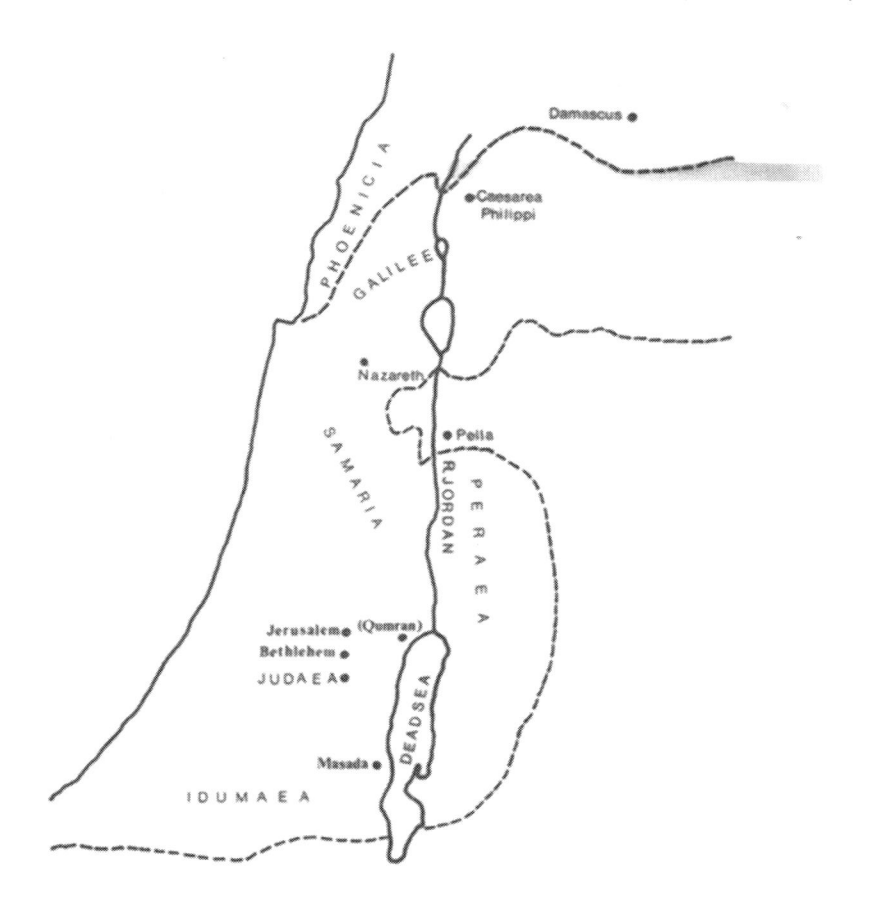

Figure 2.1 Approximate boundaries of Israel two thousand years ago indicated by broken line

The country was almost as large two millennia ago as the fabled 'Promised Land, flowing with milk and honey' said to have been given by God to his chosen people (figure 2.2)

John Larke

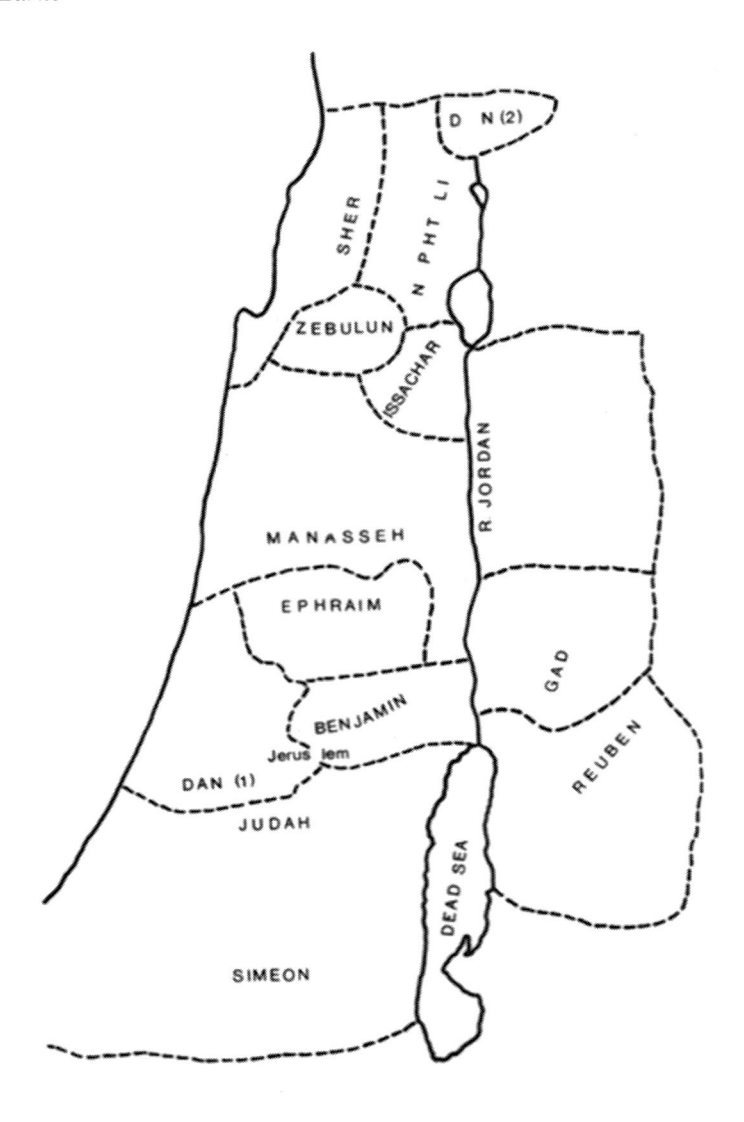

Figure 2.2 The "Promised Land" showing the approximate distribution of the twelve tribes of Judaism

The people of YHWH consisted of twelve ancestral houses: the tribes of Reuben, Simeon, Judah, Issachar, Zebulon, Manasseh, Benjamin, Dan, Asher, Gad and Naphtali. At one time these 'twelve tribes of Israel' were thought to have been semi-nomadic immigrants who entered

Canaan from outside, conquering the indigenous population by force. However, more recent archaeological surveys have shown that there were several waves of relatively peaceful settlement of the Canaanite highlands, the first occurring in the early Bronze Age, the second in the middle Bronze Age and a final wave in the Iron Age

Moreover, settlers in the highlands were probably indigenous rather than outsiders, a view reinforced by recent DNA data, which shows that many Jews and present-day Palestinians share a common Canaanite genetic inheritance. This view is in stark contrast to the biblical accounts of the heroic conquest of Canaan by Joshua and his followers. Yet if recent archaeology does not support the violent destruction of the towns such as Jericho, one finding strongly argues for an early religious distinctiveness. No pig bones dating from the early Iron Age onwards have been recovered from the villages occupied by YHWH's followers. Since the bones of pigs have been found in the surrounding areas, it would seem that not eating pork is the earliest distinctive sign of what was later to become Judaism.[12]

How did the people of YHWH arrive in this hilly and less than prosperous region? The Hebrew Bible tells how Joseph (of *'the coat of many colours'*) was sold into slavery in Egypt and of the eventual escape of one of his descendants, Moses. Moses' miraculous journey, undertaken with six hundred thousand men, accompanied by their wives and children, forms one of the most distinctive episodes of early Israelite history.[13]

The escape took place from the Nile delta in the area of Avaris, the summer palace of Ramesses II. It includes the famous parting of the 'Reed Sea', ('Red Sea' is an early mistranslation). The location of Avaris and the possible site of the Reed Sea in the Nile delta are illustrated in figure 2.3.

---

[12] Finkelstein.I. Silberman. N.A. The Bible Unearthed. Touchstone (2002) 119-120

[13] Exodus 12:37

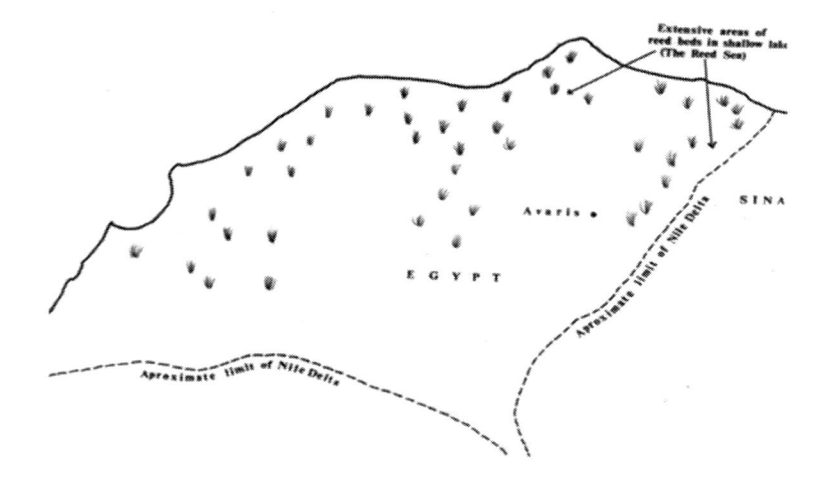

Figure 2.3 Egyptian location of Avaris and shallow reed covered lakes in the Nile Delta

The traditional route of the exodus, with possible alternatives is shown in figure 2.4.

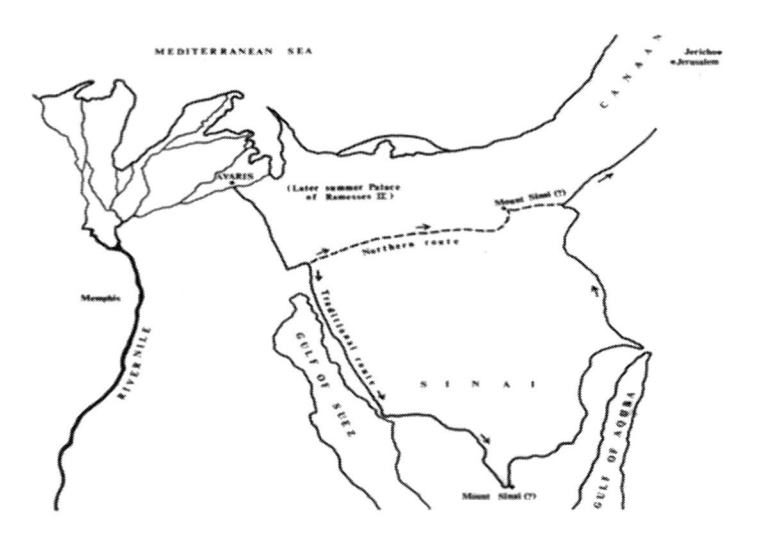

Figure 2.4 The traditional and northern routes of the Exodus

The Way to Christianity

The escape from Egypt has often been dated in the reign of Ramses II (1279-1213BCE).[14] However, the generally complete Egyptian record does not show an expulsion during this period, which is unusual, given the loss of such a large workforce to the Egyptian economy. Even if the number involved were an exaggeration, some mention would be expected; perhaps it not the number, but the timing which is incorrect?

The biblical description of the early stages of the exodus gives clues to at least one other alternative date. As the Israelites began their journey, they followed a *'pillar of cloud by day and a pillar of fire by night'*. Such a phenomenon is consistent with a large volcanic eruption. The *'pillar of cloud by day'* is probably self-explanatory, while the *'pillar of fire by night'* arises from the huge build-up of static electricity in the plume of a volcano, which discharges as almost continuous lightning. Since the Israelites are reported to have initially travelled northwards, the volcano must have been in that direction. Since there is no history of volcanic activity in the Nile delta, the eruption must have been further away. Of the potential candidates, a volcano on the present day Greek island of Santorini is the most likely.

The eruption of Santorini was one of world significance in volcanology and probably the only one to have been visible from the Nile delta. This huge explosion blew the majority of the Greek island into the atmosphere, causing climatic change that lasted for many years. The date of the explosion (approximately 1600BCE) has been deduced from the dendrochronology of trees preserved in Irish peat bogs.[15]

The initial stages of the Santorini explosion involved the generation of a powerful tsunami (tidal wave), which arriving at the Egyptian delta would have caused an exceptional outflow of water, followed by massive inundation: The same circumstances that are exactly described in the miraculous escape across the Reed Sea, where the Israelites walked across dry land, and the pursuing Egyptian army was engulfed.

The date of the Santorini eruption is interesting in that it is close to the date of Egyptian expulsion of a group of people known as the Hyksos in the lower Nile delta. Archaeologically recovered inscriptions

---

[14] Ibid 1:11

[15] Friedrich W.L. Fire in the Sea; The Santorini Volcano. English Edition Cambridge University Press. (2000)

and seals from the area of Alvaris, the capital of the Empire, show that the Hyksos were Canaanite in origin. They had slowly increased in numbers and prestige over a period of three to four hundred years, before being forcibly expelled in 1570BCE. Such a pattern parallels the biblical narrative of a people entering Egypt from outside and living and prospering there for centuries, before a dramatic departure.

Did the memories of the trauma of the Hyksos expulsion account for a strand of folk belief, which was added to even older beliefs? If so, were these events included, at a much later date, in the Hebrew Bible? We cannot of course know, but one thing is probable, the great epic tales of the bible come from remembered events, which were interpreted in a religious way by the followers of YHWH.

Although the historical basis of the exodus is difficult to reconstruct, and no archaeological evidence for the wandering of Moses and his people has ever been found, perhaps this misses the point. The exodus is the last great epic religious myth recorded prior to the entry of the Israelites into the Promised Land, and shows a God who would intervene to rescue his people from grievous suffering. It also shows a God who was capable of inflicting the most terrible punishment on the enemies of his people.

The Exodus forms the heart of Judaism and is reflected by representations of three of its definitive events in religious festivals: Passover (Pesach in Hebrew) remembers the death of the first born in Egypt when God's punishment 'passed' over the first born Jewish children who survived;[16] The Feast of Weeks (Shavuot) acknowledges the spiritual aspects of the release by celebrating the giving of the Torah on the Mountain of Sinai, whilst; Tabernacle (Sukkot) remembers God's protection and provisions during the long arduous journey across the desert from Egypt to the Promised Land.

Much of the story of the Exodus was to provide the inspiration for the scenario of the 'last days,' when many Jews believed that God would once again intervene in human affairs to rescue his people from unbearable oppression. In this 'end game' prophecy a new empire of God would be established in Jerusalem. This exclusively Jewish kingdom would replace all other earthly empires, and Jewish law would become operative worldwide, removing the need for disputes between

---

[16] Exodus. 12:13

nations. Even in the animal kingdom, predators would cease to predate and the lion would quite literally lie down with the lamb. Entry into this new perfect world, which would replicate the conditions only previously found in heaven, would be reserved for the most righteous Jews and few, if any, Gentiles would be admitted. Those who were not prepared to accept this new Jewish world order would, either live lives of misery and disappointment, or be cast into a fiery furnace in an act of unprecedented ethnic cleansing.

Early Leadership

The description of the miraculous journey following the exodus forms part of the Torah, the five books that form the bedrock of Judaism and which are attributed to Moses[17] (seemingly, at least partially, mistakenly, since the Torah contains an account of his own death.)

Before the time of Moses, God was the deity of individuals, but through Moses' part in his reinterpretation, God became the guide, saviour and inspiration to a whole people. In this conception of the relationship between worshippers and deity, to benefit and prosper under God was to enjoy his love—a love that was freely given but, in return, was one which required commitment and adherence to his law. God's law, as extensively and meticulously documented in the last three books of the Torah, provides a detailed contract, or holy covenant, between God and his people. God would never break the agreement, but if the people did so suffering and misfortune would follow—and suffering and misfortune were frequently the fate of the Jewish people.

After the death of Moses, the Hebrew Bible describes the heroic conquest of the *'Promised Land'*: Kings such as Saul, David and Solomon united the twelve tribes, and the first Temple was built in Jerusalem by Solomon. The *'Ark of the Covenant'* was brought to this Temple and placed in the *'Holy of Holies,'* a central enclosure, which in some sense was thought to contain the spirit of God.

How much of the biblical account of the settlement of the 'Promised Land' is supported by archaeology? In a magisterial work by Israel

---

[17] Orlinsky H.M. (Ed) The Torah, The Five books of Moses. English Translation The Jewish Publication Society of America. (1962)

Finkelstein and Neil Silberman,[18] the view of the co-authors is that very little archaeological evidence exists. Of Saul (1025-1005BCE) there is no trace, nor is there any evidence that the Israelites were routed in a battle with the Philistines, as the bible describes. The villages and small towns in the central Israelite highlands of this period appear continuous, with no evidence of even partial destruction.

For David, there is evidence: an inscription on a reused building stone at the biblical site of Tel Dan refers to the *'House of David'* and a similar inscription has been found east of the Dead Sea. However, there is no evidence for David's conquest of the Canaanite people. The Canaanite villages and towns appear unaffected by outside influence, and the settlement pattern of the Israelite and Judean highlands appears continuous. Jerusalem, at this time, was a village or small town.

As with Saul, there is no archaeological support for Solomon's reign. Jerusalem remained, at most, a small town, with no large buildings or a substantial Temple. In addition, the building work at Megiddo, Hazor and Gezel, which the bible attributes to Solomon, now appears to come from a later period.

Whilst the archaeologist's mantra, *'the absence of evidence is not evidence of absence'*, should always be borne in mind, there are further reasons to doubt the biblical account.

At the time of Saul, David and Solomon, Jerusalem and Judea were poor and lightly populated regions. Much of this can be attributed to geography; Judah was *'a homogenous environmental unit of rugged terrain, difficult communications and meagre and highly unpredictable rainfall.'* [19] The resources of Judah would not have supported the centre of a large empire. By contrast, the ten tribes of Israel occupied *'the northern hill country with its broad valleys and natural overland routes to the neighbouring regions,'* [20] which was very much larger and more prosperous. This does not absolutely preclude the possibility of an empire of David and Solomon dominating the surrounding land, but

---

[18] Finkelstein I. Silberrman N.A. The Bible Unearthed Touchstone, New York. (2002)

[19] Ibid. 131

[20] Ibid. 131-132

does, almost certainly, rule out the possibility of that empire being based in Jerusalem.

Yet David in particular, achieved pre-eminence in the remembered mythology of the people of YHWH and subsequently Jews worldwide. David's legacy is not that of a great religious figure such as Moses but of an outstanding military chieftain. His allegorical introduction into the bible as the slayer of the mighty Goliath, who was killed with a single sling-shot, provides inspiration for successful action against apparently impossible odds.

The followers of the Hebrew God were not simply the passive recipients of God's divine grace; they were also empowered to take action on their own behalf.

'God helps those who help themselves' is a wholly appropriate saying for this small state trapped between the Egyptian and Mesopotamian empires.

The bible describes David and Solomon leading a united monarchy of the twelve Hebrew tribes. After Solomon's death, this unity disintegrated. The ten northern tribes are reported to have formed a loose alliance, while the tribes of Judah remained unaligned.

The historical veracity of this division cannot now be established. A notable feature of the biblical account is the difference in religious observance between the two groupings. Generally, the tribes of Judah are credited with faithfully following YHWH, while the ten northern tribes are seen as falling from the *'path of righteousness'*. To what extent this reflects true adherence is uncertain, but it is probably significant that YHWH's followers in Judah were later compilers of the Hebrew Bible, which includes the religious history of the times.

Early Prophets

Following the break-up of the united monarchy, the age of the prophets was initiated with the seminal teaching of Elijah and Elisha. Unlike previous prophets, Elijah, *'this hairy man with a leather belt around his waist'*[21] was not part of a supportive royal court, but an independent nomad, commanded only by his God. His legendary trials of strength with competing religions, his healings—which included the

---

[21] 2 Kings 1:18

raising of the dead—and his eventual ascent into heaven, became so overlaid with subsequent religious writings, that little remains that is historically reliable.

Elisha, who is reported to have been present at Elijah's death,[22] seems to have played an even more intrusive role in political events. He helped, or led, a royal coup, which deposed one northern monarch and replaced him with another more acceptable to YHWH. Like Elijah, he performed miracles, which included the raising of the dead, and was credited with particular malevolence towards his detractors—on one occasion causing a group of boys who derided his baldness to be trampled to death by bears.

Elijah and Elisha may have belonged to a community of prophets who derived their political power from the support of YHWH's adherents. Their view of an omnipotent YHWH and his requirement for exclusive worship, transcending all practical considerations, is one of the earliest tenets of Jewish belief.

In the next wave of Jewish prophesy, the consequence of insufficient commitment to YHWH was spelt out. Amos, in a book of almost unremittingly gloomy predictions, turns his wrath on his own people. Their adherence to YHWH is a formal façade behind which they are prepared to debase themselves with Canaanite temple prostitutes. Although, he notes, they look forward to a *'day of judgement'*, when God will come and obliterate their enemies; God's judgement will be universal, and only a remnant of his chosen people will be spared.

This *'saved remnant'* at the 'end time' of their religion was added at a later date, in the scenario of the *'last days of Judaism.'* [23]

The Northern Tribes

The evolving richness of prophetic vision was not matched by political acumen in the leadership of the ten northern tribes of Israel.

Faced with a resurgent Assyrian empire, Israel initially became a vassal state and paid tribute to its powerful neighbour. Then, in a strategically disastrous move, Hoshea the King of Israel from 732BCE

---

[22] Ibid. 2:9-13

[23] Amos 1:9

The Way to Christianity

to 724BCE sought a military alliance with the King of Damascus and other threatened powers. Assyria learned of the plot and immediately invaded Israel. The alliance with Damascus was not supported by Judea, which, wisely, refrained from action. In the ensuing battles, which at one point involved an invasion of Judea by the north, the ten tribes and their allies were comprehensively defeated. The victorious Assyrians deported the political and religious leadership of Israel to resettlement in other parts of their empire. Many landowners were also expelled and at least two waves of Syrian resettlement of Israel subsequently occurred.

By 720BCE, Israel had effectively ceased to exist, at least as a religious entity.[24] Hopes for the return of *'the lost ten tribes of Israel'* entered into the people's religious expectations and, formed part of a more general expectation for eventual salvation. Jewish Palestine was reduced to little more than the land of Judah and Benjamin, but it contained what was to become the religiously important centre of Jerusalem and perhaps twenty to thirty villages (figure 2.5).

---

[24] Hayes J.H. and Maxwell Miller J. (Eds) Israelite and Judean History SCM(1977) 421-434

Figure 2.5 The land of Judah following the conquest of the ten northern tribes

Within this small community, traditions were preserved, perhaps only by a minority, but these were to inspire three of the world's great religions: Judaism, Christianity and Islam.

At the time of Israel's fall, Judah's position could hardly have been worse. Now surrounded by Assyrian provinces and client states, Judah faced a huge influx of refugees from conquered Israel. The result was massive expansion, not only of Jerusalem, but also of rural settlements in the surrounding countryside. Jerusalem's population doubled, and doubled again, whilst in the countryside, single farms became villages and small villages, towns. The archaeological record shows that within a few decades of Israel's demise every possible scrap of land was utilised.

The Way to Christianity

Small plots of vines, olives and figs were planted, very often on land that had previously been considered too difficult for cultivation.[25]

Judah now became, for the first time, essentially a fully-fledged state. There is evidence of an emergent state bureaucracy including a centralised processing system for olives and grapes, the development of many local administrative areas and an overall spread of literacy. Jerusalem meanwhile became a substantially defended city and the religious and administrative centre of a small state.

At some point in the late eighth century, as Judah developed, YHWH began to be seen as the only God. The worship of other Gods continued, but was increasingly condemned as sinful, whilst religious ceremonies became centred in the Jerusalem Temple. A small Temple had probably served in earlier times, but it is likely that during this period it was renovated and expanded. Also during this period the form of worship became codified and early forms of the religious laws, by which adherents were expected to live, were promulgated.

Prophecy also flourished, in particular that of one of the greatest of all prophets, Isaiah.[26] As with his predecessors, Isaiah condemned Canaanite religious practices, particularly when they had infiltrated the followers of YHWH and believed in a *'saved remnant'* in the final days. However, his chief focus was not for the condemnation of transgressors, but in attempting to convey the unimaginable holiness and universal splendour of YHWH. In language that is rarely matched in the Hebrew Bible, he sought to convey the over-arching majesty of his God.

It is perhaps fitting that amongst the archaeologically recovered material from the community of Qumran (the Dead Sea Scrolls), is a well-preserved leather scroll of the book of Isaiah.[27] It was to Isaiah, amongst others, that later Christian writers, who were seeking biblical references to the birth of Jesus, were to turn for fulfilment of prophetic vision, 'a young woman is with child and she will bear a son and you will call him Emmanuel.' [28] The child prophesised by Isaiah was

---

[25] Finkelstein I. Silberman N.A. The Bible Unearthed Touchstone (2002) 243-250

[26] Isaiah. 1:64

[27] Miller B. Et Al The Dead Sea Scrolls of St. Marks Monastery New Haven. (1950)

[28] Isaiah. 7:14

probably not Jesus, but that of a King of Isaiah's time and this suggests a desire for deliverance, from the ever-present threat from Assyria.[29]

From the period of the downfall of Israel, until the late seventh century, Judah's fortunes varied dramatically. Prudently aligning itself with Assyria was on the whole a successful strategy; however, an abortive uprising very nearly destroyed the country.

In 639BCE, King Josiah, a direct descendant of King David, succeeded to the throne at the age of eight.[30] The omens were not good. His father, Amon, had been assassinated after a reign of somewhat less than two years and the boy king probably owed his position to a group within the Jerusalem priestly elite.

Josiah ascended to his reign at a time when the geopolitical situation that determined so much of Judah's fate was beginning to change. Before Josiah's birth, a resurgent Egypt, led by King Psammetchus 1st, had thrown off Assyrian domination and Assyria was at long last in decline. For Judah, the change from Assyrian to Egyptian dominance appears to have been relatively peaceful and beneficial and religious life remained largely unchanged.

As a young man in his early twenties, Josiah is reported to have ordered a refurbishment of the Temple. During the work the high priest 'found' an ancient religious work, the 'book of the law.' [31] The book was almost certainly an early form of Deuteronomy and it was almost certainly not ancient. The 'book of the law' bears a remarkable similarity to contemporary Assyrian treaties[32] and may well have been compiled by a member of a group of priests who influenced Josiah's early upbringing. Whatever its source, the existence of the 'book of the law' enhanced the status of YHWH; for the first time, his followers were participating in a state religion. Under the 'book of the law' ritual and sacrifice were confined to the Jerusalem Temple and the surrounding countryside was largely cleansed of all other competing religions.

Under Josiah's centralised administration, the country continued to prosper as a small client kingdom of the Egyptian empire, yet it

---

[29] Grant M. The History of Ancient Israel Phoenix (1997) 147-151

[30] 2 Kings 22:1

[31] Ibid. 22:8

[32] Finkelstein I. Silberman N.A. The Bible unearthed Touchstone (2002) 281

was Egypt that brought about Josiah's demise; the circumstances are not known, but at least one possibility is that Josiah sought to regain the territory of the lost ten tribes, and this met with terminal Egyptian disapproval. Following Josiah's death, four further kings, three of whom were Josiah's sons, ruled only very briefly.

Babylonian Conquest

For some time an empire based in Babylon had been expanding and gaining in military strength. In 605BCE, the forces of the Babylonian crown prince Nebuchadnezzar overwhelmed the Egyptian army. The defeated Egyptians withdrew to the Nile and, in the power vacuum thus formed, the emerging Babylonian empire moved against Judah. After a period in which the Judean King first acquiesced and then later resisted the Babylonian advance, Jerusalem and the chief cities of Judea succumbed to sieges.[33] The Temple in Jerusalem was burned in 587BCE and, in echoes of the Assyrian conquest, the aristocracy, religious leadership and land-owning families of Judea were deported.[34] However, unlike events following the Assyrian invasion, little or no resettlement of Israel took place.

The last vestiges of the State said to have been created by David were now destroyed and the Davidic line of kingly succession, which had more or less been maintained in Judea, also came to an end. Perhaps a fifth of the Judean population were deported and resettled, mostly in the areas around Babylon.

By the time of the Babylonian conquest, the beginnings of the Hebrew Bible had been compiled and began to provide inspiration for YHWH's followers. In particular, the covenant between God and his chosen people had been amplified and detailed by the Deuteronomist historians and the inspirational lives of the prophets, particularly Isaiah, gave human expression to God's purpose.

---

[33] 2 Kings 25:1-7

[34] Ibid. 24:10-16

John Larke

Second Temple Judaism

The emerging Hebrew Bible had a profound effect on the followers of YHWH. For the first time they became the followers of a religion of 'the book;' a book that described, often in minute detail, their obligations and privileges. The Hebrew Bible became the holy literature of God, a single God who replaced the multiplicity of gods in antiquity and whose people were a chosen race residing in a territory specified by God as their homeland.

The authorship of the earliest accounts of the followers of YHWH is not known, although careful textual analysis has revealed a number of sources. As with all histories in antiquity, they were written for a purpose. In ancient Israel that purpose was to glorify God and inspire future generations with the actions of their forebears. Specifically, these histories allowed the re-casting in an heroic mould of the achievements of David and Solomon, the relocation of the centre of their 'empire' as Jerusalem and the vilification of the religious practices and leadership of the ten lost northern tribes, with their use as an illustration of God's awful judgement of those who strayed from the path of righteousness. As the prototype Bible emerged, the means of promulgating its message also evolved.

While in Babylon, the people of YHWH were unable to worship at the Jerusalem Temple and, as a consequence, religious assemblies were formed. Probably located as Sabbath meeting places in individual houses, these assemblies rapidly evolved into purpose-built structures oriented towards Jerusalem. The precursor of the Hebrew synagogue may well have been born at this time.[35] This fundamental change in Jewish religious practice, born of necessity, had far-reaching consequences, allowing Judaism to extend into a rapidly expanding diaspora (Jews who lived outside the Jewish homeland).

After little more than fifty years, the new Babylonian empire was in its turn overcome and its lands, including Judea, taken by the Persians. Persia exhibited a strategic benevolence towards the displaced people

---

[35] Ackroyd. P.R. Evans C.F. The Cambridge History of the Bible Cambridge University Press (1975) 62-102.

and encouraged a return to their homeland.[36] The followers of YHWH were known in the Persian language as *Yehuda,* or in English, Jews. Yet not all Jews wished to return—the later years of Babylonian exile having been relatively benign and with conditions in Judea having deteriorated considerably. Those who remained formed the nucleus of an expanding Babylonian diaspora, while those who returned took on the task of rebuilding the temple and of resettling their land. Even with Persian support, progress was slow and the reconstructed second temple compared unfavourably with the original. These were not the only issues arising from the reintegration.

During their sojourn in Babylon, the exiles had absorbed local customs, particularly in speaking Babylonian Aramaic rather than Hebrew, and they continued to use this language on their return. The returning aristocracy were also conscious of the rapid evolution of their religion during the years of exile and this might explain why, at this time, a further history was written, giving an account of Jewish life from Adam (in Aramaic simply 'the man') until the return from Babylon. This account, found in the book of Chronicles, is particularly critical of those who remained in Judea during the Babylonian exile.

Persian Rule

Little is known of the history of Judaism during the two centuries of Persian rule. Although there is evidence of Persian influence on the evolving Jewish religion there is little trace of events in Judea over this period. Much, however, is known of the events that brought Persian rule to an end, not only in Judea but throughout the then known world. These events were inextricably intertwined with the name of Alexander the Great.

Alexander's initial influence on Judea was limited—he passed through the country on his way to conquer Egypt, where he established a new city of Alexandria as part a military campaign to reverse the defeat of his forebears by the Persians. Whilst he was not the first attempting this, he was undoubtedly the most successful, and ultimately conquered the Persian Empire. Indeed, he is considered by many as one of the greatest military leaders of all time.

---

[36] Ezra 1: 2-3

Alexander was the King of Macedonia, which enjoyed a classical Greek (Hellenistic) culture. This influence was exported to his conquered peoples. Greek now became the new international language of the eastern Mediterranean. The first Greek translation of the Hebrew Bible, 'The Septuagint' was produced in Alexandria in response to virulent anti-Semitism.[37] This attempt to explain Judaism to the classical world met with limited success, while the influence of Hellenistic culture on Judaism was also resisted. Following Alexander's death, his empire was divided amongst his followers. Initially Judaism fell within the Ptolemaic (Egyptian) portion of Alexander's former empire; whilst at a later date it came under Seleucid (Babylonian) control.

Although the 'age of prophets' was now considered to have come to an end, Jewish literature continued to be written, and it was during this era that Ecclesiastes was compiled. This gloomy, almost cynical, work found acceptance in the Jewish apocryphal literature because it extolled the virtues of the Jewish God. It was to find a rather more exalted place in later Christian literature with Christians translating 'Ecclesiastes' as *'book of the church.'*

At first the changes introduced into the Jewish capital by the Ptolemaic empire were limited but, as the influence of Hellenistic culture grew, it found some adherents amongst the Jewish leadership. When the Ptolemaic authorities were replaced by the Seleucid Empire much worse was to come. In attempting to bring about religious uniformity, the Seleucid King Antiochus Epiphanies sought to turn Jerusalem into a Greek city and, initially with the connivance of the corrupt High Priest, Jason, Greek practices began to be introduced into the city.[38] This inflamed the populace, which unsuccessfully rebelled against their new masters. Once occupied by the Seleucid troops, all Jewish Religious practices were forbidden and the Temple rededicated to the Greek God Zeus. It is difficult to imagine an action more calculated to provoke Jewish hostility, and rebellion rapidly broke out in 160BCE.

The Maccabean rebellion, so called since it was led by members of a family of that name, should have stood little chance of success. At first this was the case and small scale skirmishes were easily repelled

---

[37] Grant M. The History of Ancient Israel. Phoenix (1984) 203

[38] 2 Macc. 4:12

by the occupying power. However, the family enjoyed increasingly popular support, and in Judas Maccabees, the revolt found a charismatic leader of great tactical skill. With great perseverance and willingness to die for their cause, the Jews succeeded in winning independence from foreign domination,[39] a situation which was to last almost unbroken for eighty years.

The effect of the Maccabean rebellion on Judaism was profound; it encouraged a deeply religious people to believe that, with God's help, they could restore their ancestral homeland. It is one of the few examples in antiquity of a successful uprising based essentially on religious belief, and may, in turn, owe its relatively unique status to the cohesion achieved in over four hundred years of subjugation.

During this period of independence, the book of Daniel was written. Daniel's book contains the familiar stories of Daniel's survival in the lion's den, and the survival of his three companions, Meshach, Shadrach and Abednego, in the fiery furnace. However, the book of Daniel is more than a collection of allegorical tales. It revives the ancient prophetic notion of the survival of a Jewish remnant in the last days, when all will be judged and only the righteous saved.[40] Indeed, Daniel goes further and, at variance with all other Jewish writers, predicts resurrection for the righteous dead, at the 'end time' of Judaism.[41] Daniel is also concerned with the appearance of a Messiah (a legitimate princely ruler) who will announce the beginning of 'the last days', but take no further part in the proceedings. Although the book of Daniel is essentially anti-gentile, its predictions influenced later Christian thinking.

During the time of independence, the structure of Jewish life began coalescing around differing religious elements. The Sadducees were, for the most part, aristocratic land-owners who included amongst their number the hereditary high priests. This small but rich and influential group gave adherence to the Torah, but resisted attempts at further religious interpretation. The Sadducees were particularly opposed to Daniel's assertion of physical resurrection and, more generally, to the idea of a Jewish 'end time' and a 'saved remnant'.

---

[39] Grant M. The History of Ancient Israel. Phoenix (1984) 210-211

[40] Dan. 7:27

[41] Ibid. 12:2

The Pharisees were a much larger and diverse group, who invested considerable effort in biblical interpretation and study. In this they were augmented by Scribes, who undertook the work of lawyers and assisted in interpretation. They seem to have played a significant role in the life of the synagogues, which were now to be found in most Jewish towns and villages. Generally held in high regard, they enjoyed only a brief period of political power, but were nevertheless revered by the general populace. Pharisees were found not only in Jewish Palestine but also throughout the Diaspora, where they controversially undertook missionary work.

In addition to the Pharisees, the Essenes formed a distinctive group centred round a largely monastic existence. An archaeologically recovered library commonly presumed to be Essene was discovered in Qumran in 1947. This library, widely known as '*The Dead Sea Scrolls,*' gives a highly detailed account of the religious practices and beliefs of the Essenes.[42] The library also details an 'end time' scenario in which the true followers of God will overcome their enemies in a concluding triumph of the 'final remnant' [43] of Judaism.

The largest single group within Judaism were the temple priests. Some twenty thousand in number, membership of the priesthood was strictly governed by heredity descent. Priests worked on a rota conducting the temple rituals two weeks in any one year and also officiated in the three great religious festivals. Their principal duty was the slaughter and preparation of animal sacrifices, which was ubiquitous in the temples of antiquity. What delineated the Jewish priesthood from all others was their professionalism: the priests were notably skilled, carrying out their temple duties in almost complete silence and with considerable reverence. As they were not allowed to work the land they were supported by a complex system of tithes. It is by no means clear how they were occupied during the majority of the time that they were not required in the temple.

The differing groupings within the body of Judaism allowed for different forms of religious adherence, yet the majority of Jews were

---

[42] Vermes G. The Complete Dead Sea Scrolls in English. Allan Lane. Penguin Press (1962)

[43] Ibid 68-69

probably unaligned. They were, however, clearly influenced, particularly by the Pharisees. By this stage in the development of Judaism, belief was widespread and deep-seated. There is no trace in the historical records of agnosticism, let alone atheism.

The principle schism within the Jewish community was between the Samaritans, descendants of those who remained in Judah after the Babylonian conquest and the great mass of the population who claimed descent from the returning exiles. Action against the Samaritans was taken during the time of Judean independence and their principal religious site was destroyed. At this time the boundaries of the Jewish state were also considerably extended to include Galilee in the north and Idumaea in the south, where many of its inhabitants were forcibly converted to Judaism.

Loss of Independence

The end of Jewish independence came with a dispute between two of the descendants of the Maccabean dynasty who—seeking Roman support—encouraged an invasion that took place in 63BCE. The victorious Roman general, Pompey, ascribed his victory to the Jewish soldier's unwillingness to fight on the Sabbath, a view reinforced by the action of Roman soldiers who forcibly entered the temple during religious ceremonies, killing the priests who offered no resistance during prayer.[44]

Jewish Palestine now entered a period of turmoil. Local resistance was encountered, particularly in Galilee for many years, and it was not until the emergence of the Idumean King Herod, that order was finally restored and the country administered as a client state of the Roman Empire. Upon Herod's death, in 4BCE, the country was divided amongst a number of his sons, but, after a period of ten years, the governance of Judah proved unsatisfactory and direct Roman rule was imposed. However, the remainder of the country, including Galilee, continued to be governed by Herod's descendants, an arrangement that continued, with some variations in territory, until the outbreak of the first Jewish uprising against Rome in 66CE.

---

[44] Hayes J.H. Maxwell Miller J. (Eds) Israelite and Judean History. SCM Press and Westminster Press (1977) 608-609

The Jewish revolt against Rome was disastrous: the leadership was fragmented and factions fought each other almost as often as they fought the Romans, whilst initial successes were not followed up. The disputes amongst the leadership led to inevitable defeat and Jerusalem fell in 70CE during which the great temple, which had been wholly rebuilt by Herod, was consumed by fire.[45] The very last remnant of resistance, besieged within the mountain fortress of Masada, ended with their mass suicide in 74CE. The Essenes, who had been so patiently waiting for the 'end time' and God's final victory, instead met their fate at the hands of the Roman army, their library remaining undiscovered until the middle of the twentieth century.

It seemed the beginning of the end of the Jewish Homeland in antiquity. A second revolt some sixty years later also resulted in disastrous defeat, after which Jews were forbidden to live in Judea and a pagan shrine was erected on the site of the Jerusalem Temple.[46] Jews were to find themselves dispossessed for almost two millennia, and it was not until 1948 that the state of Israel was re-established.

It is testament to the depth of the Jewish people's religious conviction that they survived as a distinct religious entity for almost two thousand years without a homeland—a unique achievement in the annals of religious expression. Various reasons have been advanced for this, amongst which must be counted the organic nature of the Jewish religion. Jews, unlike Christians and Muslims, do not depend on a single or even principal, iconic figure. Judaism drew inspiration from the lives of its many prophets, and its histories incorporated their lives into known events. Their numerous psalms glorified their God and gave expression to a belief system that permitted no visual art.

However, perhaps Judaism's greatest strength lay in the belief that they were God's chosen people and that this was reflected in various covenants between God and his people. On a more prosaic level, the institution of the Synagogue was fundamentally important: after the destruction of the temple, the weekly Sabbath meetings, coupled with the importance attached in Jewish life to the education (and particularly

---

[45] Josephus F. The Jewish War. English Translation: Williamson G.A. Revised by Smallwood E.M. Penguin (1981) 287-355

[46] Armstrong K. A History of Jerusalem. Harper Collins (1997) 163-164

the *religious* education) of the young, gave coherence and structure to individual lives and integrated faith into all aspects of personal development.

Over time Jewish people have been subject to countless sufferings—hardly a decade has gone by without a pogrom, an expulsion or an abuse of some kind taking place, culminating, in this generation's living memory, in the Holocaust and its unimaginable sufferings. One strand of academic debate has argued that Judaism has not only survived despite, but *because* of these atrocities. Irrefutable, however, *is its survival*, whilst many of the political beliefs of the abusers have come to be regarded as the essence of all that is evil in the human spirit.

CHAPTER 3

JEWISH HOPE AND MESSIANIC EXPECTATION

The hope for an 'end time' when Judaism would rise above its enemies and make *'captive those who were their captors and rule over those who oppressed them'* [47] was an early feature of the followers of YHWH. Even before the Babylonian conquest, the hope of the devout was for the final triumph of a completely restored Israel. (Chapter 2)

Located in a buffer zone between two ancient world powers, Egypt and Mesopotamia, Jewish Palestine was subject to both. When not falling within the Egyptian sphere of influence, Israel became assimilated by the Assyrian kingdom. When Assyrian power waned, Judah formed part of the Babylonian empire. For the chosen people of God, this was an impossible burden. Why were they so often subject to foreign oppression? The answer was not unfavourable geography. Rather, for YHWH's followers, the true cause was a chastising punishment for the sins of the people.

Isaiah

Isaiah, perhaps the most magisterial of the Major Prophets, put it succinctly: *'Ah sinful nation, people loaded with iniquity, offspring who do evil, children who deal corruptly! Who have forsaken the Lord; who have despised the Holy One of Israel who are utterly estranged.'* [48]

Yet this estrangement could be reversed, for YHWH was a merciful God, prepared to forgive his chosen people if only they would turn to him.

---

[47] Isaiah 14:4

[48] Ibid. 1:4

'Come now, let us argue it out says the Lord. Though your sins are like scarlet they shall be as like snow, though they are red like crimson they shall be like wool. If you are willing and obedient you will eat the good land, but if you refuse and rebel you will be devoured by the sword. For the mouth of the Lord has spoken.' [49]

For those who turn unreservedly to God: *'Zion shall be redeemed by Justice and those who repent by righteousness.'* [50] At the end of time, the whole world will turn to Judah; in these days: *'A remnant will return a remnant of Jacob, to the mighty God. For though your people Israel were like the sands of the sea, only a remnant of them will return.'* [51]

As discussed in Chapter 2, the 'saved remnant,' wherein in the last days of Jewish Palestine God would sit in judgement and the world would willingly submit to his will, became a widely accepted prophesy. The belief of prophets, such as Isaiah, was in spiritual rebirth as a preparatory stage for inclusion in this remnant. As such, it was an idea that captivated all the people of YHWH, delivering hope that they would become spiritually purified and cleansed of sin. In particular, it was hoped that those who had departed from the obedience of God, would see the error of their ways and return to the fold. If such a situation were to arise, the rewards would be great: Judah would be respected by all nations and its enemies would either be destroyed, or would willingly submit to the supremacy of the people of YHWH.

The yearned for supremacy of the people of YHWH would find expression in a true King of Davidic descent. Such a King would govern with perfect wisdom and justice, making no accommodation with competing Gods, and the 'high places' where Canaanite alters were found would be utterly destroyed. Complete and total subjugation by the people of YHWH to the exhortation of their prophets would ensure that the future would be perfect. In this new age, evil would have no place, and wars, which had led to the subjugation of YHWH's people would cease. Even natural disasters, so often seen as God's judgement

---

[49] Isaiah. 1:18-20

[50] Ibid. 1:27

[51] Ibid. 10:21-22

for sin, would no longer occur. This new perfect world was a world for the righteous followers of YHWH. However, it was not a hope for individual redemption or salvation—the life of an individual would still reach to its natural end.

Prior to the Babylonian conquest, death was thought to result in an ill-defined existence in Sheol, which was a shadowy continuation of a person's soul in another place. At some point, and it is by no means certain when or how, this view changed. Some, but not all, Jews began to believe in the resurrection of those judged sufficiently righteous to a blissful after-life. This was particularly applicable to martyrs, who would rise from the dead and sit in judgement on the Gentiles.

Jewish Palestine was subject to Persian dominance for two centuries. During this period the people of YHWH were exposed to the ancient religion of Persia, which had a complex religious mythology quite unlike the monotheism of Judaism. This included a belief in life after death, and at some point, many Jews seem to have exchanged the notion of Sheol for the hope of personal salvation.

Although belief in an afterlife was widespread, it was not universally accepted. The priestly aristocracy of the Sadducees wholly rejected the possibility of resurrection and much else besides. Reactionary in outlook, they insisted on the traditional precepts of the Hebrew Bible, which covered little more than circumcision and the Ten Commandments. In this they were opposed by many Pharisees who, following the hopes raised by the Maccabean revolution held that a righteous and all knowing God would sit in final judgement. Assessing the religious observance and moral conduct of an individual's entire life and the sincerity of their desire for forgiveness when they had transgressed.

Maccabeans

The remarkable success of the Maccabean uprising (164-162BCE) bolstered the hopes of many Jews.

A priest called Mattathias and his sons lead the revolt. Mattathias appears to have felt that the future glory of Israel lay in his descendant's hands, although he also foresaw the continuance of the House of David.[52] In common with some other commentators, the author of the second

---

[52] 1 Maccabees. 2:57

book of Maccabees believed that God would gather the dispersed people of Israel into one nation which would last for ever: *'Gather together our scattered people . . . plant your people in your holy place as Moses promised.'* [53]

This hope for a dominant and unified Israel did not however incorporate the figure of a Messiah. In this the Maccabean chroniclers reflected the traditional position of some of their earlier counterparts. Where they did depart however, was in accepting a belief in resurrection, as illustrated by the appalling torture and death of a mother and her seven sons. The author of second Maccabees recounts the dying speech of the second son: *'You dismiss us from this present life, but the king of the Universe will raise us up to an everlasting renewal of life, because we have died for his laws.'* [54]

In similar vein, the final speech of the fourth son is also reported: *'One cannot but choose to die at the hands of mortals and to cherish the hope God gives of being raised again by him.'* [55]

The successful Maccabean revolt and the relatively brief period of national independence which it ushered in, was not wholly without criticism. Particular condemnation was forthcoming when the role of national leader and high priest were combined. The writer of 'The Psalm of Solomon' describes the end of the Maccabean dynasty and anticipates the return of a true leader of Israel, descended from the House of David. But, these considerations aside, the Maccabean period coincides with the beginning of a remarkable epoch of hope centring on the last days of the present world. This was articulated in a large body of apocryphal writings, which were published, but, with the exception of the book of Daniel, not subsequently included in the Hebrew Bible.

Daniel

Written in about 165BCE, the book of Daniel describes a series of miracles and dreams, ostensibly experienced by the Prophet during a sojourn in Babylon. In a series of dream interpretations, Daniel foretells

---

[53] 2 Maccabees.1:27-29

[54] 2 Maccabees 7:9

[55] Ibid. 7:14

the end of the present world order and its replacement by the Kingdom of God:

> *'And in the days of those kings the God of heaven will set up a kingdom that shall never be destroyed, nor shall this kingdom be left to another people. It shall crush all these kingdoms and bring them to an end, and it shall stand forever.'* [56]

In describing the last days of Judaism and its final conquest over the Gentile forces, Daniel was reviving ancient prophetic traditions. In his allegorical tale he went further; not only would the kingdom of Babylon be destroyed, but its ruler Nebuchadnezzar would be reduced to a beast of the field:

> *'Oh King Nebuchadnezzar, to you it is declared the kingdom has departed from you, you shall be driven away from human society and your dwelling shall be with the animals of the field. You shall be made to eat grass like oxen.'* [57]

A not dissimilar fate was reserved for all those who had opposed Israel. God would come in final judgement and completely destroy all earthly empires, replacing them with a new empire governed by a human being, or in some translations, a 'son of man':

> *'I saw one like a human being (Adam one like a son of man) coming with the clouds of heaven. And he came to the ancient one and was presented before him. To him was given dominion and glory and kingship that all people's nations and languages should serve him. His dominion is an everlasting dominion that shall not pass away and his kingship is one that shall never be destroyed.'* [58]

---

[56] Daniel 2: 44

[57] Daniel 4: 31-32

[58] Daniel 7: 13-14

The Way to Christianity

Many have interpreted this human being, or 'son of man' as a Messiah who would also take the role of King in God's new world. However, as Daniel expands his vision it is clear that this is not so; the leadership of God's new Kingdom lies with the 'holy ones':

> *'The kingship and dominion and the greatness of the kingdoms under the whole heaven shall be given to the people of the holy ones of the most high; their kingdom shall be an everlasting kingdom and all dominions shall serve and obey them'.* [59]

It is clear that the 'holy ones' would have risen from the dead to take on the role allotted to them by God. At its heart Daniel's visions incorporated ideals that became increasingly, but never universally, predominant.

This kingdom of God would replace all early kingdoms and its advent would be brought about by Jews defeating their enemies—victories that would be assisted by God and the 'holy ones'. Depending upon God's Judgement, bodily resurrection would take place for those already dead. This new Empire would be centred on Jerusalem, where the Temple would be destroyed and totally rebuilt. However, this end time would not come without great anguish and suffering: *'Such as has never occurred since nations first came into existence.'* [60]

After which, at the appropriate time:

> *'Your people shall be delivered, everyone who is found written in the book, many of those who sleep in the dust of the earth shall awake, some to everlasting life, and some to shame and everlasting contempt.'* [61]

The book of Daniel reasserted the hopes of the older Jewish chroniclers and added to them. In many ways it was the ideal accompaniment to the remarkable military success of the Maccabean dynasty, introducing a

---

[59] Ibid 7: 27

[60] Dan.12:1

[61] Ibid. 12:1-2

time of hope and messianic expectation, which was to have a profound, but in many ways, disastrous influence on future events.

Wisdom of Solomon

The hope of resurrection was taken up in the Wisdom of Solomon, written at some point in the second century BCE. Here resurrection forms a true salvation after death for those who have been tested by God and found worthy, bringing immortality where the risen dead will: *'Govern nations and rule over peoples, and the Lord will reign over them for ever.'* [62] This contrasts with the fate of the ungodly who: *'Even if they live long they will be held of no account and finally their old age will be without honour.'* [63]

Enoch

The book of Enoch, (which may be somewhat later than the Wisdom of Solomon)[64] describes the final Jewish conquest of the Gentiles. Enoch foresees a massive Gentile attack launched on Jewish Palestine in which only God's intervention will secure subsequent Jewish victory. Following victory, God will then establish himself in Israel in full and final judgement and the 'House of God' will be demolished, preceding a new Jerusalem, complete with Temple, which will be brought down from heaven.

In this new and perfect world, only those judged to be sufficiently worthy will be admitted, which may include those Gentiles who accept the full majesty of the Jewish God. Although Enoch envisages an earthly kingdom of heaven, he does not subscribe to the belief in resurrection found in the Wisdom of Solomon. As such, the inhabitants of a 'new Jerusalem' can only look forward to a long and righteous life, with no possibility of resurrection after death.

---

[62] Wisdom. of Solomon. 3:8

[63] Wisdom. of Solomon l. 3:17

[64] Fragments of the oldest copy of Enoch, written in Aramaic, were found in the Qumran caves

Thus far, the development of Jewish expectation had centred mainly on the last days of Judaism. The figure of a Messiah, where encountered, is not particularly well developed—a trend which is continued in Enoch, with the Messiah envisaged as strictly subordinate to God, only appearing after God's final judgement.

As time passed, and the hope for resurrection in a new holy world order grew, the figure of the Jewish Messiah became more clearly defined. Although remaining of subsidiary importance in Judaism, the Messiah was to be of central importance to later Christianity. The Jewish Messiah, long associated with descent from the House of David as an 'anointed of God,' could play a diversity of roles. This man—in Jewish thought the Messiah was never attributed with divinity—could play a role that varied from the herald of God to a successful military King. Perhaps though, his greatest responsibility was the reunification of the twelve tribes of Israel prior to God's final judgement.

The figure of the Messiah could be preceded by the return of the prophet Elijah, amongst others. This was particularly the case in later Christian literature, but also occurs in the Hebrew Bible—in the last book of which, the writer of Malachi anticipates Elijah's return:

> *'Lo I will send you the prophet Elijah before the great and terrible day of the Lord comes. He will turn the hearts of parents to their children and the hearts of children to their parents, so that I will not come and strike the land with a curse.'* [65]

After Elijah's mission the way was prepared for the intervention by God.

Sibylline Oracles

From its beginnings, in about 140 BC, the Jewish Sibylline Oracles prophesised the last days, and the role of the Messiah. Whilst only two extracts are given here, much of the Oracles are rich in prophesy of the Jewish 'end time'.

---

[65] Mal. 4:5-6

> *'Now tell I thee a sign exceeding clear, that thou may'st know when the end of all things on earth shall be. When in the starry heaven swords shall by night point straight towards the west and east. Straightway shalt there be also from the heaven a cloud of dust borne forth to all the earth and the suns brightness in the midst of heaven shall be eclipsed and the moon beam appear and come again on earth; by drops of blood. Distilling from the rocks a sign shalt be; and the cloud shalt ye behold a war of foot and horse, like the chase of wild beasts in the dense fog. This end of all things God shalt consummate, whose dwellings is in heaven, but all must sacrifice to the great King.'* [66]

In similar vein the Sibylline predicts the arrival of the Messiah:

> *'For there came from the heavenly plains a man, one blessed, with a sceptre in his hand. Which God gave him and he ruled all things well and unto all the good did he restore.'* [67]

The successful Roman invasion of 62BCE brought to an end almost a century of Jewish independence. Although many priests were killed during the final assault on the Temple, the response of the great majority of the Jewish people was not to lose faith, but to anticipate God's final victory with ever increasing vigour. The period that followed, from 62CE to the end of the second Jewish war against Rome in 135CE, represents the apogee of hope for a new age heralded in by the Messiah. Neither before, nor for that matter since, was God's arrival so fervently hoped for and expected.

---

[66] Translation from Milton S Terry. The Sibylline Oracles. Easton and Mains, New York (1899) 3: 989-1003.

[67] Ibid 4: 566

Psalms of Solomon

The Psalms of Solomon, written in the period immediately following the loss of independence, proclaimed the arrival of a new national leader. A king of Davidic descent would defeat the Roman army of occupation, and rid Jerusalem of all impurity and the tribes of Judaism would be gathered together and judged. Once cleansed, the land of Israel would only be occupied by Jews, those Jews who 'had fainted' would be brought to Jerusalem to be incorporated into the new perfect Jewish homeland, and the Gentile nations would now recognise the righteousness of the Jewish God.

Although governed by a Davidic king, the true King would be God, who would subjugate the enemies of his chosen people. His mighty kingdom will be recognised by all:

> *'Behold, O Lord, and raise up unto them their king, the son of David. At the time in which Thou seest, O God, that he may reign over Israel Thy servant. And gird him with strength, that he may shatter unrighteous rulers, And that he may purge Jerusalem from nations that trample (her) down to destruction. Wisely, righteously he shall thrust out sinners from (the) inheritance; He shall destroy the pride of the sinner as a potter's vessel. With a rod he shall break in pieces all their substance, He shall destroy the godless nations with the word of his mouth; at his rebuke nations shall flee before him, and he shall reprove sinners for the thoughts of their heart. And he shall gather together a holy people, whom he shall lead in righteousness And he shall judge the tribes of the people that has been sanctified by the Lord his God. And he shall not suffer unrighteousness to lodge any more in their midst, nor shall there dwell with them any man that knowest wickedness, Fr he shall know them, that they are all sons of their God.'* [68]

---

[68] Psalms of Solomon. Christian Apologists and Research Ministry. SPCK (2006) M.J. XVII 23: 21-30

The Messiah, for that is what the Davidic King really is, will be holy and completely free from sin. The deliverance of his people will not come about by military means, but rather by miraculous intervention.

This hope for the restoration of Israel was widespread. It incorporated observance of God's holy dominion within a national framework, which was a long held Jewish tradition and, again, was not accepted by the aristocratic Sadducees, who were to co-operate with the Romans and their client Kings and Princes.

The Assumption of Moses

The first part of the first century CE saw one of the most poetic expressions of the last days. The Assumption of Moses describes the trauma prior to God's arrival, followed by a well-known passage in which God's new heavenly kingdom is eulogised:

> *'And then his kingdom shall appear throughout all his creation,*
> *And then Satan shall be no more,*
> *And sorrow shall depart with him.*
> *Then the hands of the angel shall be filled*
> *Who has been appointed chief,*
> *And he shall forthwith avenge them of their enemies.*
> *For the Heavenly One will arise from His royal throne,*
> *And He will go forth from His holy habitation*
> *With indignation and wrath on account of his sons.*
> *And the earth shall tremble: to its confines shall it be shaken:*
> *And the high mountains shall be made low*
> *And the hills shall be shaken and fall.*
> *And the horns of the sun shall be broken and he shall be turned into darkness;*
> *And the moon shall not give her light, and be turned wholly into blood.*
> *And the circle of the stars shall be disturbed.*
> *And the sea shall retire into the abyss,*
> *And the fountains of waters shall fail,*
> *And the rivers shall dry up.*

For the Most High will arise, the Eternal God alone,
And he will appear to punish the Gentiles,
And he will destroy all their idols.
Then you, O Israel, shall be happy,
And you shall mount upon the necks and wings of the eagle,
And they shall be ended.
And God will exalt you,
And He will cause you to approach to the heaven of the stars,
In the place of their habitation.
And you will look from on high and see your enemies in Gehenna
And you shall recognise them and rejoice,
And you shall give thanks and confess thy Creator.' [69]

Philo

In contrast to the poetic mysticism of the Assumption of Moses, the Jewish philosopher Philo provides evidence for God's judgement in the last days. For those Jews of the Diaspora who return to Israel and fully obey the law, a favourable judgement can be expected:

'When this unexpected freedom is bestowed on them who were previously dispersed in Hellas and Barbarian lands, on islands and on the mainland, they shall on one impulse hurry from all quarters to a place indicated to them, led by a divine superhuman apparition which, invisible to all others is visible only to the saved.' [70]

---

[69] Translation from the Assumption of Moses (2006) Google's cache of HTPP://www.piney.com/Testament-Moses

[70] Schurer.E. The history of the Jewish people in the age of Jesus Christ (1874) Revised English text. Vermes.G. Millar.F. Goodman M. Black. (Eds) T&T Clark (1987) 11 508

Philo sees the saved as entering a new age where universal peace will reign. Even in the animal kingdom, the previously solitary predators will form peaceful herds, which will no longer predate on other animals. For those who oppose this new era, destruction is inevitable, although it will not be brought about by human hands:

> *'Against them he shall set swarms of wasps which shall fight for an ignominious overthrow for the Saints. But the Saints shall not only have certain victory in battle without the shedding of blood, but also invincible power of government for the welfare of the subjected, who subject themselves out of love or fear or respect.'* [71]

Josephus

Further evidence for the prevalence of Messianic hope comes from Josephus. The Jewish historian reports two aspirants to Messiahdom who attracted very large groups of followers. One named Theudas,[72] and the other known simply as 'the Egyptian',[73] attracted crowds of thousands by prophesying God's imminent arrival. As so often, it was not God, but Roman auxiliary forces who arrived and dispersed the assembled with considerable bloodshed, and even worse was to follow.

The first Jewish uprising against Rome broke out in 66CE, and Josephus ascribed one cause of this rebellion to messianic hope—a prophecy that may also have helped to save his life. Having survived a suicide pact, he was brought before the Roman commander Vespasian who, as the commander of the Jewish forces in Galilee, might typically have ordered execution. However, here Josephus demonstrated his remarkable gift for survival and announced that Vespasian was the promised Messiah. Consequently Josephus' life was spared.

This intensity of messianic expectation and the imminent expected end time of Judaism had calamitous affects. In the final assault on

---

[71] Ibid

[72] Josephus F. Antiquities. XX 5, 1 97-99

[73] Josephus F. The Jewish War. Translation by Williamson G.A. Revised edition— Penguin (1981) 147.

The Way to Christianity

Jerusalem many of the survivors, particularly women and children, gathered round the Holy of Holies in Herod's Great Temple, where presumably they hoped for salvation through God's divine intervention. However, the Temple, including the Holy of Holies, was destroyed by fire and Roman troops slaughtered many of those they found in its precincts.

They were not alone, the Essene community of Qumran, having withdrawn into the desert to maintain religious purity, were probably killed or dispersed at about the same time. But not before they had hidden their library in caves in the surrounding hills.

The Essenes

The origins of the Essenes are obscure. A dissenting religious group, they maintained that the purity of the Jerusalem Temple had become irretrievably compromised. In withdrawing to the desert they sought to preserve a true and holy form of worship, which would one day be reintroduced to the Temple.

The date of the Essene withdrawal is not known with certainty, but it is likely to have occurred in the early part of the second century BCE, at some point before the settlement at Qumran was established (about 140-130BCE). The stimulus for the Essene rupture is thought to have been the Hellenization of Jewish Palestine, which reached a hiatus with the attempt by Antiochus Epiphanes to forcibly suppress Jewish worship. Yet the greatest influence on Essene religious mythology lay not in its earliest origins, but in the events leading to the establishment of the Qumran community.

Two decades after the movement was founded a 'Teacher of Righteousness' emerged in conflict with the 'Wicked Priest.' The identity of the Teacher of Righteousness, who achieved reverential status amongst the Essene, is quite unknown. Attempts to identify this religious leader with John Ben Zechariah,[74] or even James Ben Joseph[75] have all been made and in my view are entirely spurious. All that is known with any certainty is that he was a hereditary Temple Priest of

---

[74] Thiering B. Jesus the Man. Doubleday London and New York (1992) 1-20

[75] Eisenman R. James the Brother of Jesus. Faber and Faber (1997) 135

high standing. The 'Wicked Priest,' on the other hand can probably be identified as Jonathan, a son of Matthias the founder of the Maccabees revolt.[76] Jonathan's great crime, at least in the eyes of the 'Teacher of Righteousness,' was to combine the role of military leader with that of High Priest, roles that were traditionally regarded as separate and as matters of hereditary descent.

The community established in Qumran was essentially a monastic order, a rare event in Jewish history, and was strictly hierarchical, having at its head, the 'Guardian,' who also seems to have been known as the 'Master.' Below this there existed the 'Priests' the 'Elders' the 'Levites' the 'Israelites' and a group simply known as the 'Bastard.' Curiously, although a strict order was maintained, if the 'Bastard' demonstrated a higher level of learning than the 'Priests' their status could be reversed. If the probable identification of the Qumran order with the Essenes is correct—and it almost certainly is—then it is known that there existed, in addition, small groups of Essenes throughout the villages of Palestine.[77]

Within the community all property, at least in Qumran, was held in common. An initiate passed through a prolonged period of instruction before being accepted into full membership. Once admitted, the rules were strict and vigorously applied, even 'falling asleep during a meeting' earned a rebuke and thirty days 'expulsion.' This expulsion was probably from the communal meals, where teaching and discourse took place.[78]

The basis to all Jewish belief is God's covenant with his chosen people, and so it was at Qumran. The Essenes saw themselves as the only spiritually pure Jews, who would form the saved remnant at the end time of the present world. They believed that the 'Teacher of Righteousness' had been sent by God, to establish the last covenant. To this end they devoted their lives to God and the study of the Hebrew Bible.

Their form of worship was intentionally different to the Temple rituals, even going so far as to adopt a separate calendar, which divided

---

[76] For a concise summary of this hypothesis see: The Complete Dead Sea Scrolls in English. Vermes G. Allan Lane, The Penguin Press (1962) 16-20

[77] Philo Quad Ommis Probus 12 (75)-13 (91) Hypothetica in Eusebius Prae Paratio Evangelica (ed Mras, GC 43) 8 11, 1-18 Dia Vita Contemplativa.

[78] Vermes G. The Complete Dead Sea Scrolls in English. Allan Lane The Penguin Press (1962) 31.

The Way to Christianity

the year into a regular and unvarying pattern. In the life of the Qumran community the great religious festivals always fell on the same day, at exactly the same time of year and each season, and indeed each year began on a Wednesday. This unvarying chronology created a religious separateness that the Essenes asserted was based on scripture, the study of which was fundamental to the Essene way of life.[79]

In the Qumran library were excerpts of every book in the Hebrew Bible, with the exception of Esther. Very often more than one copy was available and, interestingly, these often show considerable variation, thus illustrating the scribal freedom permissible, before later textural orthodoxy was established. Alongside these accepted texts were numerous apocryphal works, which clearly provided religious inspiration for the community. Works of biblical interpretation were also present in some numbers, as were examples of hymns and psalms. All this holy literature provided the fundamental cannon of Essene belief, one which was interpreted by the 'Teacher of Righteousness,' whose decisions were binding on all. The teacher had one overriding concern, the fate of Israel in the last days:

> *'But all those who hold fast to the precepts, going and coming in accordance with the law . . . who have listened to the voice of the Teacher of Righteousness and who have not despised the precepts of righteousness when they hear them; they shall rejoice and their hearts shall be strong, and they shall prevail over all the sons of the earth. God will forgive them and they shall see his salvation because they took refuge in his holy name.'* [80]

A final battle would take place between the 'Sons of Light' and the 'Sons of Darkness.' The 'Sons of Light,' comprising the true Essene believers, would initially reoccupy Jerusalem in an attack on the 'Ungodly of the Covenant,' consisting of the Temple and Roman authorities. This initial campaign would last six years after which,

---

[79] Ibid 28

[80] Translation from the Complete Dead Sea Scrolls in English. Vermes.G. Allan Lane. The Penguin Press (1965) 85.

following the defeat of the occupying forces, Essene Temple worship would be restored in the seventh peaceful year. Following this initial victory, war would be waged for twenty-nine of the following thirty-three years. Final victory would result in the total defeat of 'the King of Kittim' (the Roman Emperor) and of Satan's 'Sons of Darkness.'

> *'O Zion, rejoice greatly!*
> *Rejoice all you cities of Judah!*
> *(Keep your gates ever open that the) host of the nations*
> *(may be brought in)!*
> *Their kings shall serve you and all your oppressors shall*
> *bow down before you;*
> *(they shall lick the dust of your feet.*
> *Shout for joy, O daughters of) my people!*
> *Deck yourselves with glorious jewels and rule over the*
> *kingdom of the nations!*
> *Sovereignty shall be to the Lord)*
> *And everlasting dominion to Israel.'* [81]

This great last victory would result in a 'new creation' when the Essene remnant of Israel would inherit the pure and holy world, only previously known to Adam before his fall and expulsion from the Garden of Eden. As with many other Jewish scenarios, all else would be swept away.

Bodily resurrection was not strongly featured in Essene religious mythology. The expectation was for spiritual release from the body after death, which for the righteous would result in: *'Eternal joy in life without end, a crown of glory and a garment of majesty in unending light.'* In sharp contrast, the ungodly would suffer: *'Endless disgrace together with shameful extinction in the fire of the dark regions.'* [82]

---

[81] The War Scroll I Q M XIX 2-8. Translation from the Complete Dead Sea Scrolls in English. Vermes. G. Allan Lane The Penguin Press (1997) 85.

[82] Vermes G. The Complete Dead Sea Scrolls in English. Allan Lane The Penguin Press (1997) 1: 8

The Essenes believed that this spiritual release began not after death, but with acceptance into the community, so that death was simply the passing away of the physical whilst the spirit continued in God's glory.

As with other Jewish end time scenarios, a Messiah, or in the Essene case, Messiahs would be expected to play a role. The community at Qumran anticipated at least two Messiahs would play separate, but mutually supportive, roles in the last days. There is also a single reference to a 'Prophet Messiah.' It has been suggested that this individual was already manifest as the 'Teacher of Righteousness.'[83] If this hypothesis is correct then it is only the two Messiahs who were involved in the last days: The first, a 'King Messiah' who was a 'branch of David,' was to lead the people to final victory and cause them to:

'Ravage the earth with your sceptre; may you bring death to the ungodly with the breath of your lips, and all Kings of the nations shall serve you.' [84]

The second, a 'Priest Messiah' or 'Messiah of Aaron', would play a wholly spiritual role. His function is to lead Israel:

'Engenders (the Priest) Messiah he shall come with them at the head of the whole congregation of Israel with all his brethren the sons of Aaron the Priests those called to the assembly, the men of renown; and they shall sit before him, each man in the order of his dignity. And then the Messiah of Israel shall come.' [85]

The priest Messiah was to take precedence in all matters other than the conduct of the final battle against the ungodly, although even here, he had a limited role in ordering certain military operations. Whilst the two Messiahs were clearly of importance, both were clearly human rather than divine. God was the supreme agent who will intervene, at a crucial junction in the final battle, to bring about the defeat of the forces

---

[83] Ibid 87

[84] Ibid 376

[85] Ibid The Messianic Rule IQSa. 159

of darkness. The Messiahs would act as his agents, but would have a relatively lowly status in the hierarchy of heaven, falling below many of the angels and the Saints.

Although the community was destroyed, or at least dispersed, during the first Jewish uprising its library, for so long undiscovered in the caves around Qumran, gives a vivid account of the depth and intensity of the Essene view of the last days of Judaism.

Roman victory in the first Jewish uprising devastated the people, but not their hopes. To judge by the surviving contemporary literature the desire for the arrival of God's new world order continued unabated.

Apocalypse of Baruch

The apocryphal 'Apocalypse of Baruch,' written after the loss of the first Jewish war, begins with God permitting the destruction of the Temple, as a punishment for his errant people. Even so, the Temple treasures would be preserved until the dawn of the last days:

> *'And the Lord said unto me: 'This city shall be delivered up for a time. And the people shall be chastened during a time, and the world will not be given over to oblivion . . . For I am sent to speak a word to the earth, and to place in it what the Lord the Most High has commanded men And I saw him descent into the Holy of holies, and take from thence the veil, and the holy ark, and the mercy-seat, and the two tables, and the holy raiment of the priests, and the alter of incense, and the forty-eight precious stones, wherewith the priest was adorned and the holy vessels of the tabernacle. And he spake to the earth with a loud voice: 'Earth, earth, earth, hear the word of the mighty God, And receive what I commit to thee, And guard them until the last times, So that, when thou art ordered, thou mayst restore them, So that strangers may not get possession of them. For the time comes when Jerusalem also will be delivered for a time, until it is*

said, that is again restored for ever.' And the earth opened its mouth and swallowed them up.' [86]

The destruction of the Temple ushers in a time of both man-made and natural disasters. In its aftermath the wars that were to be fought would result in the victory of the unrighteous, whilst many of the survivors would be destroyed in earthquakes and fire.

But when the time was fulfilled the Messiah will usher a new age:

'And it shall come to pass after these things, when the time of the advent of the Messiah is fulfilled, that He shall return in glory.' [87]

Ezra

In similar view, the writer of the fourth book of Ezra, probably written at about the same time as the Apocalypse of Baruch, foresees a time of great tribulation before the glorious arrival of the last days:

'Now concerning the signs; Lo, the days are coming when those who inhabit the earth shall be seized with great terror and the way of truth shall be hidden, and the lands shall be barren of faith. Unrighteousness shall be increased beyond what you yourself see, and beyond what you have heard formerly. And the land that you now see ruling shall be a trackless waste, and people shall be desolate.' [88]

But at the appointed time God will usher in his new age:

'For indeed the time will come, when the signs that I have foretold to you will come to pass, that the city that is now not seen shall appear, and the land that now is hidden shall be

---

[86] Charles R.H. The Apocrypha and Pseudoegrapha of the Old Testament. Oxford Clarendon Press. (1913)

[87] Ibid

[88] 2 Ezra 5: 1-3

disclosed . . . For my son the Messiah shall be revealed to those who are with him, and those who remain shall rejoice for four hundred years.' [89]

After this time all will die, but after seven days the righteous will wake in God's presence:

'The most high shall be revealed on the seat of judgement, and compassion shall pass away and patience shall be withdrawn. Only judgement shall stand and faithfulness shall grow strong. Recompense shall follow and the reward shall be manifest; righteous deeds shall awake and unrighteous deeds shall not sleep. The pit of torment shall appear; and opposite it shall be the place of rest; and the furnace of hell shall be disclosed, and opposite it the paradise of delight.' [90]

Shemoneh Esreh

The apocalypses of Baruch and Ezra did not find a place in the Hebrew Bible. That they were influential is shown by the ideas incorporated in the chief prayer of Judaism. Revised in about 100CE, the Shemoneh Esreh was, and still is, said three times a day by the devout. Of the nineteen benedictions, at least four strongly reflect the hope of the restoration of Israel, and one in particular expresses the hope for a Messiah. Verse fourteen of the Palestinian recession reads:

'Be merciful, Lord our God, with they great mercies, to Israel they people and to Jerusalem they city; and to Zion, the dwelling place of the glory; and they Temple and they habitation; and to the kingship of the House of David the

---

[89] 2 Ezra 7: 26-28

[90] 2 Ezra 7: 33-36

righteous Messiah. Blessed art thou Lord, God of David, who buildest Jerusalem.' [91]

The period after the first uprising against Rome was deeply traumatic for the Jewish people. The destruction of Herod's Temple brought daily sacrifice and ritual to an end, although the patterns of holy ritual continued to be extensively studied. During this period the Sadducees and Temple priests no longer had a function and ceased to be influential in Jewish life, whilst the Sanhedrin, the great religious court in Jerusalem, and the last vestige of Jewish independence, ceased to exist. Its functions were now wholly taken over by the new Roman Governors, who were drawn from the senatorial, rather than the equestrian ranks.

Into this void stepped the Pharisees and the beginnings of Rabbinic Judaism were born. Whilst a deep yearning for the return of Temple ritual and the priesthood remained, it was the Pharisees, in a new centre at Jamina, who now met the spiritual needs of their people. The Romans acquiesced to this situation, and it was the most respected of the Rabbis who carried out the role formally undertaken by the Sadducees.

Thus, within two or three decades Jewish religious life began to be restored, albeit in a radically different form. The certainties of Jewish belief were maintained and the calamity of the defeat in the war against Rome was seen as a just punishment for the sins of God's people. If Jews would turn from sin and worship unreservedly the one true God, then a glorious future still awaited them.

During the latter part of the first century, the situation remained generally quiet. Christian reports of the hunting down and execution of all those who claimed Davidic descent, although plausible, may not be historically reliable. But in the early part of the second century, unrest grew. Jews in Egypt and Cyrene, taking advantage of the Emperor Trajan's preoccupation with war in Mesopotamia, rebelled in 115CE, and it was not until the beginning of Hadrian's reign that order was again restored.

---

[91] The History of the Jewish People in the Age of Jesus Christ. Schurer E. (1878). Revised English text. Vermes. G. Millar F. Goodmanm. M. Black M. Eds T & T Clark (1979). II: 461

John Larke

Hadrian and the Second Jewish Uprising

Hadrian, at least by the standards of so many of his predecessors, was a benevolent and cultured ruler who was particularly impressed by physical beauty. His frequent travelling companion was a Greek youth of great beauty whose untimely death seems to have caused Hadrian great and genuine sorrow. As his reign progressed, he proved a prolific city builder, seemingly embarking on great construction programmes with an aim of unification: endowing his far flung Empire with an architectural similarity in their prominent religious and secular buildings.

At some point Hadrian announced two decrees, firstly, a ban on circumcision, and secondly, his intention to rebuild Jerusalem—which was at this time the site of a military camp[92]—as a Pagan city. The ban on circumcision, which Hadrian felt was mutilation of the male body, was not exclusively, or even primarily, directed against Jews,—the practice was quite widespread amongst Arabs and others—but circumcision was fundamental to Judaism.

The intention to rebuild Jerusalem as a Pagan city ended the deeply felt hope for the restoration of the Temple and its cultic rituals, which had formerly been so central to Jewish life. These two measures, not specifically or even intentionally directed against Jews, could not have been more calculated to offend Jewish sensibilities.

In 131-132CE, the second Jewish uprising broke out. The leader of the uprising, Simon Ben (or Bar) Kosiba, was declared the promised Messiah by Rabbi Aiciba, amongst many others. [93] Christians however, took a different view and referred to Bar Kosiba as Bar KoZiba, which translates as 'Son of the Lie.' Having bestowed Messiahdom on one charismatic Jewish figure, they were not about to tolerate a second!

The uprising lasted for about three and a half years and was probably similar in intensity and extent to the first war, almost sixty years before. The outcome was also the same. After considerable initial success, the

---

[92] The History of the Jewish People in the Age of Jesus Christ. Schurer E. (1878). Revised English text Vermes. G. Millar F. Goodman. M. Black M.(Eds) T & T Clark (1973). 1: 248

[93] The Jews in the Roman World. Grant M. Phoenix (1973) 15: 248

The Way to Christianity

uprising was eventually overcome by a superior Roman force. Those Jews not killed in the conflict were sold into slavery, and the price of a Jewish slave now fell to that of a horse.

The end of the second Jewish uprising brought about the effective end of the state of Israel. Jews were now forbidden to live in Jerusalem and a Roman Temple, dedicated to the God Jupiter, was built as a replacement for Herod's great Temple. As Hadrian and his successors reconstructed the city, it was renamed Aelia Capitolina, or more simply, Aelia. Its new population was strictly Gentile, and it was a capital offence for any Jew to attempt to enter the city.

The Jewish population of the Eastern Mediterranean, which at one time may have constituted 15% of the total, was probably now reduced in some areas to less than 5%. [94] Jews became a people apart and despite occasional attempts, they were never entirely rehabilitated into Roman society. But they had their religion, and, as such, they had hope; over time the urgent expectation of the last days dimmed somewhat, but it never went away.

In the middle of this period of desperate hope and deep trauma, a further movement came into being. At some point in the 20's CE a desert 'Holy Man' named John Ben Zechariah proclaimed that the 'last days' were imminent, and preparation should be made for God's final judgement. His message was immensely popular, and large numbers of people flocked to hear him. This alarmed the authorities, who arrested and executed John.

This could have been the end of the matter, but John came from an extended family, and his oldest male relative, who was probably a cousin, although not necessarily a first cousin, Jesus Ben Joseph took up his mantle and continued his mission. The movement came to be called 'The Way' [95] and was very much a product of its times.

---

[94] Author's own rough estimate from a number of sources.

[95] Acts 24: 14

CHAPTER 4

THE FOLLOWERS OF THE WAY

The Way was a small historically unimportant Jewish revivalist sect, which, at its peak, probably comprised of no more than a few hundred followers. The movement had two central beliefs: (a) The last days were imminent and (b) preparation must be made for God's expected judgement. A belief in the imminence of the last days was not unique to The Way, but the manner in which it was expressed set it apart from other groups. The intensity of expectation grew out of the prevailing conditions, which have been admirably summarised by Geza Vermes:

> 'The specific situation arose from the political turmoil generated by the Roman rule in Palestine, first established in 63BCE. The unrest was clearly manifest in rebellious acts following the death of Herod the Great in 4BCE, which were violently suppressed by the Romans, and in the bitter resentment caused by the census or Roman Tax Registration imposed on Judea by Quirinius, Governor of Syria in 6CE. The political unrest stirred up and nurtured a feverish longing for an impending divine intervention . . . The kingdom of God was believed to be at hand. This kingdom was a wholly Jewish issue involving Jews alone, and requiring an exclusively Jewish solution. The non-Jewish world played no active part in it.' 1[96]

This 'feverish longing' motivated a number of movements, some of which resorted to political violence.

---

[96] The Authentic Gospel of Jesus. Vermes G. Allan Lane. Penguin Press (2003) 414.

Zealots and Sicarii

The Zealot movement appears to have taken inspiration from the Maccabean uprising, which it attempted to emulate.[97] The Zealots appeared as a fully-fledged movement after Quirinius' census, which entailed the assessment of Judean property for the purpose of a poll tax. Such a count was seen as contrary to the Hebrew Bible, which required the people of Israel to be 'unnumbered.' A further insult to Jewish sensibilities was the payment of tax in Roman coinage, bearing the image of Caesar. The Zealots led the resistance movement in Jerusalem during the first Jewish war. They were responsible for the defence of the city and for much of the internecine disputes, which so weakened their cause.

The Sicarii were also notable for their violent resistance to Roman occupation.[98] They were named after the large curved dagger or Sicae with which they assassinated those they considered guilty of collaboration with the governing authorities.

At the beginnings of the first Jewish war the Sicarii took control of the mountain top fortress of Masada. Although intimately concerned with events in Jerusalem, Masada was to remain a Sicarii stronghold and it was here that the famous mass suicide, was said to have taken place, when it became clear that Roman troops were about to overwhelm the defendants.

In contrast to the unrest and turmoil surrounding it, The Way was neither violent nor overtly political. Successive leaders of the movement stressed a whole-hearted acceptance of God's love and adherence, not only to the letter, but also, more importantly, to the spirit of the law. In this they appear to have been influenced by earlier Jewish traditions, particularly those derived from a group of men known as the Hasidim.

The Way—Hasidic Traditions

The origins of Hasidism are far from clear; that they existed prior to the Maccabean revolt is shown by their eventual participation in

---

[97] Schurer.E The History of the Jewish people in the Age of Jesus Christ (1874). Revised English Text Vermes. G. Millar.F Goodman M. Black M. Eds T & T Clark (1973) 1 382

[98] Ibid 1: 463.

the uprising, however, they have also been tentatively identified with groups of poor men from the small towns and villages of rural Palestine. The most notable feature of the Hasidim was their devout and pious way of life and careful observance of both the letter and the spirit of the Torah. A well-known account describes the slaughter of a group of Hasidim, who interpreted the Hebrew Bible so strictly that they would not defend themselves on the Sabbath.[99]

Claims for the Hasidim as the forerunners of the Essenes and/or the Pharisees have been made. Unfortunately the historical record is too incomplete for this to be more than reasoned speculation. The Hasidim preached a complete dependence on God's love, and—with the exception of the Maccabeus uprising—they seem to have eschewed violence. Hasidic traditions were to form part of the inspirational ethos of Judaism, providing a role model for those who proclaimed an absolute reliance on God's munificence.[100] As such they appear to have been a particular source of inspiration for the followers of The Way.

The Way—Sources

There are a number of references to The Way in the Christian bible. The earliest relates to John Ben Zechariah and is found in all four gospels.[101] Although there are some textual variations, all four variants were taken from Isaiah: '*A voice cries out in the wilderness prepare the way of the Lord make straight in the desert a highway for our God.*' [102] It seems clear that the gospel writers saw John Ben Zechariah as the precursor of Jesus and wished to emphasize this view by citing Isaiah. Jesus, in the Gospel attributed to John, is reported to have taken this one step further by proclaiming that '*I am the way and the truth and the light.*' [103]

---

[99] 1 Maccabees 2: 31-38

[100] Ibid 2: 42

[101] Matthew 3: 3; Mark 1: 2; Luke 3: 4; John 1: 26

[102] Isaiah 40: 3

[103] John 24: 6

Of all the Christian documents that have come down to us, none contain more references to The Way than Acts. The first occurs when Paul of Tarsus was still a persecutor of Jesus' disciples: *'Meanwhile Saul (Paul) still breathing threats and murder against the disciples of the Lord, went to the High Priest and asked him for letters, so that if he found any who belonged to The Way, men or women he might bring them bound to Jerusalem.'* [104]

In this quotation the *'disciples of the Lord'* are identified with 'The Way' and this is the first occasion in which The Way appears as a title. The next quotation from Acts refers to *'Apollo's a native of Alexandria'* who had *'been instructed in the Way of the Lord'* . . . *'concerning Jesus, though he knew only the baptism of John'*. When they heard him speaking in the Synagogue two of Paul's associates, *'took him aside and explained the Way of God to him more accurately.'* [105] The views of Paul and his associates were not always so well received. *'Some stubbornly refused to believe and spoke evil of the Way.'* [106] Indeed, on occasion, proclaiming the message of The Way met with strong opposition: *'About that time no little disturbance broke out concerning The Way.'* [107]

Following an attack during his last visit to Jerusalem, Paul was arrested and taken to Caesarea. Appearing before the Roman Governor Felix who: *'was rather well informed about The Way'*. [108] Paul faced prosecution by a lawyer named Tertullus: *'We have in fact found this man a pestilent fellow an agitator among all the Jews throughout the world and a ringleader of the sect of Nazarenes'*. [109] In defending himself Paul defines his understanding of The Way:

> *'But this I admit to you that according to The Way which they call a sect, I worship the God of our ancestors, believing*

---

[104] Acts 9: 1-2

[105] Acts 18 24-28

[106] Acts 19: 9

[107] Acts 19: 24

[108] Acts 24: 22

[109] Acts 24: 5

everything laid down according to the law or written in the Prophets.' [110]

The account of Paul's trial is the last information that we have in Acts regarding The Way. It also establishes the 'Nazarenes' as an alternative title for the movement, and clearly shows that it was a Jewish rather than a Christian sect. Some of Paul's followers in Antioch were probably the first who used the term Christian,[111] but this does not necessarily imply a belief in Jesus as a divine figure; In Jewish religious thought the Messiah (Christ) was a human rather than a heavenly figure, and, although Paul clearly revered Jesus, he stopped short, if only just, in regarding him as divine (Chapter 5.)

At a slightly later date, probably post 70CE, some followers of The Way may have also been known as Ebionites, the etymology of which comes from the Aramaic for 'poor men'.[112] This, in turn, tallies with the abundant evidence for a mission to the materially and spiritually poor in the teachings of The Way.

The term 'The Way' is not limited to the movement of which Jesus' followers were a part. It is, for example, rather widely found in the Qumran literature and elsewhere, although not as a title. This implies that the term had a rather wide usage, but it appears that it was only in the movement that drew its inspiration from John Ben Zechariah that it was used as a title.

The phrase 'Jewish Christian' which is almost universally used for the family and early followers of Jesus does not appear in either the gospels or Acts. It seems clear that the use of this term is an attempt by later Christianity to claim the early followers of Jesus as their own, a claim which, in my view, has no historical support.

John Ben Zechariah

The origins of The Way lie in the teaching of a Jewish desert holy man, John Ben Zechariah, (John the Baptist)'. Although there are

---

[110] Acts 24: 14

[111] Acts 11: 26

[112] Vermes G. Who's who in the Age of Jesus. Penguin (2005) 27

The Way to Christianity

references to a number of desert holy men, the details of only two have come down to us. One is John, whilst the other was simply known as 'Bannus.'

Bannus was the spiritual mentor of the Jewish historian, Josephus, who spent three years in the desert, seeking a sense of direction in his spiritual life. Bannus depended upon what nature supplied. He wore 'no other clothing but that, which grew on trees,' and his food came from 'what grew naturally.' Bannus seems to have acted as a spiritual councillor for Josephus, helping crystallise his sense of vocation through a consideration of various religious groupings. After exhaustively examining the traditions of the Pharisees, the Essences and the Sadducees, Josephus decided to become a Pharisee, although it is as an historian that he is nowadays remembered. Josephus, who as an aristocrat, found the discipline and life-style of the desert very demanding and, at a later date, wrote with reverence of Bannus, a man who clearly had a formative influence on his early life.[113]

He also wrote of John in glowing terms:

> *'He was a good man and exhorted the Jews to lead righteous lives, practice justice towards one another, and piety towards God and so join in immersion. In his view this was a necessary preliminary if ritual immersion was to be acceptable to God. They must not use it to gain pardon for whatever sins they have committed, but as a consecration of the body, implying that the soul was thoroughly purified beforehand by right behaviour.'* [114]

How long John had been in the wilderness on the banks of the Jordan is not known. His lifestyle resembled that of Bannus, in that it was one of considerable simplicity. He relied on nature for his clothing and food, and his tunic was reported to have been made from camel's hair. In the days before the River Jordan became the over-extracted and polluted water course that is today, camels would come to drink along

---

[113] Josephus F Life 11 Translation from Josephus.1X LOEB Library

[114] Josephus F. Antiquities 5, 2 (117-119) Translation from Josephus 1X LOEB Library 82-85

its banks. Their hair would have accumulated on wild thorn bushes, in much the same way that sheep's wool collects on barbed wire in our own time. Food, however, would have been more of a problem. John is reported to have collected honey, which must have been at the cost of stings from wild bees. His diet probably consisted of all that he could forage and was allowed to eat by the Jewish dietary laws.

Unlike Bannus, John does not seem to have acted as a spiritual councillor. His central message was the imminence of the 'last days' of Judaism, and John offered practical spiritual advice on how to gain acceptance into the Kingdom of Heaven.

It has been suggested that John was an Essene, or at least strongly influenced by their beliefs. There are good reasons for rejecting this. The central tenet of the Essene movement was the rejection of Temple worship, which was thought to have been irretrievably polluted. John's father Zechariah was a Temple priest,[115] and his kinsmen Jesus and James both participated in Temple rituals. Indeed James was later reported to have become a Temple priest in his own right.

The Way and the Essenes were parallel movements, both of which reflected the hopes and aspirations of their age. In addition to Temple worship there was one further fundamental difference. The Essene's believed that with God's help they would defeat the Romans in one great final battle. The 'Followers of The Way' were pacifists, who redeemed their sins and lived in a state of 'spiritual purity' waiting for God's final judgement. This pacifism is rejected by some historians and indeed by some modern Christians—the 'religious right' in America being a notable example[116]—but it was a persistent feature of the early days of 'The Way.'

John spent most of his time on the banks of the Jordan River, probably around Beth Bara, where a number of present day shrines and churches exist.[117] (Fig 4.1)

---

[115] Luke 1: 5

[116] Balmer R. The Chronicle of High Education: Chronicle Review 2006 Washington 52. 42 B6

[117] Gibson S. The Cave of John the Baptist. Centaury (2004) 219

The Way to Christianity

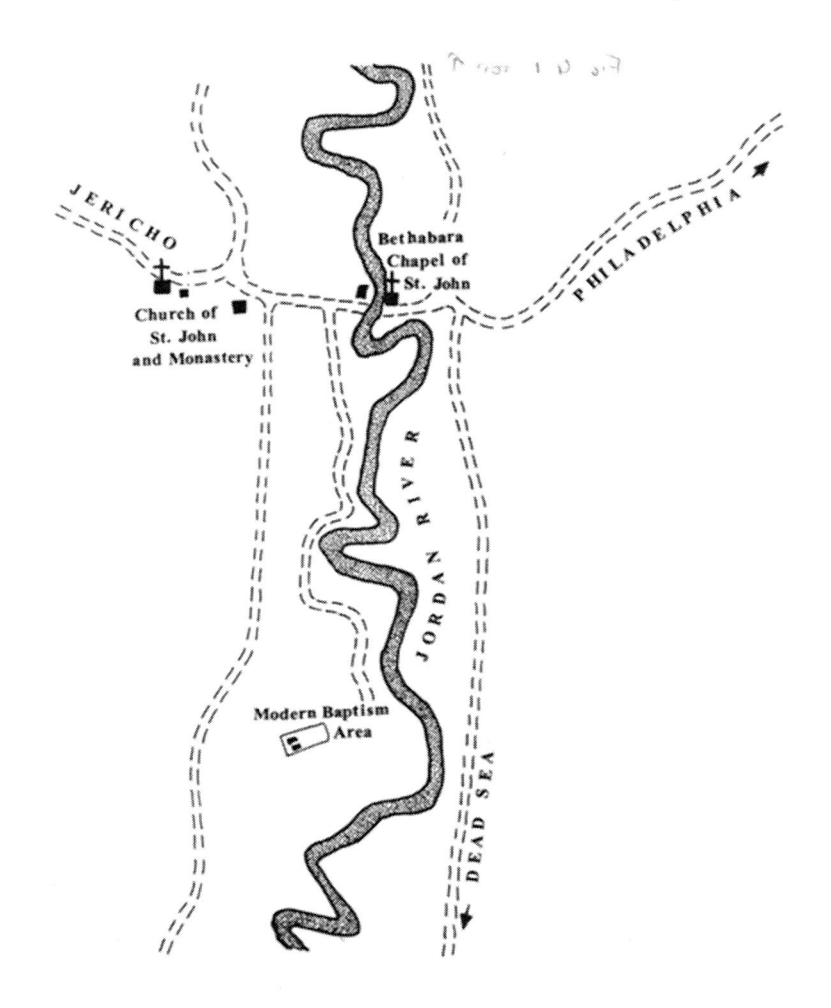

Figure 4.1 Present day shrines and Churches associated with 'John the Baptist' based on an original drawing by Gibson S. Century (2004) 219

At some point in 28 or 29CE John's fame began to spread to the outside world and particularly to Jerusalem, about two to three day's journey away. Doubtless his followers carried word of his mission, and people came to listen to him in increasing numbers. John's message was simple: The last days of Judaism were rapidly approaching and God's judgement was imminent. To use one of his few, probably authentic sayings, which have come down to us: *'Even now the axe is lying at the root of the trees; every tree therefore that does not bear fruit, is cut down and thrown on the fire.'* [118]

John's message was certainly popular—although the reports of thousands visiting the banks of the Jordan may well be an exaggeration—and implicitly begged the question of what was to be done by way of preparation. It was clear that unsatisfactory judgement would result in rejection, and that one's status as a Jew was by no means a guarantee of a place in God's new kingdom. It was here that the strength of John's teaching lay; if one wanted to be judged favourably then one must follow the *'way of the Lord.'* [119]

This 'way' was open to all, not only the supposed righteous who might pray daily in the Temple, but even those who had knowingly sinned. It is possible that in John's teachings the origins of a mission to the poor may be found. John's concern for the poor seemed to have included not only those who were financially destitute, but those who were morally corrupt as well, amongst whom tax collectors are specifically mentioned.

Tax collectors were frequently sub-contractors of a large tax district. They would bid for the tax income of an area, and any surplus that could be extracted, by whatever means, would be their profit. Tax Collectors were heartily despised, but for John even they could be admitted into the Kingdom of Heaven if they chose genuine repentance.

John's teaching also included atonement. The Jewish law gave specific criteria for atonement, for example, in the case of an unpaid debt, the amount of money, plus one fifth, must be returned to the lender. But John seems to have gone further than this, and taught that God required acts of considerable virtue, particularly towards other Jews. Such acts would put the interest of another above the interest of the self-centred individual, and this was truly what God wanted. John's teaching can be summarised in what we now call the 'Lord's Prayer', a version of which found in the Gospel attributed to Mathew:

> *'Our Father in heaven*
> *Hallowed be your name*

---

[118] Matthew 3: 10

[119] Luke 3: 4

Your Kingdom come
Your will be done
On earth as it is in heaven
Give us this day our daily bread (or bread for tomorrow)
And forgive us our debts as we
Have forgiven our debtors
And do not bring us to the time of trial (or us into temptation
But rescue us from the evil one (or from evil)' [120]

If this is indeed a short prayer used by John, as implied by the gospel attributed to Mathew,[121] it encapsulates his teachings admirably: The kingdom that John is convinced is about to happen is the 'Kingdom of Heaven,' whilst, as a gatherer of food, John prays that God will provide sufficient to sustain him. Debts and debtors clearly refer to unpaid loans and, in including the trial of temptation and asking for God's help in being rescued from evil, John is asking for God's help in living a spiritually pure life.

Once an individual had wholly committed their life to God they would undergo immersion. Ritual immersion in water was a very common part of Judaic rituals and flowing water was preferred to still, as such the Jordan must have been ideal for John's purpose. However, immersion was typically a last symbolic act, marking the culmination of a long process of spiritual renewal. One can thus readily understand John's anger with the Pharisees and aristocratic priests, who came to him for immersion only: *'You brood of vipers! Who warned you to flee from the wrath to come? Bear fruit worthy of repentance.'* [122]

In some respects, John's teaching is somewhat analogous to the modern day movement of 'born again' Christianity. John required his followers to wholly commit their lives to God and what had gone before was of little consequence.

Although announcing the Kingdom of Heaven, John did not see himself in the role of progenitor:

---

[120] Matthew 6: 9-13

[121] Luke 11: 2-4

[122] Luke 3: 7-8

> *'I baptize you with water for repentance, but one who is more powerful than I is coming after me; I am not worthy to carry his sandals. He will baptize you with the Holy Spirit and fire. His winnowing fork is in his hand and he will clear his threshing floor and will gather his wheat into the granary, but the chaff he will burn with unquenchable fire.'* [123]

There are various candidates for 'the one who is more powerful than I.' It is worth remembering that John was a pious observant Jew who was wholly concerned with Jewish traditions. In the spiritual literature of John's age, close parallels can be found in references to the prophet Elijah, who was expected to return immediately prior to God's final judgement.[124] There is a further reason for supposing that John's *'more powerful than I'* was a returning Elijah: It was in the area of John's ministry that Elijah was thought to have ascended into heaven on a 'chariot of fire,' and it was possible that his return was expected in the same location.

John's increasing popularity brought him to the attention of the ruler of Perea and Galilee, Herod Antipas, who may have had a more personal reason for acting against John: John was reported to have criticised the King's second marriage to his half-brother's former wife.

As a client King of the Roman Empire, Herod was ultimately responsible for the flow of tax revenue as well as the maintenance of order in his region of Jewish Palestine. As a successful son of Herod the Great, Antipas was very familiar with the realities of effective governance. Thus, both John's popularity and the essence of his message, in which the 'kingdom of heaven' would replace all other empires, were grounds for acting sooner rather than later. John was arrested and incarcerated in the fortress of Machaerus where, seemingly after a period of imprisonment, he was beheaded. Unusually after death his body was placed in a tomb rather than being thrown over the fortress walls, as was the normal practice.

At, or around, the time of John's arrest, many of his followers left the desert and travelled to other parts of Jewish Palestine. Doubtless the

---

[123] Matthew 3: 11-12

[124] Malachi 3: 23-24

The Way to Christianity

fear of being identified with John and sharing his fate motivated their departure.

John's execution could have been the end of his revivalist movement, but other family members continued his work.

Hereditary Leadership of the Way

Judaism incorporates strong hereditary principles: Not only was the legitimate King of Israel seen as a descendant of the House of David, but the priesthood and other temple functionaries carefully preserved their genealogies in order to justify their participation in religious rituals.[125] Recent scientific studies have revealed how strongly these traditions have been upheld. In seeking to establish the claims of two groups of present-day Jews to priestly descent, segments of DNA passed on exclusively by the male line have been examined.[126] In both groups, one African and another Indian, the hereditary principle has been upheld by a much higher than expected incidence of the appropriate marker gene.[127] Did the spiritual leaders of The Way observe a similar hereditary principle? In my view they did.[128]

John Ben Zechariah is reported to have been an only child. His oldest male relative appears to have been Jesus Ben Joseph, the oldest son of John's mother's kinswoman Mary. Jesus was therefore a cousin, although not necessarily a first cousin, of John.

After Jesus' crucifixion, his oldest surviving brother, James Ben Joseph, led The Way for the next thirty years. When James was killed in 62CE the movement was led by a further family member nephew, Simeon Ben Clopas, until his own death at the end of the first century.

The available evidence shows that the first four spiritual leaders of The Way came from the same extended family. In at least three instances: John, Jesus and James, a pattern of oldest male succession

---

[125] 1 Chronicles 24: 7-18

[126] Travis J The Priests Chromosome. Science News (1988) 154 (14) 218 (Marker Gene)

[127] Anon. Group in Africa has Jewish Roots DNA indicates. New York Times (1999) May 9th

[128] For a contrary opinion see Bauckham R. James. Routledge. (2003) 17

can be demonstrated. This inherited leadership is entirely consistent with the religious traditions of second temple Judaism.

In following a familial male line of succession, The Way was over time to become a movement. Although, in a sense, when viewed retrospectively, it was a movement by default rather than by design, since the central prophecy of God's imminent arrival would presumably result in each spiritual teacher and leader of The Way hoping that he would be the last.

Jesus Ben Joseph

As with his cousin John, Jesus proclaimed the imminent arrival of the Kingdom of Heaven and assisted in John's baptismal mission,[129] but he was to become far more than just a prophet of the last days. Amongst his activities can be listed: faith healer, folk medicine practitioner, exorcist, miracle worker, and not least as a teller of quite extraordinary parables. Yet it is clear from Jesus' reported statements that he ascribed all of these attributes to God.

At some point after the arrest of John, Jesus left the banks of the Jordan and travelled to Capernaum, a small fishing village on the shores of the Lake of Gennesaret,[130] but Jesus seems not to have stayed long in Capernaum.

A feature of his ministry was that although he did not travel widely, he seems to have travelled frequently, probably to escape the agents of Herod Antipas. On his journeys he was accompanied by his followers, some of whom, such as Peter, Andrew, James and John, had been followers of John Ben Zechariah, whilst others may have been new converts. In all, it has been claimed that Jesus had twelve disciples, although the names of fourteen close companions have come down to us. The number twelve is probably symbolic and represents the 'twelve tribes of Israel.' In the 'last days' it was hoped that the 'ten lost tribes of Israel' would be recovered and added to the remaining two tribes (Chapter 3).

---

[129] John 3: 22-24

[130] Matthew 4: 12-13

Faith Healing

The arrival of Jesus and his followers must have been a great occasion in the small towns and villages they visited. Jesus would not only have participated in the Synagogue, he would also have offered the only form of healing which country folk were likely to receive.

It is only comparatively recently that effective treatment for disease has been available. Even at the beginning of the twentieth century, whilst differential diagnosis was well-advanced, effective treatment was largely limited to herbal and folk medicine. Two thousand years ago patients had an even tougher time. Most Jews believed that disease was the result of sin. Going to a Doctor could show lack of faith in God, as it was only God who could forgive sin and alleviate sickness.

Faith healers, who could act as a conduit for God's mercy, were highly regarded. One famous example involved the revered faith healer, Hanina Ben Dossa: When the son of the noted Pharisee, Gamial, became seriously ill, Gamial sent his servant to Hanina to ask for help. After praying all night, Hanina told the servant to return as his prayers had been answered and Gamial's son would recover, which he duly did.[131] It is a measure of the stature of Hanina that the site of his dwelling is known and revered to the present day.

Hanina Ben Dossa was roughly contemporary with Jesus Ben Joseph and there are clear parallels in their healings. Perhaps the closest comparison can be found in Jesus' healing of the highly valued slave of a Roman Centurion. The officer was so deeply in awe of Jesus that he felt unworthy to have him enter his house. He therefore asked Jesus to *'simply speak the word'* and his slave would be cured, which, in turn, he was. Jesus is reported to have been amazed by the Centurion's faith: *'I tell you not even in Israel have I found such faith.'* [132]

The Centurion's slave was far from being the only example of Jesus' faith healing. A woman, who had suffered from a haemorrhage for twelve years, merely had to touch the fringe of Jesus' cloths to be cured.[133] Whilst another woman, who was *'bent over'* and unable to

---

[131] Vermes G. Who's who in the Age of Jesus. (2005) Penguin Press. 99-102

[132] Luke 7: 9

[133] Luke 8: 43-44

stand straight for eighteen years, was healed by having Jesus' hand laid upon her.[134]

In our own time, faith healing is often derided, but it is not without scientific support. In modern drugs trials, a control group is given a placebo of no therapeutic value, which, in spite of the lack of any active ingredient, will typically result in, as many as twenty percent of patients reporting an improvement in their symptoms. This recovery seemingly can only be attributed to their 'faith' in the medication that they have been given.

Folk Medicine

Not all of Jesus' cures fall into the category of faith healing. In a number of instances the treatment given reveals knowledge of folk medicine. In the case of the healing of a blind man, this is clearly the case. The description that has come down to us is revealing:

> *'Some people brought a blind man to him and begged him to touch him . . . and when he had put saliva on his eyes and laid his hands on him he asked, can you see anything? And the man looked up and said, "I can see people but they look like trees walking." Then Jesus laid his hands on his eyes again, and he looked intently, and his sight was restored and he saw everything clearly.'* [135]

It is apparent that the account describes a folk treatment for cataract: A principle factor in cataract formation is lifetime exposure to ultra violet light. Since ultra violet levels are particularly high in the Middle East, cataracts must have been a common problem.

Cataracts are caused by opacity of the focusing lens within the eye. One of the traditional treatments was to push the lens out of the line of sight. This was done by the healer placing his thumb on the eye and pushing suddenly and vigorously downwards. The aim was to break the fine ligaments which held the lens in place, and allow it to fall out of

---

[134] Luke 13: 10-13

[135] Mark 8: 22-25

The Way to Christianity

the line of sight. Jesus' first attempt was only partially successful, and *'people looking like trees walking'* is exactly what would have been expected. The partially displaced lens would have induced a prismatic effect, which would elongate the vertical image, hence 'trees walking.' The second attempt wholly displaced the lens and restored vision. Since the lens has some optical power, seeing 'everything clearly' is probably a bit optimistic and there are complications to the procedure.[136] But compared to a dense cataract, it must have been a huge improvement.

How Jesus acquired his knowledge of folk medicine is not known. The usual practice was for neophytes to be inducted through a form of apprenticeship. Since the details of Jesus' early life have not come down to us there is no way of knowing how Jesus acquired his undoubted skills.

Exorcism

Alongside his faith and folk healing Jesus was a noted exorcist. In antiquity little was known of mental illness and strange and unusual behaviour was often attributed to possession by demons, and many faith healers acted as exorcists. The gospels give a number of accounts of Jesus' exorcisms, perhaps the best known being the 'Gerasene swine.'

A naked man, who was frequently shackled, lived amongst tombs rather than in a house. Upon encountering the man, Jesus commanded the unclean spirits to come out of him and reside instead in a large herd of swine who were feeding nearby. The swine then rushed down a bank into a lake and were drowned.[137]

There are a number of other accounts of exorcisms carried out by Jesus typically involving a command for the demons to leave the affected individual. In one case this is reported to have had the additional benefit of restoring speech to a man who was previously mute.[138] The combination of faith and folk healing, together with his abilities as an exorcist, must have made Jesus a popular and respected figure. As such,

---

[136] Ademola-Popoola. D.S, Owdete J.F. Traditional couching for cataract treatment. (2004) West Afr J Med (2004) 208-210.

[137] Luke 8: 26-33

[138] Luke 11: 14

the gospel accounts of large numbers of the sick seeking Jesus' help are undoubtedly accurate, but at the heart of his mission lay his spiritual teachings.

Jesus' Teachings

All the gospels describe Jesus as an itinerant teacher, who proclaimed his message both in the open and in Synagogues. Since Jesus was not a Pharisee this may seem strange, but this was not necessarily so. Two thousand years ago Synagogues were Sabbath meeting-houses with rows of benches often facing each other (in much the same way as the seating in the British Houses of Parliament). At least part of the service seems to have consisted of a religious discussion, in which the congregation took part. Jesus' contribution to the service must have been immensely impressive. His central message was John's prophesy:

> *'But go rather to the lost sheep of the house of Israel. As you go proclaim the good news. The kingdom of heaven has come near.'* [139]

By way of preparation, Jews should obey the law with particular diligence:

> *'Do not think that I have come to abolish the law of the prophets, I have come not to abolish but to fulfil. For truly I tell you, until heaven and earth pass away not one letter, not one stroke of a letter will pass from the law until it is accomplished. Therefore whoever breaks one of the least of these commandments, and teaches others to do the same, will be called least in the kingdom of heaven; but whoever does them and teaches them will be called great in the kingdom of heaven.'* [140]

---

[139] Matthew 10: 5-7

[140] Matthew 5: 17-19

According to the traditions of the Hasidim, what was required was not simple compliance, but a whole-hearted fulfilment of the spirit of the law:

> *'You have heard that it was said to those of ancient time, you shall not murder ... But I say to you that if you are angry with a brother or sister you will be liable to judgement,'* [141]

and, in a similar manner:

> *'You have heard that it was said you shall not commit adultery. But I say to you that everyone who looks at a woman with lust has committed adultery with her in his heart,'* [142]

and, in a final example:

> *'You have heard that it was said, you shall love your neighbour and hate your enemy. But I say to you love your enemies and pray for those who persecute you.'* [143]

In one essential respect Jesus' spiritual teaching differed from John's; whilst John favoured redemption and the atonement of sin, Jesus' simpler message was 'follow me':

> *'Come to me, all you that are weary and are carrying heavy burdens and I will give you rest. Take my yoke upon you, and learn from me; for I am gentle and humble in heart, and you will find rest for your souls for my yoke is easy and my burden is light.'* [144]

The reasons for Jesus' emphasis on himself as a conduit or 'shepherd' are not clear, but may reflect his immersion experiences at the hands of John. Later accounts suggest that during his immersion Jesus underwent a transcending and life changing experience. It may have convinced him

---

[141] Matthew 5: 21-22

[142] Matthew 5: 27-28

[143] Mathew 5: 43-44

[144] Matthew 11: 28-30

that the 'kingdom of God' had begun and that he had been admitted to it. Whatever the reason, Jesus' message may have had less appeal than John's: For Jews, God's love and redemption was freely available to all, without the need of an intermediary.

Parables

In preparation for the final judgement it was important that Jews obeyed not just the letter, but also the spirit of the law. Jesus described what God wanted, not just by exhortation, but also in a series of parables. As the American scholar Ed Saunders has shown,[145] the parables, which are almost certainly correctly attributed to Jesus, are quite extraordinary. Although the immediate context of the parables has been lost, their power and vividness has transcended two millennia and they remain an unquenchable source of religious inspiration.

In a culture that had no representative visual art, the power of religious literature and oratory were highly regarded. As such, the parables illustrate the pinnacle of Jewish rhetorical expression, providing moral fables of immense vividness and clarity. Without their contemporary context some of the imagery seems obscure to present day readers, indeed, many have claimed that this was intentionally so, to provoke a questioning response in the hearer and leave space for subjective interpretation. However, the parables were clearly intended as verbal illustrations for a largely illiterate peasant Jewish audience. What is remarkable is not that, without their context, some seem 'difficult' to interpret, but rather that their power remains essentially undiminished.

Jesus' visits to the small towns and villages of Galilee and adjacent areas probably only lasted a few days, although the impact of his work there has clearly endured. The third, perhaps best-known, aspect of his mission is that which has probably contributed most to his enduring mythology, and that is his 'miracles.'

Miracles are a matter of faith, and are not really amenable to historical analysis. Many writers have observed that most, if not all, miracles have a rational basis, but this misses the point. Even if the mechanism of a miracle can be shown, the timing and the causative

---

[145] Saunders E.P. Davies M. Studying the Synoptic Gospels. SCM Press (1989) 174-186

agent cannot. This is where faith comes in. For those who believe the 'causative agent' is God, knowing the mechanism does not alter the miraculous nature of the event.

Jesus' mission lasted for a minimum of somewhat less than a year, and a maximum of three years. In that time he successfully evaded the agents of Herod Antipas, and possibly those of the temple authorities as well. Yet, in his final week, he chose to go to Jerusalem and proclaim his mission in a very public place. Why was this? Was he expecting God's arrival, or even trying to provoke it? We do not know because the religious interpretation of the crucifixion has so deeply overlaid events that the underlying history cannot be recovered.

The Last Week

All male Jews were required to attend the three major festivals at the temple each year. Probably the best attended was Passover, when the population of Jerusalem increased from approximately fifty thousand to perhaps three to four hundred thousand.[146] It was during the festival of Passover that Jesus was executed, probably in 30 or 33CE.

The great majority of people attending a festival would arrive a week early, to rid themselves of ritual impurity acquired since their last visit. There were a number of causes of impurity, amongst the most common being proximity to a corpse.[147] The accounts we have of Jesus' last visit to Jerusalem suggest that he also arrived a week early, and at least some of his preparations involved a degree of secrecy. Why this was so is not clear, although it may indicate difficulties with the Temple authorities on earlier visits.

One thing that was far from secret was his initial entry into the city. Jesus is reported to have triumphantly entered the city riding on an ass. If this is historically reliable, Jesus could have been consciously fulfilling a prophecy found in Zechariah:

---

[146] Saunders E.P. The Historical Figure of Jesus. Penguin Press (1993) 249

[147] Numbers 9: 9-10

> *'Rejoice greatly, oh daughters of Zion, shout aloud oh daughters of Jerusalem, lo your King comes to you; triumphant and victorious is he, and riding on a donkey.'* [148]

In doing this Jesus was making a public statement, which would have been understood by his fellow Jews. Put simply, it was 'the King has arrived.' This was an audacious, and, from a Roman perspective, highly provocative act. A further provocation may have been Jesus publically preaching of his message. As an illustration, he seems to have suggested that all earthly kingdoms would be swept away and even the great Temple in which he was standing would be replaced by one built by God. From the Roman viewpoint this was not just provocative, it was seditious.

Perhaps because of the high profile and potentially inflammatory nature of his arrival in Jerusalem, Jesus took some care subsequently to avoid easy detection. As preparation for the Passover meal, Jesus asked one of his followers to follow a man carrying a pitcher of water to the house where the meal was to take place. Carrying water was normally done by women, and a man would have stood out and been easy to follow.[149]

After the last meal, Jesus and his followers slept in a small cave, normally occupied by an olive press. At some point he was arrested, either by Temple guards or Roman auxiliary troops. Following arrest he seems to have been interviewed by the High Priest, Joseph Ben Caiaphas, possibly in the house of his father in law, Ananus, who was also present. However, we do not know why this interview took place; Roman standing orders almost certainly required the Jewish authorities to hand over 'trouble makers' at the first opportunity. Perhaps Jesus was being given an opportunity to escape death by repudiating his central message, or perhaps Caiaphas simply wished to confirm Jesus' identity. Either action would be consistent with what is known of Caiaphas' qualities as an administrator. In any event Jesus was held briefly, before appearing before the Roman authorities.

---

[148] Zechariah 9: 9

[149] Luke 22: 10-12

The Way to Christianity

The biblical account of what happened next is not consistent with Roman legal custom and practice and, as such, is rather implausible. From a Roman point of view, Jesus was an unimportant peasant troublemaker charged with the capital offence of sedition. Taken before Roman legal authorities in the morning, his trial would have lasted a few minutes before the inevitable sentence.

It is unlikely that the Roman Prefect Pontius Pilate was directly involved. Passover was a time of high anxiety for the Roman authorities, with the arrival of the Jewish Messiah traditionally associated with the festival. As such, Pilate was likely to have been to busy to deal personally with what he would have regarded as a minor matter, although he was likely to have confirmed the sentence before it was carried out. Prisoners were routinely tortured prior to death and forced to walk to the place of their execution.

The site of Jesus' crucifixion is not known. Prior to the first Jewish war the area surrounding Jerusalem was fairly heavily wooded. Since the Roman army did not go in for unnecessary carpentry, Jesus would probably have been crucified by being nailed or tied to an olive tree,[150] or, in the event of no suitable branch, to a cross member mounted on a tree. The partial remains of one crucified victim have been archaeologically recovered and they show that the victim had his ankles nailed to either side of a trunk.[151] Jesus may well have suffered the same fate.

During crucifixion the upper body was supported by nailing, or tying, the wrists to a branch, or cross beam. Death was agonisingly slow, each breath necessitating the body being flexed against the supporting nails. Following death it was Roman custom to leave the body to decompose and be consumed by carrion until the few remaining bones were discarded on the town rubbish heap. Since Jesus was executed by auxiliary Roman troops acting under Roman military orders, it may be a reasonable assumption that this is what happened to his remains.

There is an obvious discrepancy between what is known of Roman crucifixion customs, and the biblical account of Jesus' death. Not only is the intervention of Pilate unlikely, there is no 'cross,' no internment

---

[150] Acts 10: 39

[151] The Crucified Man from Giv'at Ha-Mivtar. Israel Exploration (1985) J 35 (1) 22-27

in a tomb, no stone rolled away from the entrance to the cave on the 'third day' and no role for Mary Magdalene or the female relatives of Jesus. If Jesus' death did indeed follow the normal pattern there is no way to 'square this circle.' Perhaps the most that can be said is that there are two viewpoints. One based on historical customs and the other on religious traditions. In the introduction to this book I outlined my view that 'Christian History' is religious interpretation based, rather loosely in places, on the events that occurred. Probably nowhere is the discrepancy more apparent than in the details of the crucifixion.

Christians may find this very brief account of Jesus' life and death puzzling and perhaps even offensive, and I should perhaps underscore that it is not my intent to appear dismissive of his significance. Historically Jesus was a remarkably charismatic Jew, who briefly led a small Jewish revivalist movement, however, *at that time*, even within the movement he was not the most significant individual. That position might be shared between the movement's founder, John, and Jesus' brother James, who developed the movement over a period of almost three decades after Jesus' death. This is not to say that Jesus was unimportant, but that his importance lies in his iconic status in the gentile religion founded in his name, rather than a particularly high profile attained within his own lifetime.

Following his death, Jesus' small group of followers left Jerusalem and returned to Galilee, doubtless taking cover amongst large crowds leaving Jerusalem. On the road to Galilee, or in Galilee itself, they experienced visions and other manifestations of Jesus' presence. How they viewed these experiences is not known. Jewish religious mythology contains a number of instances of resurrected prophets and it is likely that the visions reinforced the possibility that Jesus was indeed a great prophet. However, any hopes that they may have been nurturing of Jesus as the Messiah sent to herald the 'last days' must, at this point, have been dashed. As Geza Vermes has pointed out: *'neither the death, nor the resurrection of the Messiah formed part of the beliefs and expectations of the Jews in the first century AD.'* [152]

---

[152] Vermes G. The Authentic Gospel of Jesus. Allan Lane Penguin Press. (2003) 387. For a recent authoritative account of the Family of Jesus see Tabour J. The Jesus Dynasty (2006) Harper Element.

The Way to Christianity

The immediate events following John and Jesus' deaths are uncertain, although it would be understandable if members of the movement went into hiding. At about the same time the conditions in Galilee rapidly deteriorated when the area was successfully invaded by the Nabataean King Aretas, enraged at his daughter's betrayal by Herod Antipas. It took some time for Roman legions from Syria to reverse the occupation, and restore order. When we next meet the Followers of The Way, they are in Jerusalem under a new leader.

Leadership After Jesus' Death

There are two candidates for the leadership of The Way after Jesus' death, the disciple Simon Peter and Jesus' brother James.

Simon Peter. Claims for Simon Peter's leadership are based on three passages found in the Christian Bible:

In the Gospel attributed to Mathew, Jesus tells Peter *'You are Peter and on this rock I will build my Church.'* [153]

As with so many religious prophecies this statement was composed at a later date. At the time that Jesus is reported to have said these words there were no Christian Churches in existence. It was only some forty to fifty years later, around the time that Matthew was written, that the seminal Churches of Christianity began to evolve from Paul's House Assemblies. In short, the words about Peter's promotion should be credited not to Jesus but to Matthew, or his editor, in 80CE or later.[154]

Paul's letter to the Galatians refers to the *'three pillars'* of the Jerusalem leadership as *'Peter, John and James.'* [155] This sequence of names is held to be significant, with Peter's name appearing first to indicate leadership, whilst the first ten chapters of Acts give the impression of Peter leading the movement (although nowhere is this explicitly stated).

Set against these rather tenuous claims is the position of James:

---

[153] Matthew 16: 18

[154] Vermes G. The Authentic Gospel of Jesus. Allan Lane Penguin Press. (2003) 387

[155] Galatians 2: 9

James Ben Joseph. Following Jesus' death, the customs already referred to would suggest that James, as the oldest male heir, would assume the leadership of the movement. There is evidence that he did so. The gospel of Thomas records Jesus' followers asking about the succession should Jesus die: *'The disciples said to Jesus, we know that you will depart from us. Who is to be our leader?* Jesus said to them: *'Wherever you are, you are to go to James the righteous, for whose sake heaven and earth come into being.'* [156]

The apocryphal and largely Ebionite document known as the Pseudo Clementine Recognitions also sites James as the new leader of The Way: *'Therefore on the following day James the Bishop went up to the Temple with us, and with the whole church.'* [157] The event which is being referred to was an open-air meeting on the steps of the Temple attended by the High Priest, Joseph Ben Caiaphas. Since Caiaphas was replaced as High Priest in 36CE, James was clearly in post before that date.

Clement of Alexandria places James as the first 'Bishop' of Jerusalem after his brother's death:

> *'After the ascension of the saviour, Peter, James and John did not claim pre-eminence because the saviour had specially honoured them, but chose James the Just as Bishop of Jerusalem.'* [158]

Hegesippus, the early church historian of the second century, also records the leadership of the movement after Jesus' death: *'The succession of the Church passed to James the brother of the Lord.'* [159]

---

[156] Robinson J.M. ed The Nag Hammadi Library. Harper Collins (1990) 127

[157] Anon. The Recognition of Clement. (2006) compassionate spirit.com/recignitions/book-1.htm

[158] Clement of Alexandria: Preserved as a quotation by Eusebius Ecclesiastical History 2.1. 2-5

[159] Hegesippus. Preserved as a quotation by Eusebius Ecclesiastical History. 2.23.4.

Simon Peter or James?

The claim for Simon Peter's leadership of the movement after Jesus' death is, in my view, rather tenuous and reflected the needs of the Church rather than historical reality. The emerging Roman Church sought 'authority' for their teaching through the person of Peter and emphasised his primacy. This, however, is not to say that he was not one of the three pillars referred to by Paul. Clearly he was one of the most important, if not the most important, of Jesus' followers. Yet we lack a single source that categorically places Peter at the head of the movement. In contrast, there are four independent sources that clearly and explicitly place James as the next leader of the movement. Such numbers and uniformity of sources are unusual in the ancient literature, although their congruity is rather characteristic of references to James.

On balance, the weight of the sources lies heavily in James' favour.

The Family of Jesus and James

The relationship between Jesus and James was to cause problems for later Christianity. Their mother, Mary, is known to have had five sons and at least two daughters,[160] which made later church claims for the 'perpetual virginity of Mary' more than a little difficult. The problem was approached in two different ways: The Catholic Church opted for reclassifying Jesus' brothers and sisters as cousins rather than siblings;[161] whilst the Orthodox Church decided that Jesus' brothers and sisters must be the product of a previous marriage by Joseph, Jesus' father.[162] The position adopted by the Catholic Church is historically untenable, whilst the position of the Orthodox Church has no historical support.

James is mentioned in a large number of sources, which are surprisingly consistent in their assertions: James is clearly identified as Jesus' brother and is also reported to have been a Temple Priest.

---

[160] Matthew 13: 55-56

[161] Chilton B. and Neusner J. The Brother of Jesus. Westminster. John Knox (2001) 20-22

[162] Ibid 16-20

Priesthood, as has been noted, was at this time a hereditary position, with holders belonging to one of twenty-four courses, or extended families. A stone inscription of a somewhat later date, lists one of these courses as coming from Nazareth.

A review of the textual references to James leads to a sense of his character: He was a deeply pious and religious Jew, who in many ways had more in common with his cousin John than his charismatic brother Jesus. He is reputed to have been a lifelong celibate and, very unusually for his time, was also a vegan. He also appears to have carried these ascetic practices in his attire, and was said to have worn a cloak of unbleached linen, held in place with a woollen belt.

James appears to have lived in Jerusalem, possibly with his mother Mary. If he was indeed a Temple priest he would have been required for Temple duty for less than one month a year, yet he prayed there every day. It was said that constant prayer affected his knees to the extent that they became like those of a camel.[163] Some ideas of his spiritual life can be gained from the letter of James included in the Christian bible, which also contains a letter from another of Jesus' brothers, Jude. (Chapter 7)

Trial Before the Sanhedrin

Both John and Jesus had been executed as a matter of political expediency. If the future leadership of The Way was not to share the same fate, it needed to establish its legitimacy, which it did by appearing before the great Jewish court, the Sanhedrin, in Jerusalem. Whether this came about by the followers constantly praying in the Temple, or whether it was deliberately instigated by James, we do not know. The Christian bible describes the former, with the person of James oddly absent, but both are possible.[164] In any event, the trial duly took place, on a charge of blasphemy, for which the punishment was death.

Acts describes the noted Pharisee Gamial defending the Followers of The Way. Although the speech attributed to Gamial seems apocryphal, his support is not wholly implausible,[165] as the restoration to health of his

---

[163] Details by Hegesippus preserved in Eusebius Ecclesiastical History 2.23.3

[164] Acts 5: 27-32

[165] Acts 5: 33-39

The Way to Christianity

son by Hanina Ben Dosa, may well have inclined Gamial to movements that included faith healers.

In any event the case was dismissed and The Way became a somewhat contentious part of normative Judaism. This presented problems for the Jewish authorities, who had to accommodate a movement whose first two leaders had been executed. We have one account of an apparent attempt by the High Priest, Joseph Ben Caiaphas to achieve this end.[166] He reportedly held a public meeting on the Temple steps, in an attempt to accommodate the new movement. Such an action is plausible and consistent with what is known of Caiaphas' character. What is also consistent is a violent attack on this meeting by a man, who, it has been suggested, was Paul of Tarsus.

Circumstantial evidence suggests that the decision of the Sanhedrin was not universally accepted by the entire High Priesthood. A dominant faction, led by the former high priest Ananus, seems to have been irredeemably opposed to The Way. If this was the case, it seems likely that this was the faction that supported Paul in his initial persecution of the sect.

Whatever the validity of this argument, the immediate outlook for James was serious. During the attack he fell, or was thrown, down the Temple steps, breaking both legs. His followers took him to Mary's house in Jerusalem where it was discovered that he was not dead, as they had feared.

As soon as he was well enough to travel, James was taken to Jericho where it was hoped he would be safe. Jericho was on the ancient trade route to Damascus and thus provides a reason for Paul of Tarsus' famous journey, which otherwise seems an odd choice of destination. Fortunately for James, Paul experienced a conversion,[167] or at least a change of heart, on the Damascus road, and James suffered no further harm.

How long James remained in Jericho is not known, but it may have been some time. Not only did his broken bones have to heal, his muscles would also have had to regain their former strength. One of the duties

---

[166] The Recognition of Clement (2006) Compasionatespirit.com/recognitions/book-1 htm

[167] Acts 9: 3-9

of a Temple Priest was the slaughter and butchery of sacrificial animals as noted by the Jewish writer and philosopher Philo who witnessed the Temple ceremonies. He describes the priests carrying out their duties in silence and with great reverence.[168] The work was so arduous that teams of priests rotated between periods of sacrifice to allow periods of rest through the day.

As soon as he was fully recovered James returned to Jerusalem. At this point he began to develop the Jerusalem Synagogue and dispatched missionaries to some of the major cities of the Eastern Mediterranean. Probably the best known is Simon Peter who established a Synagogue in Antioch.

Numbers are always difficult in antiquity, but at this time perhaps 15% of the population of the Eastern Empire was Jewish. There was clearly some urgency in bringing the message of the imminence of the 'last days' to the whole Jewish community, and to facilitate the rapid spread of this central message James provided his missionaries with letters of authority. Jesus had been a charismatic holy man, but James was becoming the leader and administrator of an expanding organisation.[169] He became known as 'James the Just,' and was clearly held in considerable respect over the next twenty-five to thirty years.

As the community in Jerusalem grew, a council of seventy-two elders was appointed and other traditional features of Synagogue life began to appear.[170] The Sabbath congregation was said to number 'thousands.' This is almost certainly an exaggeration, although worshippers numbering in the hundreds are plausible (Chapter 10.) However, for James, as with his cousin John before him, success had its dangers.

In the spring of 62CE the Roman Prefect of Jewish Palestine died in office. Before his replacement could arrive, the High Priest Ananus Ben Ananus, the son of Ananus, who had been so opposed to The Way, brought a wholly fraudulent charge of blasphemy against James. In a

---

[168] Schurer E. The history of the Jewish People in the Age of Jesus Christ. (1874) Revised English text Vermes G. Millar F. Goodman M. Black M. Eds T & T Clark. (1987) 2 292-308

[169] Acts 15: 1

[170] Acts 21: 18

rigged court, the charge was upheld and James was stoned to death. As this action had not been sanctioned by Rome, Ananus may have been acting beyond his remit.[171] Upon being informed that the next Roman Prefect was approaching Jerusalem, Ananus hurried to meet him. We do not know the details of the Governor's response, but it does not seem to have been particularly hostile. However, Ananus' subsequent dismissal by King Agrippa, after only three months in office, may possibly have been as a result of his role in James' death.

The stoning of James has been given as the cause of the Jewish revolt against Rome. This is almost certainly an oversimplification. The abuse of power by a succession of Prefects and the widespread hope of God's intervention in world affairs appears more historically compelling, but the unjustified execution of James cannot have helped. In any event his death brought about a need for a replacement.

Simeon Ben Clopas

The choice of a new leader fell to Simeon Ben Clopas, a member of the extended family of Jesus and James.[172] Simeon, or Simon as he is now more commonly known, was soon faced with a crucial decision. An oracle, probably in fact a member of a Galilean resistance movement, advised Simon to leave Jerusalem, upon which Simon and an unknown number of followers left for Pella, a town some way north of Jerusalem located on the eastern banks of the River Jordan (fig 4.2). Pella was later to become an Ebionite centre after the traumas of the Jewish uprising were over.

---

[171] Josephus F. Antiquities 20. 197-202

[172] Bauckham R. Jude and the Relatives of Jesus in the Early Christian Church. T & T Clark (1990) 79-94

John Larke

Figure 4.2 Locations of Pella and Jerusalem

Shortly after 66CE an uprising against Rome broke out that has come to be known by Jews as the 'first Jewish war.' The revolt met with initial success and Rome was evicted from many parts of Jewish Palestine, including Jerusalem. However, the leadership of the uprising became increasingly fractured and internecine disputes diluted the effectiveness of the fighting forces. Gradually Rome reasserted control and, after a protracted siege, Jerusalem fell in 70CE. Whether by accident or design the Temple was set on fire and burnt to the ground.

The Way to Christianity

To this day the destruction of the second Temple remains one of the most traumatising events of Judaism. It marks the beginning of the end of a Jewish homeland for almost nineteen hundred years. It also had particular significance for the Followers of The Way, for it had not resulted, or been precipitated by, God's arrival. The imminence of this arrival, itself the *raison d'être* for The Way and its followers, must then have been thrown into dramatic question.

The two Jewish uprisings, for a second was to break out sixty-three years later, spelt the end of second Temple Judaism. Only the Judaism of the moderate Pharisees, the forerunners of modern Rabbinic Judaism, was to survive. (Chapter 2)

For Simeon and the remaining Followers of The Way the outlook was bleak. It seems likely that he returned to Jerusalem, as he is included in a list of 'Bishops' of that city.[173] The 'Bishops' were in fact all Jewish until the second uprising against Rome. The church historian Eusebius, writing in the fourth century cites an account of Roman persecution of the 'House of David' in the aftermath of the first Jewish war, however, Simeon is recorded as living until the time of the Emperor Trajan, when he was martyred, probably between 93-103CE.

This may not have been the end of the involvement of the extended family of Jesus in the leadership of The Way. At least two 'Bishops Lists' of the early Jerusalem 'Church' are extant, both of which contain fifteen names.[174] The first two names are those of James and Simeon, whilst the remaining thirteen names, up to the second Jewish war, are all Jewish. After the end of the Jewish uprising against Rome only Gentile names are found.

Richard Bauckham[175] has proposed that the third 'Bishop' of Jerusalem, who was named Justus, was a relative of Jesus, whilst the remaining twelve names were those of his followers. In my view this

---

[173] Ibid 70-79

[174] Eusebius Ecclesiastical History. 4: 5. 3-4 and 5: 12. 1-2. Also Epiphanius Pan 62: 21-22

[175] Bauckham R. Jude and the Relatives of Jesus in the Early Church. (1990) T & T Clark. Edinburgh 70-73

proposition is entirely plausible although it should be said that it lacks any ancient source.

If Justus was the last leader of The Way then a complete list of the successive leaders and disciples/missionaries of the sect can be drawn up: figure 4.3.

THE WAY:
LEADERS AND PROBABLE DISCIPLES/MISSIONARIES

Date	Names
	JOHN
23 approx.-29	**Disciples:** Jesus, James, Andrew, Simon Peter,
	JESUS
29 approx.- Either 30 or 33	**Disciples:** James, Simon Peter, Andrew, John, Phillip, Bartholomew, Thomas, Matthew, James, Thaddeus, Simon, Judas.
	JAMES
approx. 30 or 33-62	**Probable missionaries accredited by James:** Simon Peter, Andrew, Thomas, John, Phillip, Bartholomew, Mark (Paul was not accredited by James, and became a self-appointed missionary to the Gentiles.)
	SIMEON
62 to approx. 100	Names of followers are not known.
	JUSTUS (JUDAS)
100 to approx. 132	**Followers:** Tobias, Benjamin, John, Mathias, Phillip, Zacchaeus, Seneca, Justus, Levi, Ephres, Joseph, Judas.

Figure 4.3. The Way: Leaders and probable disciples/missionaries

The Decline of the Way

Even before Simeon's demise the movement was already in slow and irreversible decline, and at some point the division between the Nazarenes and the Ebionites became more pronounced, with the Ebionites probably emerging as the predominant group within the sect.

The trauma of the loss of the two wars of independence against Rome had adverse and far-reaching effects across Judaism. The movement of the Nazarenes was vilified in a Jewish daily prayer, although the date of this excoriation is uncertain.[176] Remarkably, the movement, of which Jesus was a spiritual leader and teacher, was declared heretical by emerging Christianity in the second century.

The last reference to the Ebionites in Christian literature appears in Cyprus in the fourth century. A Cypriot Bishop, Epiphanius questioned a group of Ebionites, who claimed descent from The Way. Epiphanius did not believe them and asserted that they were the followers of a heretical prophet Ebion. However, this is not the last historical reference to the Ebionites: Travelling in the eleventh century, an Arab Muslim Abd Al Jabbar came across a group of Ebionites, noting their reverence for their prophet, John the Baptist.

If the origins of Christianity are not to be found in The Way, how did they come about? For the answer to that question we must turn to the cosmopolitan town of Tarsus, situated on what is now the southern coast of Turkey. One of its inhabitants was a small unprepossessing Jew, with some form of 'affliction' who became known as 'Paul of Tarsus.'

It may be unacceptable for Christians to recognise that Jesus was not concerned, in any way at all, with the religion founded in his name. Indeed, his actions were the antithesis of those outlined in many Christian Church histories. Rather than playing a role in the creation of a new religion, he devoted his life to the 'last days' of Judaism, a religion that was already old two thousand years ago. His death resulted directly from his prophecy of the imminent replacement of the Roman Empire by a Kingdom of the Jewish God YHWH. In Roman eyes this

---

[176] Schurer E. The history of the Jewish People in the age of Jesus Christ (1874). Revised English text Vermes G Millar F.Goodman.M. Black M. Eds. T & T Clark (1979) 11 454-463.

The Way to Christianity

was nothing less than sedition and Jesus was killed in the most public and agonising way possible.

It is sometimes argued that, but for the disruption of the two Jewish uprisings, The Way would have prospered and formed a significant part of modern Judaism. This, however, appears highly unlikely given that the central prophecy of John, Jesus, James, Simeon and Justus turned out to be wrong. God did not—and two thousand years later, still has not—come. It may be uncomfortable for many Christians to acknowledge that Jesus, the inspirational and iconic figure of their religion was wrong, but in simple terms he was.

Chapter 5

PAUL OF TARSUS

Brought up in the city of Tarsus on the Mediterranean coast of what is now south-eastern Turkey; in his younger days Paul was known by his Jewish name Saul. Why he changed his name is not certain, however, whatever his reasons, he was always known to his later Gentile converts as Paul.

Then, as now, Tarsus was a cosmopolitan city of diverse cultures. In Paul's day Hellenism predominated, and the city contained temples to the numerous Gods of classical Greek antiquity. Jews were also numerous, making up a substantial minority of the population.

Paul's family were engaged in tent making, or, perhaps more accurately, in the merchandising of tents, and somewhat unusually they were Roman citizens. How citizenship had been acquired is not known. Many Jews had been taken into Roman slavery following Pompey's successful occupation of Jerusalem in 63 BC. Jewish communities were known for manumission (buying themselves out of slavery), and perhaps Paul's family acquired citizenship in this manner.

Paul's upbringing would have exposed him to a wide variety of cultural influences and, in addition to speaking Hebrew and possibly Aramaic; he also spoke Greek, the lingua franca of his day, although his Greek would have been the Greek of commerce, rather than the elegant Greek of classical literature. At some point, perhaps in his very early teens, Paul was probably sent to Jewish Palestine to study Judaism in one of the Pharisee schools. Later claims that he studied under Gamial, one of the leading Pharisees 'of his day' [177] may simply have been hubris, but it is by no means implausible. If he did study under Gamial, his teacher's tolerance and perceptive humanity does not seem

---

[177] Acts 22: 3

The Way to Christianity

to have greatly influenced Paul, for throughout his life he remained dogmatically assertive and intolerant of the views of others. This even included Jesus' brother James and Jesus' former disciples, whose first-hand knowledge of Jesus did nothing to temper Paul's assertions about the man he had never met.

Paul developed his own fiercely independent views, which radically changed Jesus' message and central teachings. In doing so Paul seems to have been untroubled by even the smallest scintilla of self-doubt. This characteristic of absolute certainty was perhaps unsurprisingly to find itself reflected in the religion as it emerged, and, over time, became a cause for great human suffering.

Initially, Paul was violently opposed to The Way and obtained some form of official remit to persecute the movement. How this came about is uncertain, but it may have been granted by a member of the family of the former High Priest Ananus,[178] who strongly disapproved of the new movement. Paul also claimed a distant relationship to the Herodian family,[179] and this may have helped him to obtain at least quasi-official status as a persecutor.

Amongst his early actions was participation in the stoning of a follower of The Way called Stephan. Since stoning to death was the punishment for blasphemy, Stephan had clearly been found guilty of this crime. The process of stoning is not wholly clear, but one likely option is that the victim was placed in a pit and a single stone of considerable weight was dropped upon them. In any event, Acts claims that, the instigators of this action laid their coats at Paul's feet whilst Stephan was put to death.[180] This and other actions would have made him a feared figure in the growing community of The Way.

The next account of Paul's activity is supported by only a single source, but it is consistent with his actions. A marginal note in an account of a debate on the Temple steps between the High Priest Caiaphas Ben Joseph and James, attributes the disruption of this event to Paul. After the

---

[178] Acts 4: 1

[179] Romans 16: 11

[180] Acts 7: 58

attack, the injured James was taken to Jericho to escape persecution.[181] As noted earlier, Jericho was on the old trade route to Damascus, and it is on the road to Damascus that we next encounter Paul.

Conversion and Aftermath

The conversion of Paul on the road to Damascus is so well known that it has entered into popular culture. The account of a 'blinding light' and the voice of Jesus asking why Paul was persecuting him can only be found in the book of Acts.[182] Paul himself suggests that *"God revealed his son to me"* [183] and that he had seen *"Jesus our Lord,"* [184] but leaves the details unclear. Whatever the circumstances, the effect was profound.

Arriving in Damascus, Paul renounced his role of persecutor and sought to accommodate himself within The Way. Unsurprisingly there was some scepticism towards his new-found faith, and, according to Acts, his life was in danger.

Paul is reported to have escaped from Damascus by being lowered in a basket from the city walls.[185] Such baskets were normally used to bring food into cities when the gates were closed at night and Paul's small size may have been useful on this occasion—indeed, one writer has suggested that Paul was a nickname for small.[186] Whatever the validity of this idea, Paul escaped and travelled to 'Arabia' for the next two or three years.[187]

Paul's time in Arabia may be equivalent to similar periods spent in the desert by John Ben Zechariah and Flavius Josephus, however, it remains a blank page for us, as he does not refer to it in his letters and

---

[181] The Recognition of Clement (2006) Compassionatespirit.com/Recognitions/Book-1htm

[182] Acts 9: 3-4

[183] 1 Galatians 1: 16

[184] 1 Corinthians 9: 1

[185] Acts 9: 23-25

[186] Wilson A.N. Paul. Random House (1997) 29.

[187] Galatians 1: 17

The Way to Christianity

there is no description in Acts. It is possible though that this time for Paul may have represented a period of inner contemplation, leading to a sense of future direction in his spiritual life.

It was probably during this period that Paul began to develop his view of Jesus: a man whom he had not met and about whose life he apparently knew very little. It may also have been during this period that Paul acquired 'secret books' which he kept with him for the rest of his life.[188] The contents and origins of these books are quite unknown; they may have helped Paul formulate his opinion of the significance of Jesus' life, but it is not possible to describe the rate at which his view of Jesus changed.

Initially, Paul seems to have come to a rapid view that Jesus was the promised Messiah. However, this immediately posed a problem, for nowhere in Jewish literature was there a belief in a crucified and subsequently risen, human Messiah. For someone assiduously schooled in Pharisaic Judaism, this presented considerable problems. Judaism was, and is, an 'organic' religion, based in large measure on religious precedent. Did Paul move outside the confines of the Jewish thought and utilise Pagan concepts to explain what otherwise seemed inexplicable? We cannot of course know, but in his birthplace of Tarsus, he would have been exposed to a wide range of Pagan beliefs on an almost daily basis.

Following the time spent in Arabia, Paul travelled to Jerusalem and met James and Peter.[189] The details of the meeting are not known, but if the account of a previous attack on James is historically reliable, then an apology would seem to have been in order, as well as assurances as to his future conduct. Curiously Paul seems not to have enquired into the details of Jesus' life, or, if he did, makes little later reference to it.

Leaving Jerusalem, perhaps accompanied by a companion, Barnabas, Paul does not appear to have immediately taken up his life's missionary work. He was perhaps preoccupied with his views of the religious significance of Jesus' death. He may also have been subject to 'experiences of Jesus.' The exact form these experiences took are not clear, and it is not known if they were auditory, visual or both, or whether

---

[188] 2 Timothy 4: 13

[189] Galatians 1: 18-19

they took the form of dreams. Whatever their form, the implication from Paul's letters is that he had a number, perhaps many, of these experiences, and that their effect was life-changing. Paul's assertion that he had been crucified with Jesus shows just how strong was the insight he felt he had into Jesus' life through these 'experiences.'[190]

The Risen Messiah

Paul's view that Jesus was the promised Messiah who would herald God's arrival at the 'end time' of Judaism was highly contentious, but not necessarily heretical. However, his view that Jesus had risen from the dead and was now communicating and guiding him, was deeply controversial and probably unacceptable to the majority of Jews of Paul's day. However, Paul went further: as a recent convert to The Way he believed that the 'end time' of Judaism was imminent, and likely to occur in his own lifetime.[191] Thus, for Jesus to play the role of Messiah in the 'end time' scenario, he would have to return to earth again. There is no precedent at all in Jewish religious literature for this 'second coming.' Thus in proposing this role for Jesus, Paul was beginning to move outside the rather broad limits of Second Temple Judaism.

There can be little doubt that Paul proposed Jesus' second coming to account for his personal experiences of what he believed to be the risen Jesus. Similarly, with hindsight, there can also be little doubt that in proposing the role of a returning Messiah for Jesus, Paul was sowing the first seeds of what was to become a new religion: Christianity. Additionally—and with echoes of the prior unwitting participation of Jesus and the other leaders of The Way in the establishment of the religion of Christianity—this was an act, which he had been aware of it, he would almost certainly have denigrated.

As with all Jews, Paul accepted God's creation of the world and all it contained. He believed that sin had been introduced as a result of Adam's disobedience in the Garden of Eden. With sin had come death, which remained man's fate since Adam's transgression.[192] Thus, as a

---

[190] Romans 6: 3-8

[191] 1 Corinthians 7: 29-31

[192] Romans 5: 12-17

man, Jesus had died when executed by Roman auxiliary forces. It is possible that Paul had been present in Jerusalem and had witnessed the crucifixion, and the subsequent putrefaction of Jesus' body. Yet now he was subject to 'experiences,' which convinced him that Jesus had overcome death. He had risen, not in a physical form, for Paul believed that 'flesh and blood cannot inherit the kingdom of heaven,'[193] but rather had transformed into a 'spiritual body.'[194]

This process was available to all if they chose to 'put on' Jesus. This conviction for Paul was fundamental, since it meant that for him that Jesus' transformation transcended all that had gone before. It was also a transformation that was available for all, both Jew and non-Jew alike since, claimed Paul, all were descended from Abraham.[195]

Paul's personal theology was attractive, since it offered a means of overcoming death, but it was incomplete. Paul clearly saw sin as a force in the world, yet God had permitted sin to enter his perfect creation. Paul seems to have believed that sin was allowed to remain in the world so that man could be 'tempted,' but his explanation of this, as with a number of other aspects of his theology, does not appear to have been wholly thought through.

However incomplete his ideas, Paul was entirely convinced of the opportunity they offered, and at some point in the late 30's or early 40's CE, Paul set out on his life's work.

The sequence of Paul's early work is not entirely clear. Following his visit to James and Peter in Jerusalem,[196] he encountered difficulties with a group of 'Hellenists' who were attempting to kill him.[197] Who these Hellenists were and why they were attempting to kill Paul is not certain, but in order to protect himself he returned to Tarsus. Sometime later he travelled to Antioch, the third largest city in the Roman Empire. Here he again encountered Peter, who had become an accredited missionary

---

[193] 1 Corinthians 15: 50

[194] 1 Corinthians 15: 44-46

[195] Galatians 3: 6-7

[196] Galatians 1: 18-19

[197] Acts 9: 29

under James. Peter had established a Synagogue of The Way,[198] which may have admitted both Jews and non-Jews.

Paul remained in Antioch for some time and at some point, perhaps encouraged by his companion Barnabas,[199] set out on his missionary work.

Missionary Travels

Paul travelled extensively in his career as a tent dealer, probably covering 10,000 miles in his lifetime, much of it on foot. As conversion took place, his followers gathered for weekly meeting in private houses, which in time became referred to as 'House Assemblies.'

The locations of a number of these assemblies are known, either from Paul's letters or from Acts. Most lay along two of the main trade routes of the Roman Empire. One was a portion of the 'Common Way,' which ran from Tarsus to Ephesus, whilst the second was the Egnation Way, which ran from Byzantium to the Adriatic coast. Paul's mission was confined to four Roman provinces: Macedonia, Galatia, Asia and Achaea. Within these provinces there were house assemblies at: Philippi, Thessalonica, Beroea, Athens, Corinth, Colossae, Laodicea, Ephesus, Hierapolis and Cenchreae, with further possible Galatian assemblies in Antioch, Iconium, Lystia and Derbe. There are some difficulties in combining the locations found in Paul's letters with those recorded in Acts.

Whatever the number and location of Paul's House Assemblies, it is worth bearing in mind that any lost Pauline letters would lead to an underestimate of their actual numbers. The trade routes, provinces and sites of House Assemblies are illustrated in Figure 5.1

---

[198] Acts 13: 1

[199] Acts 13: 2-3

The Way to Christianity

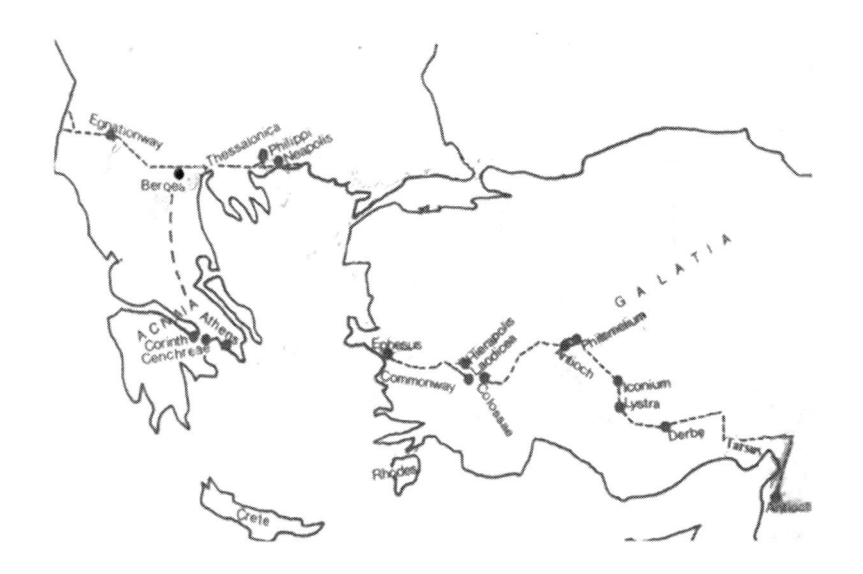

Figure 5.1 Paul's trade routes and House Assemblies

It is conventional to regard Paul as undertaking three missionary journeys.[200] A much better view is to regard him travelling for almost twenty years and making only rare visits outside his missionary area.

An Apostle to the Gentiles

Paul was later to describe himself as 'an Apostle to the Gentiles,' that is to say, to people who were not of Jewish descent.[201] This was probably by default; in his later correspondence Paul described the punishments that he had received at the hands of the Jewish authorities.[202] These punishments were ordered and administered by local Synagogues. Whilst the exact nature of his transgressions has been lost, it seems

---

[200] For an illustration see: May H.G (Ed) Oxford Bible Atlas. Oxford University Press (1962)

[201] Galatians 2: 8-9

[202] Corinthians 11: 24-26

unlikely that the Synagogue authorities would have punished Paul if he had not been attempting to convert Jews during Synagogue services. If true, it's possible that this would have been done in an assertive and repetitious way; Paul was the first to admit that he was no public orator.

If the account of his escape via the lowering of a food basket is reliable, it is likely that Paul was physically small. He also suffered some form of physical infirmity,[203] which he assumed people would find repulsive. Whether this was a skin condition, or some form of physical deformity is not known. Certainly his own description of himself as bodily unappealing, contrast greatly with his accounts of his own abundant energy and perseverance.

If Paul's attempts to win followers by public oratory met with little success, he seems to have had a greater appeal in personal contacts. Ed Saunders' scenario of Paul engaging potential converts in conversation during his dealings as a 'tent maker' is attractive, and seems more plausible than a number of other ideas that have been put forward.[204] Whatever the manner in which he converted his followers, most became members of the early House Assemblies that Paul helped establish.

House Assemblies

The nature and format of Paul's House Assemblies has been extensively examined. As a Jew, it might be expected that Paul's assemblies would follow a Jewish pattern, and to an extent this seems to have been the case. But the limited information that has come down to us also suggests that there were variants on the Jewish model. It has been pointed out that some elements of the assemblies resembled those of philosophical societies with debates and discussion taking place. Such societies were a feature of most large cities in antiquity, and Paul seems to have been attracted to them. He spent two years in Athens debating in the forum with some of the philosophers of his time. Perhaps the model of a Jewish meeting-house, combined with some elements

---

[203] Galatians 4: 13

[204] Saunders E.P. Paul. Oxford University Press (1991) 20

of philosophical societies, is as close as we will get to the nature of the House Assemblies.[205]

Constituency

By his own admission, Paul had little success in converting Jews, and, on the face of it, his conversion of Gentiles seems somewhat improbable: Why should a non-Jew be converted to a Jewish revivalist movement by a Jew? However, there was one group who may have been particularly susceptible to Paul's persuasive powers. 'God-fearers' were Gentiles who were attracted to at least some elements of Judaism, many of whom lived within Jewish areas and attended Synagogue services—some men even going so far as to be circumcised. That they formed an extensive and widespread group is attested to by a number of sources.[206] However, it should be said that the theory of god-fearers as 'low-hanging fruit' for Paul's conversion constitutes a reasoned speculation, rather than a historically supported view.

The Weekly Meal

Weekly gatherings were a feature of Paul's assemblies and an important feature of these meetings was a communal meal. Later chroniclers were to claim that this was in remembrance of the 'last supper' eaten by Jesus and his followers prior to the crucifixion. Whilst this is by no means implausible, the communal meal may have been no more than a reflection of the pattern of life of Jesus and his followers, who presumably ate together on a regular basis. Whatever its origins, the weekly meal would have helped to bind the small, early groups of Paul's followers together.[207]

There are suggestions that early converts held at least some of their possessions in common. Although it seems unlikely that new members gave everything to the group on joining, some form of contribution,

---

[205] Meeks W.A. The First Urban Christians (1983) 74-84

[206] Josephus F. Antiquities 7.2.20; Cassius D 10 XXXVII; Seneca De Civitate Dev VI 11

[207] Ibid 157-162

which went considerably beyond a 'church collection,' seems to have taken place. Beyond this, little is known of these early House Assemblies; the nature and content of any service that took place has been entirely lost, although it is likely to have followed a Jewish pattern. However, we do know of some of the problems encountered in the early days, as Paul refers to them in his surviving letters.

Some converts in a House Assembly in Thessalonica had died, which was clearly an unanticipated event. Paul, ever resourceful in the face of novel problems, sought to reassure his followers:

> *'But we do not want you to be uninformed brothers and sisters about those who have died, so that you may not grieve as others do who have no hope. For since we believe that Jesus died and rose again, even so through Jesus, God will bring with him those who have died. For this we declare to you, by word of the Lord, that we who are left until the coming of the Lord will by no means precede those who have died. For the Lord himself, with a cry of command with the archangels call and with the sound of God's trumpet will descent from heaven and the dead in Christ will rise first.'* [208]

Perhaps nothing more clearly encapsulates Paul's proselytising efforts in turning a potential problem into a triumph; not only will the dead be resurrected and transformed, but this will happen before the living. Had Paul lived in a later age, political 'spin doctors' would have recognised their own craft in his work. As the number of Paul's converts grew, he was summoned to Jerusalem to discuss his mission.

Appearing Before James and Peter

Characteristically, Paul defined his decision to visit Jerusalem as a 'revelation.' [209] The only account we have of the meeting is Paul's: He claims that discussion took place between himself, James and Peter and agreement was reached. Paul's mission to the Gentiles reportedly

---

[208] Thessalonians 4: 13-16

[209] Galatians 2: 2

received approval from James, who decided that as far as Paul's converts were concerned:

> '... I have reached the decision that we should not trouble those Gentiles who are turning to God, but we should write to them to abstain only from things polluted by idols and from fornication and from whatever has been strangled and from blood.' [210]

This gave clear guidance as far as dietary issues were concerned, and reinforced Paul's own views on 'fornication,' but made no mention of circumcision. That no guidance was given is highly improbable; James was an observant and righteous Jew, who would have rightly regarded the law as central to Judaism, and circumcision as a necessary symbol of the faith. However, James, like his crucified brother and indeed Paul, regarded the 'last days' as imminent, and may have felt that this overrode other considerations. However unlikely this may seem, it cannot be completely ruled out.

What is rather more certain is that Paul received no letter from James authorising his activities. This remained a source of resentment, as James had issued letters to other missionaries who were preaching the message of The Way. Thus, Paul left Jerusalem to fulfil a self-appointed, or in his eyes, a Jesus-inspired, mission.

The issue of circumcision was again raised after Paul had left Jerusalem. Someone had attempted to persuade some of Paul's converts in Galicia to be circumcised. This led to Paul's most vitriolic letter:

> 'You foolish Galatians! Who has bewitched you ... they make much of you, but for no good purpose; they want to exclude you, so that you may make much of them ... Listen! I Paul am telling you that if you let yourselves to circumcised, Christ will be of no benefit to you ... I wish those who unsettle you would castrate themselves!' [211]

---

[210] Acts 15: 19-20

[211] Galatians 3: 1-4: 12

This venomous letter shows that the topic of circumcision was far from resolved. Although Paul was to support the large Jerusalem Synagogue of The Way, particularly during the severe famine that afflicted Jewish Palestine in the 50's CE, the seeds of dissent had been sown.

An Argument with Peter and Barnabas

After some years of travel and missionary work, Paul and Barnabas returned to Antioch. There they again met Peter, who seems by nature to have been a rather amiable individual who, when occasion required it, ate in the company of Gentiles.

In the world of antiquity, animals were commonly offered as a sacrifice in a local Temple, and consumed shortly afterwards. A Jew dining with Gentiles ran the risk of eating food that had previously been offered to one of the numerous Pagan Gods. On one occasion, Peter's tolerant attitude was rapidly curtailed when he heard that people from James were coming to visit him. He then sat apart from the Gentiles who were present, eating his own food.[212] This inflamed Paul, who accused Peter of hypocrisy. In the row that ensued, Barnabas, Paul's long-time companion, took sides with Peter, and this probably made matters even worse. Paul now abandoned Barnabas and continued his life's work with one of his own Gentile followers called Silas.[213]

Further Travels

After Antioch, Paul travelled widely in what are today Turkey and Greece. His proselytising efforts were now wholly confined to Gentiles, although his capacity for upsetting people remained undiminished. In Philipas, he and Silas exorcised a slave girl who had acted as a fortune-teller, causing her to lose her talent for prophecy. The girl's owner complained, and Paul and Silas were brought before the city magistrate and imprisoned.[214] In Ephesus some of Paul's followers were attacked

---

[212] Galatians 2: 11-14

[213] Acts 15: 40

[214] Acts 16: 16-24

by a crowd led by a silversmith, called Demetrius, who complained that Paul's activities were reducing the sale of religious souvenirs of the Goddess Artemis, who had a large Temple in the city.[215]

Paul and Misogynism

If Paul's urgency and unremitting proselytising occasionally brought about problems, it also brought converts. In this he was aided by a number of female patrons; In Philippi, Paul's work was supported by Lydia, a widow fluent in Greek, whose business in the purple dye trade brought her a comfortable living. She was baptised by Paul and insisted that the rest of her household, including her slaves, did the same. Thereafter, she allowed her house to be used for weekly meetings.[216]

In Corinth, Paul converted a married couple, Priscilla and Aquila, who also allowed their house to become a weekly meeting place for worship.[217] This couple became close friends of Paul, and it is notable that he mentions them in his letter to the Romans.

It is ironic that later Christian writers, notably Tertullian and Augustine, were unashamedly misogynistic. In part they based their views on opinions expressed in letters attributed to Paul by later writers. This practice of attributing authorship to a great master was widespread in the world of classical antiquity and was seen as a form of homage. However, it could lead to misunderstandings. This was almost certainly the case where Paul's attitude to women was concerned.

Judged by the standpoint of contemporary Judaism two thousand years ago, Paul was not as enlightened in his treatment of women as Jesus may have been, but his views were on the whole 'liberal.' He valued women converts as helpers and friends in his cause and even entrusted the delivery of his remarkable letter to the Romans to a female deaconess named Pheobe.

Given that communications in Roman times had—with the exception of missives from Rome itself—to rely on delivery by trusted associates, who were prepared to undertake arduous and often dangerous journeys,

---

[215] Acts 19: 23-41

[216] Acts 16: 14-15

[217] Romans 16: 3-4

Phoebe's task was one likely to have only been entrusted to someone considered to be a resourceful and reliable follower.[218]

Problems with Converts

The small number of House Assemblies that Paul had established continued to grow, perhaps increasing in membership by about fifty percent every ten years (Chapter 10.) However, with modest growth came problems, which were often far from modest. One convert was living with his father's wife, a form of immorality that Paul claimed was: *'Not even found amongst Pagans.'* [219]

Other converts were overeating and some were drunk at the weekly communal meals, yet others were dominating the weekly proceedings by 'speaking in tongues.' Paul received a letter from members of the Corinth congregation asking for guidance about these and other matters.[220] In his reply he sets out the ethical guidelines, to which he expects his converts to adhere: Under Paul's guidelines husbands and wives should be faithful to one another and meet each other's needs exclusively; The unmarried should be celibate, but if they find this too difficult they should marry;[221] If someone is hungry before the weekly communal meal, they should eat at home to avoid taking someone else's share;[222] When speaking in 'tongues,' Paul advised his followers to take care that it was tongues from God, and that it should be done decently and in order.[223]

Perhaps Paul's best-known exhortation was to love one another. It is his poem on the topic of love, which is probably the most famous part of his letter to the Corinthians:

'Love is patient; love is kind; love is not envious or boastful, or arrogant or rude. It does not insist on its own

---

[218] Romans 16: 1-2

[219] 1 Corinthians 5: 1

[220] 1 Corinthians 7: 1

[221] 1 Corinthians 7: 2-39

[222] 1 Corinthians 11: 33-34

[223] 1 Corinthians 14: 2

The Way to Christianity

way; it is not irritable or resentful; it does not rejoice in wrong doing, but rejoices in truth. It bears all things, believes all things, hopes all things. Love never ends . . . and now faith, hope and love abide, these three; and the greatest of these is love.' [224]

Despite these now familiar and moving words, Paul's converts could still be attracted to other missionaries. He was particularly concerned with other 'Followers of The Way,' whom he refers to as 'false apostles.' To counter this, Paul boasted of his own antecedents:

'Are they Hebrew? So am I. Are they Israelites? So am I. Are they descendants of Abraham? So am I. Are they ministers of Christ? I am talking like a madman? I am a better one; with far greater labours, far more imprisonments with countless floggings and often near to death. Five times, I have received from Jews the forty lashes, minus one. Three times I was beaten with rods. Once I received a stoning. Three times I was shipwrecked; for a day and a night, I was adrift at sea, on frequent journeys in danger from rivers, in danger from bandits, in danger from my own people, danger from Gentiles, in danger in the city, danger in the wilderness, danger 'at sea,' danger from false brothers and sisters.' [225]

With his combination of religious letters, coupled with abundant energy, Paul kept Corinth and his other small 'house assemblies' together to form what would become the seedbeds of later Christianity.

As Paul was engaging in facing the problems of his small House Assemblies, the Synagogue of the 'Followers of The Way' in Jerusalem faced an even greater emergency. The famine of the 50's CE had intensified, and starvation was rife, particularly for the widows and orphans whom the Synagogue supported.

---

[224] 1 Corinthians 13: 4-13

[225] 2 Corinthians 11: 22-26

Paul collected money from his congregation and wealthy patrons and decided to travel to Jerusalem to deliver it personally.[226] Before doing so, however, he wrote his letter to the Roman assembly: a community that Paul had not established or even visited. Paul's letter was probably written in Corinth.[227]

The Letter to the Romans

Since Paul was not dealing with the problems in his own small House Assemblies, the letter to the Romans presented him with an opportunity to describe his own religious beliefs. His letter reasserts Paul's central conviction—formed some twenty years prior—that Jesus' resurrection and transformation after death created the opportunity for personal salvation. Paul also emphasises his conviction that faith in Jesus replaced all that has gone before, in particular replacing the law by which observant Jews lived. But this created difficulties as it left Paul's followers without a clear guide to acceptable behaviour.[228] As we have seen, this led some of his followers into doing things that were clearly immoral. In his letter to the Romans Paul returns to this theme:

> *'All who have sinned apart from the law will also perish apart from the law, and all who have sinned under the law will be judged by the law. For it not the hearers of the law who are righteous in God's sight, but the doers of the law who will be justified. When the Gentiles, who do not possess the law, do instinctively what the law required these, though not having the law are a law to themselves. They show that what the law requires is written on their hearts, to which their own conscience also bears witness; and their conflicting thoughts will accuse or perhaps excuse them on the day when, according to my gospel, God through Jesus Christ, will judge the secret thoughts of all.'* [229]

---

[226] Romans 15: 25-28

[227] Romans 1: 1-7

[228] Romans 5: 18-21

[229] Romans 2: 12

The Way to Christianity

At this juncture, Paul's thoughts had clearly evolved since the time when he simply advised his followers to 'put on Jesus' as a replacement for 'the law.' It would fall to later Christianity to develop Paul's ideas on moral behaviour into a written code of conduct. As has been noted, this code would strongly resemble many aspects of the Jewish law.

Paul also argued that 'putting on Jesus' also replaced the need for the ubiquitous symbol of Judaism: circumcision. Paul claimed that Abraham received God's grace before he was circumcised,[230] thus establishing God's grace above the need for circumcision. In particular, Paul wished the assembly in Rome to live in the spirit, rather than in the flesh:

> *'For those who live according to the flesh set their minds on the things of the flesh, but those who live according to the spirit set their minds on the things of the spirit. To set the mind on the flesh is death, but to set the mind on the spirit is life and peace. For this reason the mind that is set on the flesh is hostile to God; it does not submit to God's law—indeed it cannot, and those who are in the flesh cannot please God.'*[231]

Running through Paul's letter to the Romans is his central theme: Jews and Gentiles are equal before God. For those reborn in Jesus, race does not matter; the only requisite is to 'die in Christ' and thus be reborn free from sin. Thereafter the individual would live in the spirit rather than in the flesh, as this is what God truly wanted.

Although Paul's letters were seminal for later Christian theology, there is no evidence that Paul was attempting to start a new religion. Indeed, Paul presents his ideas from Abraham to Jesus as a Jewish discussion, supported by a highly selective and occasionally spurious use of Jewish literature. Paul's argument for Jesus as the fulfilment of God's promise to his chosen people was wholly unsupported and contradicts one of the central covenants of Judaism.

Paul believed that he was 'making the Jews jealous' by converting Gentiles, and this would lead to the whole of Judaism adopting his personal ideas of Jesus. This may seem strange, or even perverse, but

---

[230] Romans 4: 10

[231] Romans 8: 5-8

Gentile conversion had a precedent, for Pharisees had on occasion engaged in missionary work amongst non-Jews. It is one of the ironies of Christianity that Paul, a man who was born a Jew, should be seen as the bridge to a new religion, when in reality he was attempting to persuade his fellow Jews to adopt his own, deeply heretical, views.

The Last Journey to Jerusalem

Paul left Corinth in the spring of 57CE and travelled overland to Troas, before embarking on a ship to Jerusalem. Fears of a plot, either real or imagined, caused him to change boats.[232] He arrived safely in Tire some weeks later, having travelled directly across the Eastern Mediterranean. In Tire he again received further warnings of an assassination plot and his friends urged him not to travel to Jerusalem.[233] Ignoring the warnings, Paul travelled by boat to Caesarea Maritime, where he again received further warnings, before travelling on to Jerusalem. On the final overland stage of the journey Paul was accompanied by a group of his followers, probably for his own protection. On arriving at the city they stayed at the house of a convert, and the following day Paul visited James and the elders.[234]

The meeting between Paul and James must have been a little strained, to put it mildly. We only have a partial account in Acts, which naturally enough reflects Paul's position. The money, which Paul had collected and brought with him, was very welcome; the harvest had failed yet again, and misery and starvation were widespread. Money to buy grain from Egypt must have been a great relief to 'the poor Saints in Jerusalem,' to use Paul's phrase.

The financial relief that Paul brought to James and Peter's followers was likely to have been less an act of altruism, than a symbol of Paul's desire to stay within the fold of the larger movement and, as a form of persuasion, to convince its leaders of his view of the significance of

---

[232] Acts 20: 5

[233] Acts 21: 5

[234] Acts 21: 18

The Way to Christianity

Jesus' death. But there were problems, as some followers of The Way had heard of the substance of Paul's teachings.[235]

To abandon the law and the practice of circumcision were no small matters in themselves, but Paul had also come perilously close to declaring Jesus divine, and any suggestion of Jesus' divinity was unthinkable: Deeply religious Jewish men who sought to do the will of God could legitimately regard themselves as 'sons of God,' but construing this in a literal sense was deeply blasphemous. Perhaps to reassure other members of The Way of Paul's Jewish loyalty, James encouraged Paul to enter the Temple and participate in a Passover festival. Unfortunately he was recognised, accused of illegally taking a Gentile companion into the Inner Temple court, and a riot ensued.[236] Despite Paul's attempts to defend himself, he was arrested by Roman troops and taken to the Antonia Fortress to be flogged. As he was being tied up, Paul protested that he was a Roman citizen and that it was illegal to beat him. He was untied and held overnight prior to appearing before the Sanhedrin court the following day.

Trial and House Arrest

The disturbance that had occurred was almost certainly the result of the underlying conflict between Paul and other 'Followers of The Way.' Whilst Paul was able to discuss matters with James and the rather affable Peter, there were others who were prepared to offer more vigorous opposition.

Certainly Paul's abandonment of the law and the lack of circumcision of Gentile converts would provide ammunition for those Jews who were opposed to The Way, and the followers of James may have felt vulnerable as a consequence. They had good reason to be concerned, as the later execution of James on a trumped up charge of blasphemy was to show.[237]

Paul's appearance before the Sanhedrin the next day could well have brought about his downfall. Certainly, had the contents of Paul's letter

---

[235] Acts 21: 21

[236] Acts 21: 27-30

[237] Josephus F. Antiquities xx 9, (200)

to the Romans been known, his life would have been in danger, but Paul was nothing if not politically astute and intellectually adroit.

The court was composed of two groups: the Pharisees and the Sadducees; the former believing in the possibility of personal resurrection, whilst the latter did not. Paul, therefore, chose to defend himself, by describing his belief in Jesus' resurrection, rather than in the areas of the law and circumcision, where he was vulnerable. The tactic worked, and the court descended into an increasingly acrimonious argument over the question of resurrection. After a while, Paul became a mere spectator at his own trial.[238] The Roman authorities grew increasingly exasperated, and eventually took Paul back into custody. He was then transported to Caesarea Maritime with a returning cohort of auxiliary Roman cavalry.

In Caesarea Maritime Paul was imprisoned whilst the procurator Marcus Antonium Felix waited for a deputation from the High Priest Ananias. The High Priests deputised the advocate Tertullus, to put the case against Paul:

> *'We have, in fact found this man a pestilent fellow, an agitator amongst all the Jews throughout the world, and a ringleader of the sect of the Nazarenes. He even tried to profane the Temple and so we seized him.'* [239]

Paul defends himself in his now familiar way: portraying himself as a pious and observant Jew, who happened to believe in the resurrection of Jesus, and decrying the charges against him as entirely false.

Those who brought the original charges against him: 'some Jews from Asia,'[240] were not present, and Paul clearly hoped to be discharged. Felix, who was facing growing unrest in Judea, was clearly disinclined to do this, and found a convenient way to put the case 'on hold' by placing Paul under house arrest, where he was to remain for two years.[241]

During this time, it is probable that Paul communicated with the House Assemblies that he had established. It is also possible that the

---

[238] Acts 23: 6-10

[239] Acts 24: 5-6

[240] Acts 24: 19

[241] Acts 24: 27

'letter to the Philippians' represents a compilation of a series of letters sent at this time. In Philippians, Paul rages against the Jerusalem leadership and their requirements for circumcision:

> *'Beware of the dogs, beware of the evil workers, beware of those who mutilate the flesh. For it is we who are of the circumcision who worship in the spirit of God, and boast in Christ Jesus, and have no confidence in the flesh.'* [242]

Paul also extols his own interpretation of the 'end time' of Judaism remembering that 'the Lord is near.'

> *'Therefore God also highly exalted him and gave him the name that is above every name, so at the name of Jesus every knee should bend, in heaven and earth and under the earth, and every tongue should confess that Jesus Christ is Lord to the glory of God the Father.'* [243]

After two years, Felix was replaced by Porcius Festus, who, upon arriving and finding Paul under confinement, reopened his case. The proceedings were heard in the presence of King Herod Agrippa, a great grandson of Herod the Great, together with the Temple authorities who had again travelled to Caesarea Maritime to prosecute Paul. At some stage, and presumably because his case was not going well, Paul claimed the right of Appellatio, the entitlement of every Roman citizen to have his case heard by the Emperor. Festus acceded, and Paul was dispatched to Rome.[244]

The Journey to Rome

The journey by ship to Rome is described vividly in Acts, and is illustrated in figure 5.2.

---

[242] Philippians 3: 2

[243] Philippians 2: 9-10

[244] Act 27: 1-32

John Larke

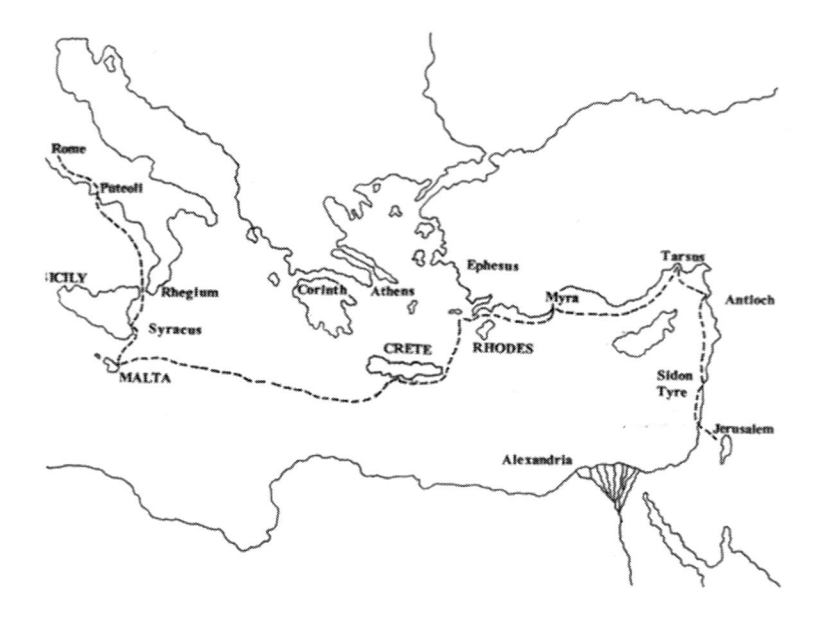

Figure 5.2 Paul's last journey to Rome

It included unfavourable winds, a violent storm, a ship-wreck, and a winter spent in Malta. Although a good deal of the description of this journey has been said to be allegorical, a recent examination of prevailing weather conditions in the Eastern Mediterranean, has shown that it is entirely consistent with an autumnal journey under sail.[245]

Upon arrival in Rome, Paul was again placed under house arrest whilst waiting for his case to be heard. This is the last we hear of him, with one possible exception: 'the second letter to Timothy.' Although at one time thought to have been written by the author of the first letter to Timothy, many scholars now see 'Timothy 2' as Paul's last letter. A last testament was a practice followed by a number of ancient writers when approaching death. If Paul is correctly identified as the author of the second letter to Timothy, it shows a changed man. The tone is

---

[245] White J. Evidence and Paul's Journeys. Presaged (2001)

sombre, Paul's life being: *'Poured out as a libation, and the time for his departure has come.'* [246] Many have deserted him:

> *'All who are in Asia have turned away from me including Phygelus and Hermogenes.'* [247]

> *'Demas in love with this present world has deserted me; Crescens has gone to Galatia, Titus to Dalmatia.'* [248]

But Luke is with him, and Paul begs Timothy to visit him, and bring Mark. Perhaps his greatest sadness is that Jesus has not yet returned. Yet even in the last days of his life, he remains loyal to the man he has 'put on,' and whose life replaced all that had gone before. Paul has no regrets:

> *'For this gospel I was appointed a herald and an apostle and a teacher, and for this reason I suffer as I do. But I am not ashamed, for I know the one in whom I have put my trust, and I am sure that he is able to guard until that day, what I have entrusted to him.'* [249]

Paul's Death and Legacy

The place and date of Paul's death are not known; Church tradition has him either continuing his journey from Rome to Spain, or being beheaded in Rome—with his bouncing head causing the emergence of three springs. However, other historically documented, synchronous events might provide clues to the nature of Paul's death.

In 64CE a fire broke out in Rome and much of the city was destroyed. Suspicion for the start of the fire fell on the Emperor Nero, who later substantially expanded and embellished the Imperial Palace. Although Nero was not in Rome at the time of the fire, it appeared to start in a slum quarter adjacent to the palace wall, and suspicion fell on Nero's agents.

---

[246] 2 Timothy 4: 6

[247] 2 Timothy 1: 15

[248] 2 Timothy 4: 10

[249] 2 Timothy 1: 11-12

Upon returning to Rome, Nero was faced with popular unrest and sought a scapegoat by persecuting the followers of 'Chresus'—a term widely thought to refer to early Christians—who made their homes in the slum. In true imperial tradition, Nero arranged for games to be held in which a proportion of the followers of 'Chresus' were consumed by wild animals. The remainder were soaked in tar, and used as human torches to illuminate Nero's gardens during elaborate evening celebrations. If Paul was caught up in this barbarity, he was martyred in one of the first Christian persecutions.

However Paul died, it seems likely that he was martyred at, or around, the time that James was stoned to death in Jerusalem. Thus, Paul joined the first three leaders of the 'Followers of The Way' in meeting a violent and untimely demise.

There are those who claim that Paul was a lifelong Jew, whilst others proclaim him as the first Christian, however, on reflection, neither of these positions appears sufficient to capture the nuances of Paul's faith.

Born into a Jewish family and raised as a Jew, Paul's time in Jewish Palestine training to be a Pharisee would have given him a thorough knowledge of the Torah and other religious works. However, his experiences of what he believed to be a risen Jesus altered his world completely and he spent the rest of his life trying to accommodate Jesus within normative Judaism. This presented him with several problems: Paul clearly believed in the" election of Israel", that is to say that Jews were God's chosen people. He also believed that God, as part of a binding covenant, had given the law to Jews. However, Paul 'knew' that God had also raised Jesus from the dead, which, to his interpretation, offered the promise of life after death for all. Why then had it been necessary for God to provide the example of Jesus' life and death, when he had already provided the law?

Paul's view that the law had led the people of Israel into sin is difficult to follow. The example he gives is of covetousness: It is possible that Jews would not have seen covetousness as a sin, unless it had been defined as such. The argument cannot be extended to aspects such as murder or theft, which would have been seen as sinful even without the law. As Ed Saunders has pointed out, Paul never entirely resolved this problem.[250]

---

[250] Saunders E.P. Paul. Oxford University Press. (1991) 84-100

The Way to Christianity

Clearly God could not have changed his mind, nor could he—in sending Jesus as a replacement for the law—have acted in a less than a perfect way. Perhaps the fault lay with the 'people of Israel,' who simply obeyed the law without immersing themselves in its spirit. Paul seems to have believed that God sent Jesus as an example to all; that it was only by 'putting on Jesus' that God's will could be fulfilled. In this sense Jesus had replaced the law, which had led people into sin by encouraging simple obedience rather than through a full spiritual acceptance of God's will.

Perhaps an even greater problem was that Paul seems to have had greater success in converting Gentiles than Peter did in converting Jews. After all, as God's chosen people, it was natural for Jews to be converted and saved before everyone else. Yet Paul reversed this natural order of things, and proclaimed his own Gentile followers as the first to enter the 'Kingdom of Heaven.'

Why did Paul develop this novel and in some respects deeply heretical view of Jesus? That Paul experienced what he believed to be the risen Jesus is clear in his writings and would explain his belief in the resurrection of the dead, a view shared by many of his fellow Jews. Combining Jesus' resurrection with the hope for the promised Messiah was unprecedented in Judaism, but not necessarily heretical. The same can be said for Paul's assertion that he was in some form of continuing communication with his risen spiritual mentor. But why the claim of 'putting on Jesus' as a replacement for the Jewish law and circumcision? It is difficult to avoid the conclusion that there were pragmatic and rather personal reasons for these heretical views.

Had Paul allowed or encouraged his followers to observe the Jewish law—which was entirely reasonable since they had become part of a Jewish revivalist movement—then they would have been accountable to James in Jerusalem rather than Paul. Had Paul required circumcision, then the numbers of his male followers would likewise have sharply declined; before the age of anaesthetics and antibiotics adult circumcision was painful and carried a high risk of infection.

It seems clear that having converted his followers, Paul wished to independently control them to avoid anything which might reduce their numbers or threaten his position as their sole leader.

To support his case, Paul turned to the book of Genesis and the figure of Abraham. Arguing that, since the law had not yet been promulgated,

Abraham had received God's love on the basis of faith alone, Paul then took a huge step and claimed that just as Abraham's faith alone had brought God's love, so faith in Jesus was sufficient to bring God's love to those who believed. This of course, ignored everything that had happened to the Jewish people between the time of Abraham and that of Jesus; in essence Paul was abandoning almost all of the Hebrew Bible.

Paul also cited Genesis over the question of circumcision; In Genesis, Chapter 15 verse 18 there is no mention of circumcision in God's first covenant with Abraham. However, there is a fundamental flaw with this approach, for although God promised to make Abraham the 'Ancestor of a multitude of nation'—which implies both Jewish and Gentile communities—in Genesis Chapter 17 verses 10 and 11, God confirms that circumcision is a 'sign of the covenant between you and me.' Thus, like so many others, Paul was entirely happy to use highly selective quotes from scripture to support his personal beliefs.

Whatever criticism may be levelled at Paul, he clearly cannot be accused of a lack of ambition: Ultimately he wished to convert not only the leadership of The Way, but also the entire Jewish people, to a new Torah-free religion which would be Jewish in name only. This new inclusive faith would admit both Gentiles and Jews who would venerate Jesus whilst waiting for the 'Kingdom of God.' Again, one can only guess at the irony that Paul would have felt had he lived to witness the evolution of exclusively Gentile Christianity, with its iconic divine figure of Jesus 'Christ' standing in opposition to Judaism and increasingly promoting anti-Semitism.

Whilst alive, Paul remained a 'Follower of The Way,' although he was probably regarded by the leadership as a 'loose cannon' who only nominally accepted the leadership of James in Jerusalem. No doubt this led to the opposition he experienced and the separation from his own people, which troubled him so much. Yet he never seems to have considered that he may have been, even partially, at fault. In Paul's world there were only his own beliefs; no one else understood the significance of Jesus' death and resurrection in the same way that he did. As has been mentioned, this hallmark of intolerance and a marked lack of self-doubt was later to resonate in Christianity, leading to a reappraisal—seemingly without qualms—of the central meaning of Jesus' mission, as understood by his apostles. Yet how had these followers and relatives,

The Way to Christianity

such as James, seen the man who had played such an inspirational role in their movement?

Whilst Christianity has preserved a great deal which supports its own viewpoint, relatively little documentation survives from 'The Way.' In total this amounts to the two letters of James and Jude, some extracts from the gospel of the Ebonite's and Nazarenes quoted by later Christian historians, and parts of the Pseudo Clementine Homilies and Recognitions, which have been shown to have Ebonite origins. Taken together, these documents present a different view from Paul's; rather than a crucified and returning figure, Jesus is portrayed as a great Jewish holy man and prophet.

The gospel attributed to Matthew in part supports this view, and even goes so far as to have Jesus taken to Egypt as a young child, so that he can come out of Egypt, in the manner of Moses. Yet, even if Jesus' family and followers regarded him as wholly human, they did agree with Paul in one respect: Jesus was quite remarkable. The Way was founded by John, and James became its long standing spiritual leader and guide, but Jesus remained its most charismatic prophet. Perhaps the only point of contact between Paul and The Way was the reverence that they all had for the memory of Jesus.

The death of James and Paul brought to an end the first chapter of what, in time, was to become Christianity. The Way's fundamental belief in the imminence of the 'end time' of Judaism and God's arrival was wholly misplaced, yet out of the ashes of this failure was born a new religion: Christianity. How did this come about? For the answer to this question we must leave the world of Judaism and enter the all-pervading Hellenistic culture of the Roman world.

CHAPTER 6

CHRISTIAN GENESIS

The end of the first Jewish uprising against Rome brought to a close the first phase in the evolution of what was to become Christianity. The loss of the Temple traumatised Judaism and brought about far reaching change. For The Way the effects were, if anything, even worse. The central prophecy of the imminence of God's arrival was thrown into considerable doubt when the Holy of Holies in the Temple was destroyed and God did not come. Only Paul's House Assemblies prospered; free from Jewish influence, they developed independently in a Gentile environment.

Judaism

For the Jewish people defeat brought the end of Second Temple Judaism. The loss of independence curtailed the activities of the Sanhedrin, the central Jewish court in Jerusalem,[251] and the semi-independent judiciary no longer functioned.

With the Jerusalem Temple destroyed there were no Temple rituals. The Sadducees who had overseen temple administration no longer had a role to play and rather rapidly disappeared from Jewish history.

For a time the temple rituals were described as though they were continuing, but in reality they were not.[252] This led to the decline of the priesthood, who, like the Sadducees, had lost their religious function.

---

[251] Schurer E. The History of the Jewish People in the age of Jesus Christ (1885). Revised English text. Vermes G. Millar F. Goodman M. Black. M (Eds) T & T Clark (1973) 1. 521

[252] Ibid 522-523

The restoration of the temple and its rituals now became incorporated into the more general and long-standing hope for the 'last days,' and the final triumph of Judaism. Perhaps the greatest concern of the Jewish people was to account for what had happened. It seemed to all that, once again, the ungodly had triumphed over God's chosen people. How could this have come about?

The answer, at least in terms of a response from the Pharisees, was the traditional one: The loss of the war was God's chastising punishment for a people who had strayed from the true path of righteousness. Jews needed to redouble their efforts, particularly in observance of the law. To this end those Pharisees who had survived the Roman re-conquest, established new centres of study. A principle one was at Jamnia (Yaveh), where, by the end of the first century, a succession of outstanding Pharisees provided renewed leadership. A second centre at Lydda came into being at about the same time.

A group of notable scholars, under the leadership of Yohanan Ben Zakkai, including the Rabbis Eliezer Ben Hyrcanus, Simon Ben Nathanael, Eliezer Ben Arkh and Joshua Ben Hanania, began the process of religious renewal. At a slightly later date Gamalial Ben Gamaliel, the grandson of the Gamalial referred to in the Acts of the Apostles, became the leader of the Jamnia scholars.[253] Their efforts were highly regarded, and they soon began to carry out a number of functions previously undertaken by the Sanhedrin. The work undertaken at Jamnia established the basis of what, in time, became Rabbinic Judaism. The movement more clearly delineated what it meant to be a Jew: a consequence of which was a greater separation between Jews and the other peoples of the Mediterranean. This process was in turn accelerated by the break out of further uprisings, both in Alexandria and in other parts of the Roman Empire, reaching a climax in 115CE

Even worse was to follow. The greatest calamity of all was the final Bar Kokba uprising against Rome (132-135CE).[254] The frustrated hopes of the rebuilding of the temple, and the ban on circumcision, decreed by the new Emperor Hadrian, were too much to bear. The final revolt appears to have been free of the damaging infighting of the first

---

[253] Ibid 11 369-380

[254] Ibid 1 535-557

uprising, but so much had already been lost that final Roman victory was all but inevitable.

The Way

There is only sporadic information on 'The Way' after 70CE. As Christianity evolved, it viewed its precursor sect with increasing unease. The Way's failure to regard Jesus as divine, and its exclusive emphasis on the 'last days,' was not well received. Similarly, within Judaism, God's non-arrival, particularly when the Holy of Holies was destroyed, was seen as a failure of prophecy. Thus, neither Christian nor Jew wrote at any length on the movement during this period, although, given the remarkable preservation of the material from Qumran and Nag Hammadi, there will always be hope for further discoveries.

The Prayer

The 'Shemonah Esreh' is the principal prayer of Judaism, and is often known simply as 'the prayer.' Originally intended to be recited three times a day by every Jew and his family; the composition of the prayer is unknown, but clearly ancient. Of the various versions that exist, a form found in Cairo at the end of the nineteenth century, is probably closest to the prayer said by Jews in the first three decades of the first century CE. The opening verse begins with recognition of the unique position of God:

> *'Blessed art thou, Lord God of our fathers, God of Abraham, God of Isaac and God of Jacob, great mighty and fearful God, and most high God created heaven and earth, our shield and the shield of our fathers, our trust in every generation. Blessed art thou, Lord shield of Abraham.'* [255]

Of the eighteen verses, verse 12 is of particular interest:

---

[255] Schurer.E. The History of the Jewish People in the Age of Jesus Christ Revised English text Vermes G. Millar F. Goodman M. Black M. (Eds). T & T Clark (1973) II. 459

> *'And after the apostates let there be no hope; and may the insolent kingdom be quickly uprooted in our days. And may the Nazarenes and the heretics perish quickly; and may they be erased from the Book of Live; and may they not be inscribed with righteous. Blessed art thou, Lord who humbles the insolent.'* [256]

Although there is a degree of agreement about the date of the entire prayer, the date of verse 12 is more problematic. There is a Jewish tradition that dates the verse condemning heretics to the time of Gamaliel, but it is not clear if this tradition relates to the material discovered in Cairo. The phrase: *'And the apostates, let there be no hope,'* [257] may have a particular relevance.

Viewed from a Jewish perspective, Paul, and therefore his followers, were certainly seen as apostates from the law. But widespread Jewish condemnation of Christianity did not take place until later. However, the phrase: *'and may the Nazareens and Heretics perish quickly,'* may be historically significant. The phrase 'Nazareens' was used by the lawyer representing the Sanhedrin for the 'Followers of The Way' at Paul's appearance before the Roman Governor, Felix.[258] Since The Way was in progressive decline from the death of James onwards, it seems unlikely that an execration of The Way would be declaimed at a later date, when the movement was clearly failing. If the case can be made for a relatively early date of the condemnation of The Way, what effect would it have had on the movement?

Being a Jew brought considerable practical advantages. When the renowned Rabbi Hillel was asked to summarise the law, he replied: *'Doing nothing to your fellow man that you would hate to be done to you.'* [259] This sentiment encapsulated the many detailed requirements of the law, which were observed by the Jewish people.

---

[256] Ibid 11 461

[257] Ibid 11 462

[258] Acts 24: 2-5

[259] Schurer E. The History of the Jewish People in the Age of Jesus Christ. Revised English text, Vermes G. Miller F. Goodman M. Black M. (Eds) T & T Clark (1973) 11 467

In essence, Jewish law provided recourse to 'human rights', which could be enforced in legal proceedings. This was not true of much of the classical world, where the untrammelled power of high position was invariably dominant. Jews also exercised a form of medical and social insurance. Paul's contribution towards famine relief on his last visit to Jerusalem was not unique; Jews frequently helped each other in adversity, as enshrined within the duty of all Synagogues to provide support for 'widows and orphans'. Jews also valued their position in their communities. The various offices within a Synagogue were widely recognised, and much sought after. Following the condemnation in the Shemoneh Esreh, the followers of The Way would have faced great difficulties. Adherents could have been barred from Synagogue office, whilst their own Synagogues may not have been recognised. In such circumstances, it would have been easy to have felt an alienation from Jewish life.

The 'Followers of The Way' were not only meeting with opposition from their fellow Jews, but also encountered hostility from evolving Christianity, which, towards the middle of the second century, denounced The Way as heretical.[260] That emerging Christianity should decry the movement of which Jesus had been a spiritual leader and teacher may seem extraordinary, yet there is little doubt that this was so.

From Jesus to Christ

Jesus became divine with remarkable speed. The gospel attributed to Mark, probably written about 70CE opens with: *'The beginning of the good news of Jesus Christ, the son of God.'* [261] Within a few years the gospels attributed to Luke and to Matthew were describing Jesus' miraculous conception brought about by the Angel Gabriel in a 'virgin' named Mary who had *'not known a man.'* [262] How did this transformation in Jesus' status come about with such alacrity? The cultural and religious background to the rapidly changing view of Jesus has been eloquently described by Geza Vermes:

---

[260] Chadwick H. The Early Church. Penguin (1993) 23

[261] Mark 1: 1

[262] Luke 1: 4

> 'Within decades of his death, the message of the real Jesus was transferred from its Semitic (Aramaic/Hebrew) linguistic context, its Galilean/Palestinian geographical setting, and its Jewish religious framework to alien surroundings. In other words, the emigration of the Jesus movement from its Jewish home territory to the primarily Greek-speaking pagan Mediterranean world of classical cultural back-ground occurred at too early a stage. The aims, ideas and style of life of Christianity had no time properly to crystallize and develop. The clay was soft and malleable; it could still be easily moulded into any shape the potter cared to choose. As a result the new Church, by then mostly Gentile, soon lost its awareness of being Jewish; indeed, it became progressively anti-Jewish.
>
> Another fundamental twist exerted an adverse effect on the appeal of the Christian message to Palestinian and Diaspora Jews. Jesus, the religious man with an irresistible charismatic charm, was metamorphosed into Jesus the Christ, the transcendent object of the Christian religion. The distant fiery prophet from Nazareth proclaiming the nearness of the Kingdom of God did not mean much to the average new recruit from Alexandria, Antioch, Ephesus, Corinth or Rome. Their gaze was directed towards a universal saviour and even towards the eternal yet incarnate Word of God who was God.' [263]

Jesus the Jew, to employ one of the titles of Vermes' books, was a wholly human figure. Even Paul of Tarsus, an apostate from the law, could not quite bring himself to regard Jesus as divine. Yet there was no such reticence on the part of the earliest Christians. Having lost their Jewish inheritance they began to see Jesus in ways that were wholly inimical within Judaism yet wholly acceptable in a Gentile context.

The greatest change lay not in the totality of the religious lexicon but in the meanings of individual words and phrases as belief transposed from one religious milieu to another. Four are of particular relevance: 'Son of God,' 'Messiah,' 'Virgin' and the 'Kingdom of Heaven.'

---

[263] Vermes G. The Changing Face of Jesus. Allan Lane, Penguin (2000) 26

SON OF GOD

The Hebrew Bible utilises the term 'Son(s) of God' with respect to three distinct groups:[264] Angels, Jewish men, and the succession of Davidic Kings who ruled ancient Jewish Palestine.

Angels acted as one of the intermediaries between God and man. When God wished to destroy the corrupt cities of Sodom and Gomorrah, but save the life of Lot and his family, it was two Angels who urged Lot to leave the doomed cities. Angels were commonly regarded as heavenly beings but on occasion could also be identified as 'Sons of God.'

The Hebrew Bible describes God creating the first man Adam from the 'Dust of the Ground.' [265] Since all Jewish men considered themselves to be descended from Adam there was a widespread acceptance that they could be 'Sons of God.' In practice the phrase was restricted to those Jewish men who submitted themselves wholly to the will of God: *'When the Israelites do the will of the holy one blessed be he, they are called sons; but when they do not do his will they are not called sons.'* [266]

The most consistently recognised 'Sons of God' were the Davidic Kings of Israel. In describing King David, the Hebrew bible records God's admiration: *'I will make him my firstborn highest among the Kings of the earth.'* [267]

Although it is widely recognised that these three groups were designated as 'Sons of God', in no instance does this imply divinity. Rather the term relates to the recognition of exceptional status, but this was not the case in the Greco-Roman world.

The Pagan world in which the first Christians lived was full of Gods; even modestly sized towns contained Temples to the numerous Gods of antiquity, whilst individual houses contained images of a household deity to which regular small offerings would be made. Alongside these ubiquitous manifestations of the 'Pagan' Gods of the Roman world, the Emperor was also worshipped.

The origins of Emperor Worship are somewhat obscure. There is general agreement that towards the end of his reign Julies Caesar was

---

[264] Vermes G. Jesus the Jew. SCM Press (1994) 194

[265] Genesis 2: 7

[266] Vermes G. Jesus the Jew. SCM Press (1994) 197

[267] Psalms 89: 26-27

The Way to Christianity

increasingly seen as divine, a practice which continued during the reign of Augustus, although the Emperor disparaged the erection of statues to himself during his lifetime. This reticence was largely existent up to the reign of the deranged Caligula, who not only considered himself divine, but meted out punishment to those who did not recognise his elevated status. By the time that Christianity began its remarkable ascendancy, the practice of worshipping a divine Emperor was formalised and widespread. Indeed, it formed the single most important part of Roman religious practice, far exceeding the worship of any other single deity within the Empire. Of even more relevance to Christianity was the practice of declaring new Emperors 'Sons of God.'

The designation of 'Son of God' was not restricted to the Emperors, but could also apply to some of the best-known figures of classical antiquity. Whilst in Egypt, Alexander the Great found it politically expedient to claim his conception was the result of a union between his mother and the Greek God Zeus.

Alongside the worship of Emperors and notable figures from antiquity were the religious practices and beliefs of the 'Pagan' religions. Some bore a remarkable resemblance to evolving Christianity, with Mithraicism in particular bearing many features in common. The followers of Mithras claimed that he was the product of a virgin birth and remained a life-long celibate. Initiation involved baptism, whilst the central feature of religious sacrament was the consumption of bread embossed with a cross, as well as the drinking of wine symbolically representing blood. The followers of the cult believed that Mithras was born on the 25th December and regarded Sundays as a Holy Day. Co-religionists called each other brother and addressed their priests as father. Although possibly older than Christianity, it later met with criticism from those who felt that it was imitating the religion of Jesus' followers.

> *'Let us recognise the devices of the Devil, especially when he creates imitations of divine rites so as to shame and condemn us with the faith of his followers.'* [268]

---

[268] On the Soldiers Crown 15: 3-4 Cited by Goodman M. The Roman World. Routledge (1977)

To what extent did Christianity draw on Emperor Worship and 'Pagan' religions to formulate its religious ideas? Because of the paucity of sources there can be no definitive way of knowing. But the similarities between the differing religious beliefs are too close to have arisen purely through chance. As a number of writers have shown, the cross fertilisation of religious ideas and practices was widespread in antiquity, and it is unlikely that Christianity was immune to this process.

However it arose, the amalgam of Jewish and Pagan beliefs caused great problems for early Christianity. A religion which claimed a belief in a single God had in fact two: God and His Son, together with an ill-defined entity known as the 'Holy Spirit.' Resolving this central contradiction was to take over three hundred years of increasingly acrimonious and occasionally violent debate. (Chapter 9)

Jesus' elevation to the divine 'Son of God'—which had been so unthinkable in the Jewish world—was wholly acceptable in a Pagan context, and may have occurred quite naturally as belief transferred from one religious culture to another. However, the concept of 'Son of God' was not the only thing that changed with the cultural shift.

MESSIAH

It is highly probable that Jesus' followers used the title 'Son of God' for their charismatic leader who wholly submitted himself to the will of God, but this was not necessarily the case with the designation 'Messiah.' [269] In Jewish religious thought the Messiah could be associated with both military and spiritual leadership, although in common with Jewish tradition these roles were usually separated.

Whatever the nature of Messiah-ship, there was one overriding function which was *'the restoration of Israel.'* In practical terms this meant the reunification of the lost ten tribes of Israel with the remaining two.

There are virtually no authentic references to Jesus accepting the designation 'Messiah' [270] in the Christian bible. His reported response when such claims were made was at best ambiguous, at worst derogatory. Two examples illustrate this point: While Jesus was teaching in the Temple he said *'How can the Scribes say that the Messiah is the son of*

---

[269] Mark 8: 29

[270] Vermes G. Jesus the Jew. SCM Press (1994) 141-153

David. David himself calls him Lord so how can he be his son,' [271] and, rather more directly, *'Many will come in my name and they will lead many astray.'* [272]

Perhaps the most apparent conclusion, from the admittedly limited amount of information that is available, is that whilst at least some of his followers hoped that Jesus was the promised Messiah, Jesus was reluctant to accept this designation. But if Jesus demurred, then Paul of Tarsus did not.[273] Indeed the scenario of Jesus as the promised Jewish Messiah who was resurrected from death, ascended to Heaven and would return in the near future was central to Paul's theology. How Paul came to this view is not known, (see Chapter 5), but it was to form the bedrock of later Christianity.

Jesus' Messianic status is most explicitly and frequently found in the fourth gospel and in Acts. Very rapidly Jesus became 'Jesus the Messiah' then 'Jesus Messiah,' which when translated into Greek became Jesus Christ, or simply 'Christ.'

VIRGIN

Within a Jewish context, the concept of virginity was associated with a person, who has not had sexual intercourse or begun menstruation. Thus a girl was a virgin until the time of her first menses, and later, as a woman, regained her virginal status once she was post-menopausal. Since Jewish girls were frequently married in their middle teens at the first sign of puberty, the possibility of a 'virgin birth' was ever present, although probably rather uncommon: A newly married bride who had not yet menstruated could conceive at the time of her first ovulation, and since this suppressed further menstruation could remain a virgin until the birth of her child. We have no way of knowing if this was the origin of Jesus' mother's 'virgin birth,' but it cannot be discounted. An alternative explanation lies in the early Christian examination of Jewish literature, which described a number of examples of apparently infertile women who with God's aid, but not his direct intervention, bore children. In addition the mistranslation of a prophecy in Isaiah 7: 14

---

[271] Mark 12: 35-37

[272] Mark 13: 6

[273] Acts 8: 18 17: 26: 23

'Look the young woman (mistranslation virgin) is with child and shall bear a son' may have added to the stories of Jesus' miraculous birth.

KINGDOM OF HEAVEN

The Jewish Kingdom of Heaven was ruled over by God. Its' earthly counterpart was the Jewish nation, subject to God's Holy law and ruled by a succession of Davidic Kings. This succession was broken in the seventh century by the Babylonian conquest; whilst the subsequent successful Persian campaign against the Babylonians restored the land of Jewish Palestine the uninterrupted line of Davidic Kings had been lost. As replacement the people hoped for a Messiah of Davidic descent, who would restore Israel's fortunes and once again bring it under God's divine governance. It was not only Jews who would be honoured by God's presence. The Prophets foresaw a time when all God's creation, including the Gentiles would acknowledge the Jewish God, *'Nations shall come to your light and Kings to the brightness of your dawn.'* [274]

The hope for the restoration of Israel led by a Messiah of Davidic descent was—and for Orthodox Jews, still is—seen as the culmination of Jewish hope. Yet not all Jews would be admitted to God's perfect Kingdom, nor for many commentators would the Kingdom of Heaven on earth be achieved without a final and traumatic conflict, a scenario particularly well developed by the Essenes.

Entry into the Kingdom of Heaven was dependent on God's favourable judgement on an individual's life; if this was satisfactory, admission to the earthly kingdom could be granted. Yet after a blissful earthly life, death was still inevitable. Persistence of the soul after death—for Jews did not believe in physical resurrection—initially took place in a shadowy world called Shoel. After a further period the soul could then ascend into the spiritually perfect Kingdom of God, where the 'life of the soul' could be everlasting.

Not unnaturally the 'final judgement' was of great importance to individual Jews. Many envisaged the presence of a ledger detailing the good, and not so good, actions of an individual, upon which the final judgement would be based. Many, but not all, anticipated the final judgement taking place at the end of time. The Essenes in particular

---

[274] Isaiah 60: 3

The Way to Christianity

foretold of judgement before a final battle, in which the unrighteous would be defeated.

The Essenes prophecy was a detailed and clearly defined account of the final conflict. The war scroll recovered from the Qumran caves covers the final days:

> *'On the day when the Kittim (Romans) fall, there shall be battle and terrible carnage before the God of Israel, for that shall be the day appointed from ancient times for the battle of destruction of the sons of darkness. At that time, the assembly of gods and the hosts of men shall battle, causing great carnage; on the day of calamity, the sons of light shall battle with the company of darkness amid the shouts of a mighty multitude and the clamour of gods and men to (make manifest) the might of God. And it shall be a time of (great) tribulation for the people which God shall redeem; of all its afflictions none shall be as this, from its sudden beginning until its end in eternal redemption.'* [275]

This battle presaged the final and complete victory of the Jewish people, which would establish a new perfect world order. All conflicts would cease as nations saw the glory of Judaism and obeyed God's holy law. But what of those who did not, or did not wish to seek entry into the Kingdom of God? Here the prophecies are somewhat mixed. The more benevolent envisage a time when most would come to see the justice of the new religious autocracy, whilst the remainder would lead lives of misery and disappointment. The more trenchant foresaw the unbelievers being cast into the fiery furnace in an act of unprecedented global ethnic cleansing.

THE KINGDOM OF GOD

As with the Jewish Kingdom of Heaven, which had both a heavenly and earthly component, very early Christianity claimed a celestial region which initially had seven heavens based on the seven visible planets, and an earthly Kingdom of the Christian God. But all of this hoped for

---

[275] Vermes G. The Complete Dead Sea Scrolls in English. Allan Lane the Penguin Press (1997) 164

change was dependent upon a single event: the anticipated return of Jesus. The immediacy of the 'second coming' was central to Christian hope and expectation and, as has already been observed, singularly failed to happen. Nevertheless, the death, resurrection and return of Jesus was, and indeed still is, a central tenet of Christianity.

The failure of the second coming to eventuate did not inhibit Christian speculation on the nature of heaven and, more particularly, hell. The author of the visionary Book of Revelation described a heaven peopled by angels who resided in a Temple containing the heavenly throne of God.[276] *'And there in heaven stood a throne with one seated on the throne .... around the throne are twenty four thrones .... Coming from the throne are flashes of lightening and peals of thunder and in front of the throne burn seven flaming torches.'* [277]

This remarkable view of heaven was located in a 'new Jerusalem', which would eventually become the centre of a new holy order. In the eyes of many Christians the hope for a new Jerusalem was brought significantly closer with the defeat of Jewish forces at the end of the second uprising against Rome in 135CE. Jews were forbidden to live within sight of the city, and many Jewish sights began to be occupied by Christians.

Alongside the Christian visions of heaven were many more traumatic and lurid visions of hell. In the Synoptic Gospels, hell is described as the final resting place of anyone who is unreservedly angry with a 'brother or sister': *'You will be liable to the hell of fire.'* [278] In similar vein it was better to tear out an eye that *'causes you to stumble'* rather than to enter the Kingdom of God with two eyes and be *'thrown into hell where the worm never dies and the fire is never quenched.'* [279]

Initial descriptions of Hell grew in terrifying detail as Christianity developed. Sinners were condemned to suffer unquenchable fire, burning, brimstone and boiling pitch and many other kinds of appalling suffering. Specific sins also warranted particular forms of punishment:

---

[276] Revelation 4 1-4: 5

[277] Luke 16: 24

[278] Matthew 5: 22

[279] Mark 9 44-48

blasphemers were suspended by their tongues, whilst male adulterers were hung from their genitals.[280]

The conceptual differences so far discussed between the Judaism of The Way and early Christianity are summarised in Table 6.1

---

[280] Himmelfarb M. Tours of Hell. Philadelphia (1983) 26 1-6

THE WAY	EARLY CHRISTIANITY
SON OF GOD	
Term of respect and admiration for: (1) A Jewish King of Davidic descent; (2) Angels and; (3) a righteous Jewish man who seeks to do the will of God. Does not imply divinity.	Applied to Jesus, and Roman Emperors amongst other in the classical world. The phrase was always taken literally as denoting divinity
MESSIAH	
Hoped for Jewish redeemer anointed by God, the principle task of whom was to reunite the 'twelve tribes' of Israel. Exulted but always human.	Jesus, in Hebrew the Messiah, (Greek translation, Christ). Believed to be the divine Son of God whose death and resurrection offered the only possibility of personal salvation.
VIRGIN	
Two meanings: (1) a person, usually a woman, who has not had sexual intercourse; (2) a non-menstruating woman, either pre-pubescent or post-menopausal.	A person, usually a woman who has not had sexual intercourse.
KINGDOM OF HEAVEN (GOD)	
Two components: the first, heavenly and spiritual, directly presided over by God; the second, earthly, governed by King David or his descendants, and, after the demise of the Davidic line of descent, by a hoped for Jewish Messiah.	The kingdom that would be created after the hoped for arrival of Jesus at the time of second coming.

Table 6.1. DIFFERING MEANINGS OF PHRASES USED BY MEMBERS OF THE WAY AND EARLY CHRISTIANITY.

The Way to Christianity

The transformation of Jesus the Galilean Jew into Jesus Christ, the divine Son of God, was arguably the result of a change in religious environment.

Within Judaism, Jesus Ben Joseph, the extraordinary Holy Man, healer and failed Prophet was a largely acceptable figure. His assertion that the last days of Judaism were imminent was clearly misplaced, but his remarkable life and extraordinary parables illustrating his insistence on observing not just the letter, but the spirit of the law, was an important contribution to Jewish religious thought. Had he lived, there can be little doubt that he would have become a revered Jewish figure. This was not so in a Gentile environment.

Jesus the Galilean Jew did not correspond to Paul's teaching of a crucified, risen and returning figure, who would herald the arrival of the Kingdom of Heaven on earth. The opportunity that belief in Jesus provided for personal salvation and everlasting life was so much more than that offered by the Gods of classical antiquity that his divinity must have been unquestioned, particularly when his Jewish compatriots were known to have referred to him as 'Son of God.' Yet this rapidly emerging divine figure was deeply objectionable to Jesus' fellow Jews.

It is difficult to envisage anything more offensive to the religious sensibilities of any Jew that the notion of God fathering a child. In a religious culture where even for a child to speak the name of God by accident was a capital offence, a divine 'Son of God' was untenable. It offended one of the most fundamental tenets of Judaism. *'I am, the Lord your God . . . . You shall have no other Gods beside me.'* [281] And so the division between Judaism and Christianity was born at an early stage, with neither side being able to accommodate the other.

Early Converts

Into this new religion transposed from its origin in Judaism, came those attracted to its *'metaphysical speculation on the incarnate Christ's person and nature.'* [282]

---

[281] Deuteronomy 5: 6

[282] Ibid 264

Initially a potential convert would attend some, but not all, of the activities of a house Church. Christianity for the most part, conducted its business, if not in secret, then at least behind closed doors, and new entrants were carefully screened. The newcomer would be a friend or trusted acquaintance of at least some members of the congregation. There were good reasons for these cautious introductions; Christianity was viewed with some suspicion by the general populace, and on occasions, by city magistrates and Governors.

Christianity's claim of a single powerful God was at a variance with the multiplicity of Gods in the Roman world. The 'Pagan' viewpoint of the general populace was one of awe for their Gods, who could be easily offended by the Christian failure to recognise the Roman panorama of deities.

Whereas Judaism could claim great antiquity for its beliefs, Christianity was an entirely new phenomenon. Tertullian's exasperated cry of: *'If the Tiber reaches the walls, if the Nile does not rise to the fields . . . if there is famine, if there is a plague, the cry is at once, the Christians to the lions.'* [283] is perhaps an over-reaction, but graphically illustrates the fragility of early Christian's footing within the wider population at the time. It also serves well to illustrate the salience of trust and less-than-overt displays of religiosity within the movement; Christianity for the most part, conducted its business, if not in secret, then at least behind closed doors, and new entrants were carefully screened.

Initially a new convert was treated as a 'catechumen', that is a Christian under instruction. This educational experience seems to have varied somewhat, but could last as long as two to three years. It may later have involved attending a catechetical school, although in the earliest days, instruction was probably given by a member of the community. The period of training completed, the successful neophyte would be admitted to full membership of the Church by undergoing baptism.

The Didache

Early baptismal customs may well be described in a document known as the Didache, a complete copy of which was discovered in a

---

[283] Stevenson J. A New Eusebius. SPK 158

monastery library in Istanbul in 1873. Probably dating from the turn of the first century, the Didache gives an account of baptism that is remarkably similar to the customs of Jewish ritual immersion.

It was not only the traditions of Jewish ritual immersion that were followed by early Christians. Within a short time of Paul of Tarsus abandoning 'the law' the early Church had begun the process of creating its Christian equivalent.

The Didache begins with a statement of principle, which is identical to that mentioned earlier by the great Rabbi Hillel, when he was asked to reduce the law to its essentials. It stipulates:

> *'Thou shallt love the God who made thee, thy neighbour as thyself and all things that thou wouldest not should be done unto thee, do not though unto another.'* [284]

As with Judaism, elaboration of these fundamental principles gave a guide to the Christian way of life in a manner reminiscent of the Manual of Discipline, recovered from the Qumran caves.

Christians were advised to choose between two paths: one of life and one of death. The way of life is clearly desirable, and indeed represents the only path for a Christian. As such, it involves following the principles laid down by Jesus, as described in the 'sermon on the mount' wherein it is important not just to love one's neighbour, but to love one's enemies as well, and in so doing:

> *'Do ye love them that hate you . . . ye will not have an enemy. It is important to aim for an almost superhuman level of perfection. To offer the other cheek if one is struck on the first; To go two miles if someone compels you to travel the first; to give your coat to someone who has taken you cloak. Because . . . Blessed is he who giveth . . . but woe unto him that receiveth.'* [285]

---

[284] Ibid, Chapter 1

[285] Ibid, Chapter 1

The way of death is contrasted in some detail to the desirable attributes of the way of life: amongst the followers of this undesirable path will be found those guilty of murders, fornication, sorcery, arrogance and much else besides.

In addition to the details of baptism and the delineation between the ways of life and death, the Didache provides the earliest details of important Church rituals: the Eucharist is described, together with the treatment of prophets and apostles and the election of Bishops.

It is not clear why the Dichache was written. It is possible that it was an instructional booklet, written for the general guidance of Christians and particularly for the instruction of Catechumens. In emphasising the contrast between the way of life and the way of death this early Church document might have underscored the potential consequences facing a new convert; to be Christian in the first century was by no means an easy choice, nor indeed was it a choice without risks.

The Didache very clearly describes what is expected of a newly converted Christian and the standards to which they will be expected to aspire. It is also interesting for what it does not contain: the document as a whole is relatively free of doctrinal details, although a good deal is implied. The only direct reference to doctrine is given towards the end of the document, where in addition to avoiding teachers who proclaim alternative doctrine the true Christian should: *'Do ye according to the doctrine of the gospel.'* [286]

It may be significant that 'gospel' is singular rather than the plural. The writer of the Didache may have had in mind a gospel used in his local Church before the evolution of the Christian bible.

Further insight into the development of Christian thinking can be gained from a series of letters written around the turn of the first century. The first is 'the letter of the Romans to the Corinthians' attributed to Clement, the Bishop of Rome, whilst the remainder were written by Ignatius, the Bishop of Antioch in Syria.

---

[286] Ehrman B.D. After the New Testament. Oxford University Press. (1999) 320-323.

Clement of Rome

The letter traditionally ascribed to Clement was sent from the Church of God in Rome to the Corinthian Church.[287] It deals with problems that were probably a continuation of the difficulties encountered by Paul.[288]

Corinth was subject to numerous disputes and occasional instances of immorality. Paul had dealt with these issues by writing letters and making visits, but never to their full resolution and, by the turn of the century, the old problems had resurfaced. At the time of Clements's letter, the established leadership of the Corinthian Church had been usurped by a group of dissidents. This situation had captured the attention of the 'Church of God in exile in Rome,' which led to the missive, directed to 'the Church of God exiled in Corinth,' in which Clement deals with the problem with great vigour.

> *'We refer to the abominable and Holy schism, so alien and foreign to those whom God has chosen, which a few impetuous and headstrong have fanned to such a pitch of insanity that your good name, once so famous and clear to us all, has fallen into the gravest repute.'*

The appropriate course of action is to: *'Bow the neck and adopt the attitude of obeisance.'* [289] In promoting this Clement draws extensively and at length on the Hebrew bible. Quoting Cain and Able, he illustrates that rivalry can lead to brother killing brother. Expanding upon his theme he goes on to cite further Biblical examples of the negative impacts of rivalry: Joseph fleeing from the presence of his brother Esau and his subsequent persecution and sale into slavery, and of Moses fleeing from the Pharaoh.

These aspects of his letter are illuminating. Clearly at this early stage in the development of Christianity, the Hebrew bible was held in high regard. As such, the moral lessons contained therein applied not only to Jews, but also to Christians and could be quoted at length.

---

[287] Corinthians 1: 4-17

[288] Ehrman B.D. After the New Testament. Oxford University Press. (1999) 320

[289] Ibid 323

But perhaps there is an even more fundamental point regarding the relationships between the early Churches. The fact that Clement felt empowered to write his letter in the first place points to his belief that the events affecting one early Christian Church were felt legitimate concern for the comment and advice by another. This sense of community seems to have been a feature of the early Church as does an egalitarian approach to status: Clement was not claiming any superiority for the Church in Rome, or at least if he did so it was merely implicit. Put simply, for Clement, what was happening in one Church was of legitimate interest to another.

Clement made a further point: In verses 42-44 of his letter Clement begins to expound what was to become known as the 'Apostolic Succession'.

> *'The Apostles received the gospel for us from the Lord Jesus Christ; Jesus Christ was sent from God. Thus Christ is from God and the Apostles from Christ. In both instances the orderly procedure depends on God's will. And so the Apostles received their orders . . . appointed their first converts, after resting them by the spirit to be Bishops and Deacons of future believers.'* [290]

This is the first instance of a claim for a direct succession of authority from Jesus to the Bishops. At a later date it was to be of particular interest for the Roman Church, which was unable to rest its claim for apostolic succession on Paul, so instead relied on Simon Peter.

> *'Peter who by reason of wicked jealousy, not only once or twice but frequently, endured suffering and this bearing witness went to the glorious place which he merited.'* [291]

Peter's position as one of the principal disciples of Jesus was sufficient to become an essential element in what was to become the 'authority' of the Roman Catholic Church.

---

[290] Ibid 42: 1-44: 6

[291] Ehrman B.D. The New Testament. Oxford University Press (1998) 398

The Way to Christianity

At about the same time as Clement was writing to the Corinthian Church, Ignatius, the Bishop of Antioch, was writing a series of seven letters. Six of which were to Churches in the Eastern Mediterranean,[292] whilst the seventh was to his friend and fellow Bishop, Polycarp.[293] The occasion for writing was Ignatius' arrest and transfer as a prisoner to Rome. Ignatius' letters are important for early Christianity, since they give insight into both the divisions in the early Church and Ignatius' understanding of his role as Bishop.

Ignatius

Ignatius believed that the Kingdom of the Devil was present alongside the heavenly Kingdom of God and, as a consequence, God had sent his son to earth to destroy death and sin. As such, only through belief in Jesus could any Christian similarly overcome death.

In Ignatius' system of belief man does not have an existence independent from God, therefore, man is wholly unable to atone for his sins. The central problem facing man is that his relationship with God has been distorted by the Devil; a malaise that he cannot remedy by himself and one that can only be cured through establishing a new covenant with God, since man's position has been irredeemably corrupted.

The only restitution that man can make is through participation in the resurrection of Jesus: only in this way can man restore a proper relationship with God and re-acquire immortality and freedom from sin. Thus, man must live in Christ, and the only way that man can do this is through the Church, which is the 'body of Christ'.

Ignatius' conception of the Church lies at the centre of his beliefs, and he saw the Church as a community of believers. A Christian may be baptised, but this does not guarantee protection from the Devil: only when Christians gather together can they overcome sin. This is particularly so when individual members of a congregation partake of the 'blood and body of Jesus' in the Eucharist. This ritual, performed by their Bishop, is the great communal act in which the devil can be defeated.

---

[292] Ibid 318-321; 322-324; 325-327; 328-330; 332-333; 334-336

[293] Ibid 337-339

However, the Devil remains an ever-present risk, constantly seeking to divert believers from the path of true righteousness. As such, the power of evil is never completely banished, and it is only through continual communion with one another in Jesus that salvation is assured. Only when a congregation comes together with their Bishop in the presence of Jesus can sin and death be overcome; anyone attempting to practice his beliefs outside the community of the Church is doomed to failure.

The position of the clergy was of great importance to Ignatius. He firmly believed that there was only one body and blood of Jesus, together with one Bishop in the Eucharist. These elements were inseparable, as was the position of the Bishop with the Presbyters and Deacons. Submitting to the person of the Bishop was the same as submitting to God.

Although Ignatius does not seem to have believed that God directly selected Bishops, he does see the Bishops as God's representatives. This was especially true when the Bishop, the Deacons and the congregation joined together in the Eucharist. Indeed, the Eucharist performed without the Bishop was not as valid as one with the Bishop present. For Ignatius this formed a central tenet of his belief and he saw no greater power than the Bishop in communion with his congregation.

This view seems to suggest that Ignatius viewed the power attainable through the presence of a Bishop as something transient—attained at its peak through their role as a conduit in facilitating a relationship between God and the congregation—rather than an inherent, permanent power. As such, a gathering of Bishops was of no greater significance than the presence of an individual Bishop, whilst if the congregation were not present, then it was diminished.

Although Ignatius believed that a community worshipping without its Bishop was worshipping the Devil, he does not see the Bishop as superior to the congregation. Clements's non-hierarchical perspective on inter-Church relationships is also reflected in Ignatius' views on structure and practice: each Church following these principles was spiritually equal to all other communities.

Appointment of a new Bishop was not to be under the purview of other Bishops, but instead was the result of an election by a council of the community of which he was part. Writing to his friend Polycarp,

Ignatius suggests the steps that should be taken to appoint a new Bishop after his death:

> 'So my dear Polycarp, (and how richly God has blessed you), you ought to call a most religious council and appoint somebody whom you regard as especially dear and diligent, and who can act as God's messenger.' [294]

Church Rituals

The first description of early Church rituals comes from Justin Martyr. Although written in the middle of the second century, it seems reasonable to assume that the account probably provides a fair description of even earlier Church practices.

Once baptised, the newly admitted Church members would take part in their first Eucharist, repeating the words:

> 'We thank you our Father for the holy line of David, your child which you have revealed through Jesus your child to be glory forever.'

Then in connection with the piece of bread:

> 'We thank you Father for the life and knowledge which you have revealed through Jesus your child. To be glory forever.' [295]

In addition to bread, the cup of wine mixed with water would also be drunk, and a kiss of spiritual love exchanged with each member of the community. The newly baptised Christian would enter a world of considerable piety, and would be expected to pray at least three times a day, to fast on Wednesdays and Fridays, and to attend a Church service

---

[294] Ibid 338

[295] Ehrman B.E. After the New Testament. Oxford University Press. (1999) 347-349

every Sunday. The days of fasting and service mimic the patterns found in Synagogues, but seem to have been consciously set on different days.

Worship consisted of a reading from the 'memoirs of the Apostles' or 'the writing of the Prophets', a sermon was given and prayers and thanksgiving said. A collection was taken, probably of both food and money, which was distributed to the 'orphans and widows and those on account of sickness, or any other cause are in want.' This distribution of goods and money was a common feature of a number of religions in antiquity, where almost the only form of 'social security' was by membership of a religious assembly.

Church Structure

No aspect of the early Church has been examined as exhaustively as its structure. The 'Apostolic Succession' and the position of Peter as the 'first Bishop of Rome' were early concerns, particularly of the Catholic Church. During the reformation and at other revivalist times, there was a desire to return to a time when: *'Christians lay under obedience to no ordained officers, but were led by the Holy Spirit.'* [296]

The difficulty with such an undertaking is that so little is known of the first and second century Church. James Tunstead Burtchaell,[297] amongst others, has argued that the structure of the earliest Christian Churches was similar to that of the Synagogue. There is considerable force in this argument. Paul of Tarsus was a Jew and it was highly likely that the 'House Assemblies' he founded followed, in part, a Jewish pattern. As Christian Churches began to develop from Paul's House Assemblies this pattern was likely to persist, with one notable exception.

In the early Churches considerable reverence was accorded to visiting charismatic preachers, whilst in contemporary Synagogues this was not so. The reasons for this are readily apparent. The traditions of Paul, one of the most energetic itinerant religious teachers ever known, were revered, and it was natural for others to emulate his approach as well as to afford respect to others who did so.

---

[296] Tunstead Burthaell J. From Synagogue to Church. Cambridge University Press (1992)

[297] Ibid

Whilst the structure of the early Christian Churches was essentially that of Judaism, the nomenclature was not. The use of the term 'Synagogue' to denote a Jewish Sabbath meeting place is early, although it may not predate the destruction of the Great Temple in Jerusalem, but Christians avoided the term. Initially the first Christians may have only referred to 'meeting places' to denote the location of their weekly worship, although this is by no means certain.

If the descriptive title of early Christian 'House Churches' is not wholly clear, the day of worship was. From earliest times Christians met on a Sunday, not on a Saturday, to commemorate the day of the resurrection, which was regarded as taking place on the day after the Sabbath. It also helped to distinguish themselves from Jews.[298] In a similar manner, Muslims were later to utilise Friday as a day of communal worship, to distinguish them from both Jews and Christians.

The early Christian Churches were organised and run by a group of 'elders' or Presbyters who were assisted in this task by Deacons, who could be either male or female. This structure is essentially similar to that of the Synagogues, with the exception that women were not allowed to hold office in Jewish places of worship.

A further system of appointment found in Synagogues may arguably have had its equivalent in early Christianity. In Judaism, a board of notables drawn from elders of the assembly would elect a president who would hold ultimate responsibility for the Synagogue, this position of 'President' would find its equivalent in the title 'Bishop' in a Christian gathering.

That the position of Bishop was to be imbued with great status and power at a somewhat later date is incontestable, however, the position of 'Bishops' in the very early Church is far from clear. If Bishops were yet to realise significant status and influence over their congregations, then who ultimately held influence over these scattered small House Churches? The answer is that it was probably the itinerant charismatics. Paul's legacy lived on, the memory of the 'Apostle to the Gentiles' remained strong, and congregations revered travelling teachers and Prophets, who followed in his footsteps.

---

[298] Ibid 278

Differing Emphases

Central to the new religion of Christianity was the possibility of personal salvation after death. Belief in Jesus was the necessary prerequisite for the prospect of eternal life, whilst, since the Devil was ever-present to lead the unwary astray, Christians were encouraged to gather together regularly with their Bishops and symbolically partake of the 'blood and body of Christ'.

However, even in this early stage, potential differences were present. Clement the Bishop of Rome had proposed what became known as the 'Apostolic Succession'. In the second and third centuries this became increasingly important, and in time was incorporated into 'Roman Catholicism' with the position of Pope as the symbolic inheritor of the mission of Jesus. By contrast, Ignatius had forcibly proposed the supremacy of the individual Bishops, with no other authority above them. His ideas were to eventually be incorporated into the Orthodox Church—which could claim direct descent from Paul's original House Assemblies—and, although modified by national boundaries and Patriarchal structures, this remains the structure of the Orthodox Church to the present day.

Although the first great schism in Christianity between the Catholic and Orthodox Churches was not to occur for many centuries, it is possible to see differences in emphasis arising at a very early stage.

The greatest achievement of the early Church was to overcome the failure of prophecy. The central prophecy of The Way was the imminence of the 'last days.' Even Paul, a robustly independent member of The Way, believed in the imminence of God's arrival. With the destruction of the Holy of Holies in Jerusalem, it was apparent that God was not coming, or at least he was not coming in the near future. Early Christianity, which appears to have been remarkably adaptable, simply downgraded The Way's prophecy and replaced it with a deeply mystical account of Jesus' life and death. In so doing Christianity denigrated its Jewish inheritance and created fertile soil for the seeds of anti-Semitism.

The Way to Christianity

Christian Anti-Semitism

The virulent anti-Semitism, which has so disfigured Christianity, is often attributed with early beginnings, particularly in the oft-repeated charge: that 'The Jews killed Jesus.'

That a small group within the High Priesthood was vigorously opposed to The Way is undeniable; that they were acting under Roman standing orders to arrest trouble makers during the time of Passover is highly likely, however, much else is not.

The account in the Gospel, attributed to Matthew, of Jesus' appearance before Pilate is highly suspect. The claim that Pilate addressed a crowd saying: *'Then what should I do with Jesus who is called the Messiah?'* [299] seems wholly implausible. Pilate would have been too busy at Passover to concern himself with an insignificant troublemaker from Galilee, and Roman Prefects did not leave decisions over capital offences to conveniently gathered crowds. The spectacle of Pilate washing his hands whilst the crowd chanted *'Let him be crucified'* [300] followed by *'His blood be on us and our children'* [301] seems highly unlikely, as well as somewhat illogical.

Far more likely was that a small group of Sadducees who were not representative of Judaism as a whole, collaborated with the Roman authorities, as they were bound to do if they wished to maintain their position within the High Priesthood. The responsibility for Jesus' death lies with Pilate, who as the representative of Rome ultimately signed the warrant to crucify Jesus after had had been found guilty of the Roman crime of sedition.

The misplaced belief in Jewish responsibility for Jesus' death was not the only factor inciting Christian anti-Semitism. Paul's intemperate attacks on the Jerusalem leadership of The Way and his occasionally derogatory remarks about the 'Jews' cannot have helped. But other factors were also at play.

The Emperor Vespasian and his son Titus had led the legions during the first Jewish campaign, and both had good reason to dislike the

---

[299] Matthew 27: 22

[300] Matthew 27: 24

[301] Matthew 27: 25

rebellious Jews. Many of the privileges which had previously been extended to the *'Tribe of David'* were revoked after the Roman victory[302] and subsequently to be a Jew was to be viewed with intrinsic suspicion by the Roman authorities. The great Jewish historian Josephus, from whom we know so much of this period, wrote his accounts both to explain his fellow countrymen, and to blame Roman maladministration for the first Jewish uprising.

For the small groups of early Christians life was far from easy. To die for one's beliefs might well be considered glorious, but to die as a result of being confused with a rebellious Jew was not. The anti-Jewish tone of much early Christian literature reflects these immediate circumstances in which it was written.

The effects of Christian anti-Semitism have been horrendous. As Christianity became the dominant European religion, Jewish persecution grew ever more widespread. From the Christian inspired Roman pogroms against Jewish communities, through the medieval Spanish persecution instigated by the Royal leadership of Ferdinand and Isabella, to the Holocaust, which was met with an appalling silence from Rome, millions have died. Many more have been displaced and suffered unimaginable hardship.[303]

Perhaps the greatest cause of Christian antipathy towards The Way and Judaism in general stemmed from the failure to recognise Jesus as divine; that Jesus' family and earliest followers did not regard him as anything other than human was well known. The Christian response was, as far as possible, to remove these individuals from the accounts of the earliest days of their religion. Where this was not possible, because they were too well known, they were portrayed as incompetent or dim-witted. Yet this must have left lingering personal doubts; whilst Jesus' family and first disciples could be largely written out of the earliest accounts, as is the case with the Acts of the Apostles, this did not resolve the central question: Why wasn't Jesus' divinity recognised by his own family? A question that Christianity has never satisfactorily answered.

---

[302] Dunn J.D.G. The Partings of the Ways. SCM Press (1991) 231-238

[303] Wilson B. How Jesus Became Christian. Wiedenfeld and Nicolson. (2008)

CHAPTER 7

THE LITERATURE OF THE WAY AND EARLY CHRISTIANITY

The earliest literature of The Way, and the only material which can be dated pre-70CE, are the letters of two of Jesus' brothers.

The Letters of James and Jude

The letters of James and Jude are probably the least well known of the epistles in the Christian Bible and are also amongst the shortest. Jude consists of a single chapter and twenty-five verses, whilst James is somewhat longer at five chapters and one hundred and eight verses. Both use Jesus' name and give him a number of titles such as Lord, Master etc., however, questions remain over the letters' authenticity.

Prior to the invention of the printing press, publication was done by hand, with groups of writers slowly recopying original documents. These writers would, in turn, be overseen by redactors who would check their work and compile component parts into scrolls or books. Over the years, further hand written copies would be repeatedly remade from older copies. There is now a general consensus that in at least one instance a document was altered by Christian copyists, to the extent that the original cannot now be recovered.

Much of the works of the Jewish historian Josephus were preserved by Christianity on the basis of a single paragraph found in only one version of his writings:

'At about this time lived Jesus, a wise man, if indeed one might call him a man. For he was one who accomplished surprising feats and was a teacher of such people as accept the truth with pleasure. He won over many Jews and many

> *of the Greeks. He was the Messiah. When Pilate, upon an indictment brought by the principal men amongst us, condemned him to the cross, those who had loved him from the very first did not cease to be attached to him. On the third day he appeared to them restored to life, for the holy prophets had foretold this and myriads of other marvels concerning him. And the tribe of the Christians, so called after him, has to this day still not disappeared.'* [304]

This paragraph provides the only independent, non-biblical, evidence for Jesus' life. However, it now appears that Christian scribes were not able to resist altering what they were preserving.

Josephus was known to be a devout Pharisee without any Christian sympathies, as such, it is nowadays widely accepted that he would not have written the phrase *'he was the Messiah'* in relation to Jesus. There are also other aspects of Josephus' reference to Jesus where omissions and changes are thought to have occurred. Whilst few doubt that Josephus referred to Jesus, very few believe that what we now have is an accurate copy of the original document. Do similar considerations apply to the letters of James and Jude?

It is widely accepted that James was a particularly righteous Jew who fully accepted the Jewish law: *'You do well if you really fulfil the Royal law according to the scripture.'* [305] It was also the case that Jews unlike later Christians considered the Messiah to be human rather than a divine figure (Chapter 3). In the introduction to this letter James uses the phrase: *James a servant of God and of the Lord Jesus Christ.'* [306]

How plausible is it that James wrote these words? As Richard Bauckham has pointed out, this shows that: *'Jesus shares the divine throne in heaven.'* [307] Whilst this is no more than a statement of belief for a Christian, in my view, it is quite unthinkable that a devout Jew such as James would have used these words. If the names and titles of Jesus are removed from the letters what is left are two characteristically

---

[304] Josephus F. Antiquities XV111 3,3 63-64

[305] James 2: 8

[306] Ibid 1: 1

[307] Bauckham R. James. Routledge (1999) 138

Jewish documents. Since Jude describes himself as: *'Brother of James'* [308] they probably stand or fall together. [309]

The Letters of James

James' letter was written to the *'Twelve tribes of the dispersion.'* [310] That this refers to the twelve tribes of Judaism is, in my view, incontrovertible. It has clearly been shown that the apparently unconnected elements of James' letter are characteristic of wisdom literature.

Wisdom literature takes the sayings of a wise sage and re-presents them, in a somewhat different form, to cast new light on the power of the original. This type of literature was quite widespread amongst the cultures of antiquity. As might be expected, Jewish wisdom literature was always considered to be derived from God. In the case of James, the original sage has been seen as Jesus, but the reverse could also be true. It is also possible that both Jesus and James could have been drawing upon the now lost sayings of a previous sage, perhaps John Ben Zechariah? There is of course no way of knowing. In his letter James advised his followers to follow a clearly defined path:

> *'If any of you is lacking in wisdom ask God . . .'*
> *'Blessed is anyone who endures temptation . . . Every generous act of giving, with every perfect gift is from above . . .'*
> *'Religion that is pure and undefiled before God the Father is this: to care for orphans and widows in their distress and to keep oneself unstained by the world . . .'*
> *'Listen my beloved brother and sisters, has not God chosen the poor of the world to be rich in faith . . .'*

---

[308] Jude 1: 1

[309] For a discussion of the authorship of the letters of James and Jude see Bauckham R. Jude and the Relatives of Jesus in the Early Church. T & T Clarke (1990) 171-178 and Bauckham R. James. Routledge (1999) 16-19

[310] James 1: 1

> *'You do well if you really fulfil the royal law according to scripture . . .'*
>
> *'Do you want to be shown your senseless person that faith without works is barren. Was not our ancestor Abraham justified by his works . . .'*
>
> *'Submit yourselves therefore to God. Resist the devil and he will flee from you . . .'* [311]

As more than one writer has observed, taken together, these and the other exhortations in James' letter are a call for *'perfection before God.'* [312] This seems to beg two related questions: Why place so much emphasis on the need for perfection, and; what was driving the urgency implied in its content and tone? The answers are to be found in the last chapter of James' letter:

> *'Strengthen your hearts for the coming of the Lord is near. Beloved do not grumble against one another so that you may not be judged. See the judge is standing at the door!'* [313]

The message of James's letter is the central teaching of The Way, and clearly reflects the situation that existed prior to the destruction of the Jerusalem Temple in 70CE.

As a leader of The Way, James is advising his followers to prepare for God's arrival and imminent judgement. Tellingly, there is no Christian element to this message, indeed, contrary to one of the central tenets of early Christianity 'faith' in Jesus is not enough: *'you see that a person is justified by works and not by faith alone.'* [314] James does not advocate 'faith' in his brother as the route to the Kingdom of Heaven, nor does he suggest that his brother's death was an atoning sacrifice for sin. Neither is there any suggestion that the Followers of The Way should 'put on Jesus' as a replacement for the law, as was the case with the teaching of James' contemporary Paul of Tarsus. As such, James'

---

[311] Extracts from Hames 1: 2-4: 7

[312] Hartin P.J. A Spirituality of Perfection. Liturgical Press Minnesota (1999)

[313] James 5: 7-9

[314] James 2: 24

message is wholly Jewish; the examples he gives are taken exclusively from the Hebrew Bible. In my view what we have, quite remarkably, is the central thesis of The Way set out by one of its leaders, preserved as Christian literature.

How this came about is quite unknown, there is no historical source of which I am aware, which gives us a clue. But I would like to offer a speculation. James' letter was sent to the 'Twelve Tribes of the Dispersion.' In practical terms this means to the missionary leaders of The Way. The best known, and certainly the most highly regarded by emerging Christianity, was Simon Peter. Was James' letter found amongst Peter's effects after his death, and did this lead to its preservation by Christianity? We will, of course, never know.

The Letter of Jude

Unlike the letter of James, Jude's letter clearly belongs to the Jewish tradition of Pesharim writings, examples of which have been recovered from the Qumran caves.[315] Pesharim documents draw on biblical traditions to support a particular view-point. As such, Jude's letter was a warning not to be led astray by false teachers, using as its principal source the book of Enoch.

> *'Woe to them! For they go the way of Cain and abandon themselves to Balaam's error for the sake of gain and perish in Korah's rebellion. It was also about these that Enoch . . . prophesised saying. See the Lord is coming . . . to execute judgement on all.'* [316]

Why were these warnings necessary? The answer is found in verses 4 & 8:

> *'For certain intruders have stolen in among you, people who long ago were designated for this condemnation as*

---

[315] Bauckham R. Jude and the Relatives of Jesus in the Early Church. T & T Clark (1990) 149-154

[316] Jude 1: 5-14

ungodly. Yet in the same way these dreamers also defile the flesh, reject authority and slander the glorious ones.' [317]

Jude does not say who these ungodly people are, but clearly the most obvious candidate is Paul, who advised his Gentile followers to abandon the law and refuse to be circumcised.

Taken together the letters of Jude and James provide a remarkable and unsuspected insight into The Way. It is difficult to imagine a more complete description of the religious ideas of The Way than James' letter. There is one further point that can, and perhaps should, be made. The letters of James and Jude do not 'fit' into Christianity, as they fail to recognise that exclusive faith in Jesus had replaced the need for the Jewish law—but they do fit seamlessly into the Jewish expectation of the 'last days.'

It is not clear why the letters of James and Jude were written. James' letter may be the Jewish equivalent of an Episcopal letter sent from Jerusalem to Synagogues established or affiliated to The Way, but, as is so often the case with the history of early Christianity, the context has not come down to us. James' letter, and perhaps that of Jude, predates James' demise in 62CE.

'Jewish Christian' Literature

There a number of quotations from documents which are usually chronicled under the heading of 'Jewish Christian' literature.

THE GOSPEL OF THE EBONITES derives its name from the Aramaic word for 'poor men,' and appears to have been written in the first half of the Second Century. The gospel itself is no longer extant, but quotations are contained in the Fourth Century book of Epiphanies. These fragments show that whilst the Ebonite's did not subscribe to Jesus' divinity, they did believe that his death was an atoning sacrifice for sin.

THE GOSPEL OF THE NAZAREENS was also written in Aramaic, probably in the first half of the second century, and places particular emphasis on strict observation of the Jewish 'law'. Many scholars have suggested that it is the Hebrew form of the Gospel of

---

[317] Jude 1: 4 & 8

Matthew, but, as the original is no longer in existence, it has not been possible to test this claim.

THE GOSPEL OF THE HEBREWS also failed to survive the passage of time, and is only known from passages quoted by early Church historians. One in particular describes James, Jesus' brother, fasting until he (Jesus) rose from the dead.[318]

THE LETTER OF PETER TO JAMES AND JAMES' RESPONSE are to be found in the introduction of the Homilies of Clement. Peter's letter accompanied a selection of his sermons, which the apostle was anxious should not fall into the wrong hands, particularly those of his 'enemy,' who is generally considered to be Paul of Tarsus. In response, James agrees to Peter's request and limits the reading of Peter's sermons to worthy members of The Way.[319]

PAUL'S LETTERS: Not all the letters attributed to Paul are thought to have been written by him; of the fourteen letters, only seven or possibly eight are generally accepted as being written by the Apostle. The letter to the Thessalonians is probably the earliest, written around about 50CE.[320] Whilst the second letter of Timothy, if it can be correctly attributed to Paul, was written in Rome whilst Paul was under house arrest, perhaps in 64CE. Of the remaining five or six letters some are thought to represent compilations of more than one letter. The second letter to the Corinthians and Philippians falls into this category. The remaining letters: Romans, first Corinthians and the letter to Philemon, probably represent single compositions.

Of the further letters attributed to Paul: the second letter to the Thessalonians, the first letter to Timothy, the third letter to the Corinthians and the letter of Titus are thought to have been written at some point after Paul's death. For the most part they deal with problems encountered by the emerging Church. It is not clear when the letters were collected together, but it may have been towards the end of the first century. Thereafter, they were to appear in every list of canonical writings until the final compilation of the Christian Bible.

---

[318] Elliot J.K. The Apocryphal New Testament. Oxford University Press (1993) 9-10

[319] Ehrman B.D. After the New Testament. Oxford University Press. (1990) 22-25

[320] Ehrman B.D. The New Testament. Oxford University Press (1998) 244

Paul and the Law

If the gospel writers were successful in replacing the imperative of the 'last days' with the religious significance of Jesus' life and death, they faced greater problems with the Jewish law. Whilst Paul had clearly claimed that a belief in Jesus superseded the need for the law, the writers of the gospels had considerable difficulties in tracing this assertion to Jesus. In only two instances were they able to assert a rather tenuous claim that Jesus had not observed the full requirements of the law.

In the first, and perhaps the best known, Jesus' disciples are encountered by a group of Pharisees eating *'ears of corn on the Sabbath.'* [321] In this instance Jesus defended his followers by citing a precedent attributed to King David. This was a wholly valid Jewish approach: if an individual could show that his actions were consistent with Hebrew scripture then no breach of the law was considered to have taken place. It should be said that Jesus' precedent was somewhat disingenuous, King David had been feeding his troops prior to battle, and this was clearly not the case with Jesus' followers. Nevertheless, a precedent had been claimed and doubtless Jesus and the Pharisee who had questioned his follower's actions had a thoroughly enjoyable time debating the issue!

In the second instance, which also involves the laws governing food and its consumption, the gospel attributed to Mark has Jesus declaring all foods clean.[322] However, Mark precedes this apparent breach of the dietary law, by citing Jesus:

> *'Whatever goes into a person from outside cannot defile, since it enters not the heart but the stomach and goes out into the sewer . . . it is what comes out of a person that defiles.'* [323]

As Geza Vermes has pointed out:

---

[321] Matthew 12: 5

[322] Mark 7: 19

[323] Mark 7: 19-20

> *'The patent meaning of the words is that defilement is caused not by the foodstuff as such, but by the heart's disregard of a divine prohibition.'* [324]

Thus, whilst the writers of the Christian Bible clearly sought to substantiate Paul's claim that Jesus had replaced the law, they were generally unable to attribute this position to Jesus. Indeed, they recorded a series of statements in which Jesus flatly contradicted any suggestion of not obeying the law, the best known of which is probably: *'Till heaven and earth pass away not one letter, not one stroke of a letter, will pass from the law.'* [325]

This rather obvious conflict between the view attributed to Jesus, and that expressed by Paul, is still a matter of scholarly debate. Perhaps the best recent contribution has come from Ed Saunders, who has clearly shown that Jesus was an observant Galilean Jew, who sought not only to observe the law, but more importantly to uphold its spirit.[326]

The Synoptic Gospels

Perhaps no feature of the Christian Bible has been as thoroughly researched as the Synoptic Gospels: Matthew, Mark and Luke. In 1989, Ed Saunders and his wife Margaret Davies published an authoritative textural analysis of the three gospels that is unlikely to be surpassed for some time.[327]

There is an almost universal view that the Synoptics, and indeed much of the emerging Christian Bible, was written in Greek. There is also consensus that, unlike the letter of Paul, the authors of the three gospels, and indeed of John, are unknown. Indeed, as has been shown,[328]

---

[324] Vermes G. The Changing Face of Jesus. Allan Lane, Penguin Press (2000) 196-197

[325] Matthew 5: 18

[326] Saunders E.P. Jewish Law from Jesus to Misnah. SCM (1990) Chapters 1-4

[327] Saunders E.P. and Davies M. Studying the Synoptic Gospels. SCM Press (1989)

[328] Ibid 7-15

it was not until the middle of the second century that the authorship of the gospels was attributed to named individuals.

Although we cannot establish the authorship of the gospels with any certainty, we do have some idea of when they were written. For a variety of reasons, there is fairly general agreement that the gospel attributed to Mark was written about the year 70CE. The gospels attributed to Matthew and Luke were written in the latter part of the first century, whilst the gospel attributed to John can probably be dated to the turn of the century. They were written by authors who lived two or three generations after Jesus' death, who may have had three potential sources for information which will be considered in turn: The Hebrew Bible; An—as yet unidentified—'source book' and; By word of mouth.

1) THE HEBREW BIBLE

Paul's seminal contribution to Christianity was the establishment of Jesus as its single religious iconic figure. But Paul had gone further than this: for Paul, Jesus' life, death and resurrection, had been foretold in Jewish religious literature.[329]

The writers of the New Testament assiduously searched the Hebrew Bible for references to Jesus. It is apparent that they used the Greek translation for this purpose, rather than the original Hebrew, since Greek mistranslations were carried forward into the gospels. To an outside observer it would seem that the Hebrew Bible contains very little that was relevant to Jesus' life and death. However, the writers of the gospels were not to be deterred, and even the smallest reference, particularly to the Messiah, was closely examined for any Christian reference that it might contain. The earliest reference, at least in terms of relevance to Jesus' life was his conception: *'Look the young woman (translated in Greek as virgin) is with child and shall bear a son'* [330] The passage comes from the Greek translation of the Old Testament, rather than the original Hebrew, where the words *'young woman'* (in Hebrew almah), rather than virgin, are found. [331]

---

[329] Romans 1: 1

[330] Isaiah 7: 14

[331] Vermes G. The Changing Face of Jesus. Allan Lane, Penguin Press. (2000) 212

The Way to Christianity

Although born the *'son of a virgin'* it was important for the writers of Matthew and Luke to trace Jesus' antecedents to King David, and, utilising the Hebrew Bible, two genealogies were derived. The writer of Matthew traces Jesus' descent through David, to Abraham.[332] Whilst the writer of Luke went even further, ending his list with the first man created by God, Adam.[333] Both trace descent through male lineage, including Jesus' father Joseph—in apparent contradiction of his wife's *'virginity.'* For a detailed discussion of the Lucan Genealogy of Jesus see Bauckham (1990).[334] In addition to his descent, the Hebrew Bible also supplied the place of Jesus' birth: Bethlehem.[335] The city of King David was regarded as the expected birthplace of the Jewish Messiah.

Both Matthew and Luke placed Jesus' birth in Bethlehem, with Luke utilising a *'registration'* in 6CE by the Syrian Governor Sulpicius Quirinius for this purpose.[336] The writer of Luke was apparently unaware that the registration was for the purpose of a poll tax, which would have required Joseph and Mary to remain in Nazareth whilst their tax liability was assessed. In addition to details of the nativity, the gospel writers may also have utilised the Hebrew Bible as a source for later episodes in Jesus' ministry.

Some of the activities attributed to Jesus follow a pattern found amongst the seminal Prophets of the Hebrew Bible, and can be summarised in the following manner:

---

[332] Matthew 1: 2-16

[333] Luke 3: 23-38

[334] : Bauckham R. Jude and the Relatives of Jesus in the Early Church. T & T Clarke (1990) 315-373

[335] 1 Samuel 17: 12-25

[336] Luke 2: 2-4

John Larke

FEEDING MIRACLES

Jesus:

'Taking the five loaves and two fish he looked up to heaven, he blessed and broke the loaves . . . and all ate and were filled and they took up twelve baskets full of broken pieces.' [337]

Elisha:

'A man came . . . bringing . . . twenty loaves of barley . . . in his sack. Elisha said, give it to the people and let them eat. But his servant said how can I set it before them, they ate and had some left over.' [338]

HEALINGS

Jesus:

'As he entered a village, ten lepers Approached him, keeping their distance they called out saying, Jesus Master, have mercy on us. When he saw them he said to them: Go show yourselves to the priests . . . they were made clean.' [340]

Elisha:

Elisha sent a messenger to him saying:
Go wash in the Jordan seven times and your flesh shall be restored and you shall be clean.' [339]

RAISING THE DEAD

Jesus:

'When he had entered he said to them . . . the child is not dead but sleeping . . . He took her by the hand . . . and immediately the girl got up and began to walk.' [341]

Elisha:

'He carried him and brought him to his mother, the child sat on her lap until noon and he died . . . When Elisha came into the house he saw the child lying on his bed . . . Then he got on the bed and lay upon the child . . . and while he lay bent over him, the flesh of the child became warm.' [342]

---

[337] Mark 6: 41-42

[338] 2 Kings 4: 20-24

[339] 2 Kings 4: 20-34

[340] Luke 12: 14

[341] Mark 5: 39-40

[342] 2 Kings 5: 10

Elijah:

'After this the son of the woman . . . became ill . . . there was no breath left in him . . . he laid him on his own bed . . . The Lord listened to the voice of Elijah: and the life of the child came into him.'[343]

In the similarities between Jesus, Elijah and Elisha, it is tempting to see the hand of the gospel writers, who, having examined the Hebrew Bible, felt that these were the type of activities that Jesus would have been involved in, but this was not necessarily the case. It may have been Jesus who was consciously following some of the traditions of the early Prophets, in which case the writers of Mark and Luke were simply recording what had taken place. Of course this may be simple coincidence, although the number and closeness of the similarities rather argues against it.

2) A SOURCE BOOK

We owe the concept of an, as yet unidentified, *'source book'* to nineteenth century German scholars. This theoretical collection of material relating to Jesus was called 'Q' after the German word 'quelle' for source. The notion of 'Q' was based on the observation of similar elements appearing in different sequences in the gospels, particularly those attributed to Matthew and Luke. The German scholars appear to have envisaged the writers of Luke and Matthew, utilising Mark, in conjunction with some other source book to write their gospels.

But how realistic is it to envisage the first and second century gospel writers compiling their work in the manner of later nineteenth century scholars? Ed Saunders has proposed a pattern that much more closely reflects the realities and likely practice of Jesus' followers and the early Christian writers.[344]

---

[343] 1 Kings 17: 17-22

[344] Saunders E.P. The Historical Figure of Jesus. Allan Lane, Penguin Press (1993) 57-76

3) WORD OF MOUTH

Saunders' scenario sees a gradual accumulation of material—beginning in the period immediately after Jesus' death, with the disciples initially recalling some of the things that Jesus had said, and then discussing it amongst themselves. This was, in turn, passed on to the people whom they were trying to convert, often in the form of a saying, accompanied by an introduction and conclusion. This conception allows for a transmission of narrative that preserved many of Jesus' words, but in which the context of the original sayings were often lost. In time, these brief sayings began to accumulate into longer passages and, at some point, they became written down.

At an even later stage, passages were linked to form a single episode of a longer story, and it was only after 70CE that the episodes were compiled into a complete account and the gospels were written. This approach has the advantage of plausibility—providing a model that 'fits' the common origins evident in some of the Gospels—and also accounts for no trace of the 'Q' source book ever being found.

The Gospel of John

Paul had two overriding principles:[345] firstly, the unique significance of Jesus' life and death and secondly, the embodiment of Jesus as a replacement for the Jewish law.

The unique significance of Jesus' life and, more particularly, his death, find wholehearted and extensive expression in the Christian Bible, in particular in the gospel attributed to John, which eulogises Jesus in a way not found in the synoptic gospels.

On encountering Jesus, John Ben Zechariah declares: *Here is the lamb of God who takes away the sin of the world'* [346] and, somewhat later: *'For God so loved the world that he gave his only son, so that everyone who believes in him may not perish but may have eternal life'* [347]

These, and the numerous other descriptions of Jesus, place the gospel attributed to John in a special category and, taken together with

---

[345] Romans 3: 21-26

[346] John 1: 29

[347] John 3: 16

Paul's letters, form the bedrock of much Christian belief. John is usually regarded as the most theologically developed of all the gospels, written at some point after the turn of the first century.[348] In many ways, the gospel attributed to John represents the natural culmination of Paul's view of Jesus: Whilst Paul had stopped short, but only just, in declaring Jesus divine, there is no such reticence in John, who sees Jesus as the fulfilment of God's purpose: *'Now the son of man has been glorified and God has been glorified in him'* [349]

One other notable feature of the gospel attributed to John is the almost complete absence of any hope for the imminence of the 'last days'. If whoever wrote John was writing at the beginning of the second century, then this gospel may be representative of a time when belief in Jesus had almost completely replaced the expectation of the early arrival of the Kingdom of God.

The Acts of the Apostles

In the New Testament, the Acts of the Apostles follows the synoptic gospels and the gospel attributed to John. Whilst the title is suggestive of several apostles, the book is principally concerned with just two: Peter and Paul.

Ostensibly, the Acts of the Apostles is an historical account of the events that occurred after Jesus' execution. In fact, it is a proselytising tract that shows the continuity of the Holy Spirit passing from Jesus to Paul: other apostles are mentioned in the first portion of Acts, but the only significant other actor besides Paul is Peter, whose principal contribution is to declare all food clean. The most notable person missing from Acts is James, who is only briefly mentioned in relation to Paul.

Robert Eisenman, amongst others, has argued in an exhaustive account that James' role in Acts has been removed by later Christian editors and copyists. He points to the disjointed nature of the early part of Acts, and suggests that this is indicative of rather brutal editing. In particular, Eisenman argues that the election of a twelfth disciple after the death of Judas was originally a description of the election of James

---

[348] Vermes G. The Changing Face of Jesus. Allan Lane, Penguin Press (2000) 9

[349] John 13: 31

as the new spiritual leader of The Way.[350] Whilst entirely plausible, we have no historical source to support this contention.

Also speculative is the role of Peter in the early Church: Acts gives no credence to the role of Peter as the first 'Bishop of Rome', and indeed states that his 'Church' was at Antioch. What is not speculative is the role of Paul, whose character and energy permeate the second part of Acts.

Paul's last journey from Caesarea Maritime to Rome has been shown to be consistent with an autumnal boat trip under sail (Chapter 5) and some of the other episodes in Acts also appear historically reliable. The trial of the disciples by the Sanhedrin accords with ancient legal practice, in which a powerful 'friend in the court' would speak for the accused.[351] The episodes of James' judgement of Paul's activities, is also consistent with what is known of the character of 'James the Just.' But, in the end, the most powerful impression of Acts is Paul of Tarsus, accepting the mantle of Jesus, and sowing the seeds of a new religion in his name.

Letters of the Christian Bible

In addition to the letters of James and Jude, there are six further letters included in the 'New Testament,' although the first of these, Hebrews, resembles a book rather than a letter. Originally attributed to Paul, it is now widely accepted that it was not written by the apostle. Rather, it may represent a sermon, or series of sermons, delivered towards the end of the first century.

The purpose of Hebrews is to chastise those members of a Christian community who are also attending a Jewish Synagogue. The writer of Hebrews clearly sees emerging Christianity as superior to Judaism: *'Yet, Jesus is worthy of more glory than Moses.'* [352]

The remaining five letters of the Christian Bible: Peter1, Peter2, John1, 2 and 3, have two similarities with Hebrews: firstly they deal with problems encountered by the emerging Church and secondly they

---

[350] Eisenman R. James the Brother of Jesus. Faber and Faber (1997) 154-213

[351] Acts 5: 33-39

[352] Hebrews 23: 3

were not composed by their putative authors. Whilst the dates of these letters are uncertain, it is unlikely that they predate the end of the first century, and some might originate from as late as the third.

The Revelation of John

The final component of the New Testament is usually referred to as Revelation, and is easily the most mystical book in the Christian Bible. The book records a number of visions experienced by a writer called John, who is otherwise unknown, and apparently lived on the Greek island of 'Patmos', off the coast of Turkey.

In these visions the number seven is both significant and recurrent. The first vision is of the 'son of man' sending letters to seven Churches. There are a number of disasters outlined in further visions, which include the blowing of seven trumpets, the breaking of seven seals, the seven bowls of God's wrath, and the destruction of Rome, which was built on seven hills. These catastrophic events are a prelude to the arrival of the Kingdom of Heaven, which will first be inhabited by the souls of those who have been beheaded for their testimony to Jesus. Concurrently with the Kingdom of Heaven, the Devil and Satan will be bound in a bottomless pit for a thousand years, at the end of which death will be defeated and a new heaven and earth created.

To modern readers, Revelation must seem a strange conclusion to the New Testament. However, this type of visionary book was well known and popular in antiquity, both amongst Christians and Jews. Three other Christian apocalyptic mystical books are known: 'The Shepherd of Hermas' [353] the 'Apocalypse of Peter' [354] and the 'Apocalypse of Paul,' [355] but none found a permanent place in the New Testament.

The 'Holy Bible,' now has a deep and revered place in Christian consciousness, however, this was apparently not so in the very early Church. The gospels, although not named until the middle of the second century, were probably read in Church services.[356] The process by which

---

[353] Ehrman B.D. The New Testament. Oxford University Press (1998) 386-406

[354] Ibid 296-301

[355] Ibid 301-308

[356] Saunders E.P. and Davies M. Studying the Synoptic Gospels. SCM (1989) 3-24

the gospels were attributed to Matthew, Mark, Luke and John is not known, but it seems to have been part of a desire for authority, at a time when the early Church was rather fragmentary. The only reasonably reliable authorships are the majority of the letters of Paul, and the letters of James and Jude.

Even at a time when the canon of the New Testament was beginning to emerge, it was not held in unquestioning regard. Justin Martyr, by no means the first 'Martyr,' regarded the gospels merely as memoirs.[357] He does not seem to be alone in this; indeed some early literate Christians disliked the written word so much that they preferred to depend instead on the stories of Jesus, which had been passed down by word of mouth.

If the New Testament did not initially have widespread acceptance, its definitive composition was even more of a problem. The earliest list describing the contents of the New Testament was discovered in the eighteenth century by an Italian, L.A.Moratoi.[358] The list comprises the gospels and much of the present day canon and was probably originally composed during the second century. However, excluded from the list are: Hebrews, James, Jude and the third letter of John, as are two of the letters attributed to Paul. Included are: 'The Wisdom of Solomon' and the 'Apocalypse of Peter'.

At a slightly later date, Irenaeus, writing against the 'heretics,' defends the use of all four gospels: *'It is not possible that the gospels can be either more or fewer in number than they are ... There are four zones of the world ... and four principal winds.'* [359]

The Christian scholar Origen of Alexander, does not provide a complete list of canonical books, but agrees with Irenaeus on four gospels, to which he adds the Pauline epistles, one letter each of Peter and John, and the 'Apocalypse of John.'

Eusebius, the noted early Church historian, writing in the first part of the Fourth Century, describes the debate continuing on the composition of the New Testament:

---

[357] Stevenson J.A. A New Eusebius. SPCK London (1987) 117

[358] Ehrman B.D. After the New Testament. Oxford University Press (1999) 311-312

[359] Stevenson J. A New Eusebius. SPCK London (1987) 117

> 'We must of course, put the holy quartet of the gospels, followed by the Acts of the Apostles. The next place on the list goes to Paul's epistles and after that we must recognise the epistle called John, likewise Peter, to these may be added, it is thought proper the Revelation of John . . . these are classed as the recognised books. Those that are disputed, yet familiar to most, include the epistles known as James, Jude and Peter two, and those called two and three John . . . Amongst spurious books must be placed the Acts of Paul, the Shepherd and the Revelation of Peter, also the alleged Epistle of Barrabas, and the teachings of the Apostles, together with the Revelation of John.' [360]

Even after Eusebius the debate still continued, and it was not until 367CE that the first list of twenty-seven books, now found in the Christian Bible was published.[361]

Apocryphal Literature

Besides the twenty-seven books that were eventually incorporated into the Christian Bible, there are many that were not. In some instances a published work did not correspond with emerging Christian orthodoxy, in others a book might be seen as largely fictitious, and in a few it is difficult to escape the impression that personal preferences played a part.

The Homilies and Recognitions of Clement

Ostensibly written by Clement, the Bishop of Rome, towards the end of the first century, both the Homilies and Recognitions were probably written at a later date, perhaps in the third century. Both depend on an earlier common source, which purports to be an account of Clement's travels with Simon Peter, and particularly his disputes with Simon Magnus. The Homilies and Recognitions were supposedly sent to Jesus'

---

[360] Ehrman B. After the New Testament. Oxford University Press. (1999) 311-312

[361] Ibid 5

brother James in Jerusalem, and are a somewhat curious amalgam of the beliefs of The Way and early Christianity.[362]

Gnostic Literature

In the summer of 1945, a library of fifty-two tracts was discovered close to the Egyptian village of Nag Hammadi.[363] The majority of the library was Gnostic (Chapter 9) and, of the total of fifty-two works, forty were previously unknown. Although there were considerable early difficulties, and a great delay in publication, the entire library is now available translated into English.[364]

The burial of the library may have been deliberate: a number of early Christian Bishops were known to have been Gnostic, and it is possible that the Library was interred to preserve its contents during the widespread suppression of Gnosticism by the Christian Church in the fourth and fifth centuries. For this reason, this date is usually given for the burial of the documents. The literature varies somewhat in style and religious orientation and is thought to have been collected over a period of time. Of the various documents, perhaps the best known is the Gospel of Thomas.

THE GOSPEL OF THOMAS[365] is a 'sayings book' containing one hundred and fourteen statements attributed to Jesus. Some replicate sayings found in the gospels, whilst others are wholly unknown. Although there is a pervasive Gnostic theme throughout Thomas' gospel, other books contained within the library are more characteristically Gnostic, and many individual sayings contained in the gospel are only mildly Gnostic. Whilst the gospel has been widely researched, there is, as yet, no general agreement as to the authorship, or indeed the date of composition.

---

[362] Roberts A. and Donaldson J. The Anti-Nicene Fathers. Erdmans. (1995) Volume 8.

[363] Robinson J.M.(Ed). The Nag Hammadi Library. Harder, San Francisco (1990) 22-25

[364] Ibid

[365] Ehrman B.D. After the New Testament, Oxford University Press (1999) 237-244

THE SECRET BOOK OF JOHN[366] presents discussion between Jesus and John, taking place after the former's resurrection. The writer of the secret book gives a particularly clear account of Gnosticism, describing the juxtaposition of two Gods. One is portrayed as a pure spiritual God, whilst the other is the wholly impure creator of the physical world, who is seen as the God of the Hebrew Bible; Jesus' role is described as providing knowledge (Gnosis) of the higher spiritual God, so that the enlightened may escape from their mundane physical existence.

Unacceptable Works

THE SECRET GOSPEL OF MARK was 'discovered' in 1958, by the American scholar Morton Smith, who found it at the end of a letter recovered from the library of a Greek Orthodox monastery outside Jerusalem. Longer than the gospel of Mark, it contains an apparently homoerotic encounter between Jesus and a young man who has been raised from the dead. Highly controversial, only copies of the original documents have been made available, leading to doubts regarding the document's authenticity.[367]

THE GOSPEL OF PETER[368] was popular in many Churches in the second century, and is one of the most virulently anti-Semitic works produced by any Christian writer. Notable anomalies, when compared to the New Testament, include a depiction of Jesus dying without pain on the cross and rising on the third day as a giant, accompanied by two equally large angels. The gospel is only known in fragmentary form, from material recovered from the tomb of an Egyptian monk. It may have been written in the second century.

THE EPISTLE OF THE APOSTLES[369] lacks clarity regarding its author and date of composition, although the second century has been suggested, and takes the form of a Gnostic text, in that it is a

---

[366] Ibid 146-154

[367] Smith M. Clement of Alexandria and a Secret Gospel of Mark. Cambridge. Mass. (1973)

[368] Ibid 259-262

[369] Ibid 259-262

post-resurrection account of Jesus addressing his eleven remaining disciples. But whilst the form is Gnostic, the contents are not. Jesus argues against the ideas found in the Secret Book of John by insisting that the crucifixion and resurrection took place with a physical body. He also emphasises the importance of the flesh: *'Truly I say to you, the flesh of every one will Rise with his Soul alive and his spirit.'*

Letters Falsely Attributed to Paul

It is nowadays recognised that Paul was not responsible for authoring some of the letters attributed to him in the Christian Bible; even as early as the third century some of these letters were seen as inauthentic, and were not considered for inclusion in the emerging Christian Bible. Three letters all fall into this category: Paul's third letter to the Corinthians,[370] the letter to the Laodiceans[371] and correspondence between Paul and Seneca.[372]

In the third letter to the Corinthians, the author argues strongly against a number of Gnostic teachings, and emphasises that only those who oppose the tenets of Gnosticism will find salvation

The author of the very short—only twenty verses long—letter to the Laodiceans sends a series of exhortations to the Laodicean assembly. Although exhibiting no underlying theological purpose, the letter was included in many early copies of the Christian Bible.

The correspondence between Paul and the noted Philosopher Seneca purports to be fourteen letters exchanged between the two notable figures. Although the purpose of these pseudonymous letters is clearly to enhance Paul's reputation by showing him corresponding with the most noted Philosopher of his day, there is little of real substance on either side of the correspondence.

Alongside the rather numerous documents that were considered for inclusion in the emerging Bible is one notable exception: there are almost no authentic accounts of Jesus' childhood.

---

[370] Ibid 290-292

[371] Ibid 295

[372] Ibid 292-294

Jesus' Early Life

After the miraculous birth narratives recorded in Matthew and Luke, there is an almost complete break in the accounts of Jesus' early life, and it is only in the gospel attributed to Luke in which we find any record of an incident from Jesus' boyhood.

As they return from a religious festival in Jerusalem, Joseph and Mary are horrified to find that their son is missing. Returning to Jerusalem, they find Jesus in learned discussion with the 'teachers' (Pharisees) at the Temple, and *'all who heard him were amazed at his understanding and his answers.'* [373]

It is only in the apocryphal literature that further accounts of Jesus' early life and that of his mother are found. In 'The Protevangelium of James' Mary is described as a 'perpetual virgin' whose intact state was not altered by the birth of her son. Mary's descent from David is also described, as is an assertion that Jesus' brothers were in fact his stepbrothers. Although this account is historically implausible, its style is restrained and it was greatly influential, particularly in medieval times, when Mary was elevated to the iconic status of 'Mother of the Son of God.' [374]

Rather more details of Jesus' early life are provided by the Infancy Gospel of Thomas, which should not be confused with the 'Gospel of Thomas,' an entirely separate work. The infancy gospel provides a highly fanciful account of a precocious child given to capricious and even vengeful acts: At one point Jesus *'withers up a child'* completely for scattering water that had previously been purified. In similar manner, *'a child ran and knocked against his (Jesus') shoulder'*, and Jesus was so angered and said to him: *You shall go no further on your way, and immediately he fell down and died.'* [375] However, within the Infancy Gospel, and juxtaposed against these destructive episodes, are instances where Jesus intervenes to raise both a child and a building labourer from the dead.

---

[373] Luke 2: 47

[374] Ehrman B.D. After the New Testament. Oxford University Press. (1992) 248-255

[375] Ibid 256

Although these oddly opposed and impetuous actions fail to draw a coherent picture of Jesus' character as a child, they do echo episodes in the Hebrew Bible. Once again there are parallels with the prophet Elisha, who both raised the dead and caused bears to maul a group of small boys who had mocked his baldness.[376]

The Protevangelium of James and the Infancy Gospel of Thomas were both popular in the early Church, and probably went some way to satiating a natural curiosity amongst believers by describing Jesus' early years. Both works were copied and widely available, giving rise to considerable derivative literature including, *inter alia*, the Gospel of Pseudo Matthew, the Arabic Infancy Gospel, the History of Joseph the Carpenter and the Gospel of the Birth of Mary. Although of no historical value, these works give insight into the religious curiosity and beliefs of many early Christians and, although considered for inclusion, were never accepted as canonical literature.

Apocryphal Acts

In addition to the literature concerning Jesus, apocryphal descriptions of some of his followers were also compiled. The authors of these apocryphal acts are quite unknown, but most are thought to date from the second and third centuries:

THE ACTS OF PETER[377] is a highly fanciful account of the Apostle resembling the Pseudo Clementine Recognitions and Homilies. A series of Peter's miracles and sermons are described, as is a contest with the magician Simon Magnus.

THE ACTS OF JOHN[378] take place in Ephesus, where John carries out a healing which amazes the inhabitants of the city. He then engages in a contest with the Pagan authorities, which results in both the death of their priests and the destruction of the City Temple.

---

[376] 2 Kings 2: 23-24

[377] Elliott J.K. The Apocryphal New Testament. Oxford University Press (1999) 278-284

[378] Ibid 303-347

THE ACTS OF THOMAS[379] recounts Thomas' journey to India. The rewards of a virtuous life are also contrasted with the terrors of hell, which is the fate of those who fail to repent of a life of sin.

THE ACTS OF PAUL[380] describes a series of miraculous episodes from Paul's life. A lion converted by Paul spares his life in the arena, whilst during his martyrdom, milk rather than blood flows from his severed head and body.

THE ACTS OF THECLA.[381] Following her conversion by Paul, Thecla converts other female followers to a chaste form of Christianity, which leads to conflicts with husbands and fiancées, who complain to the authorities. Although condemned as a Christian, Thecla is saved from martyrdom by a series of miraculous events, after which she shares equally in Paul's missionary work.

Apocryphal Apocalypses

Apocalypses were popular amongst Jews and early Christians, where they served as grave warning for those who strayed from the paths of righteousness. They often take the form of a celestial traveller, who visits both heaven and hell:

THE APOCALYPSE OF PETER[382] records an account of a discussion between Jesus and his loyal followers. Typical of its type, it stresses the horrors of hell to a greater extent than the wonders of heaven.

THE APOCALYPSE OF PAUL.[383] Paul had once claimed to have been taken into heaven,[384] but could not bring himself to describe what he had seen. This reticence did not extend to the writer of the apocalypse

---

[379] Ibid 350-356

[380] Ibid 439-442

[381] Ehrman B.D. After the New Testament. Oxford University Press (1999) 278-284

[382] Elliott J.K. The Apocryphal New Testament. Oxford University Press (1993) 593-612

[383] Ibid 619-644

[384] 2 Corinthians 12: 1-7

attributed to Paul, who gives a fairly stereotypical account of heaven and hell, which in many ways follows the pattern found in the apocalypse of Peter.

The Shepherd of Hermas[385]

This book is an account of the mystical experiences of an early Christian, Hermas, who experience a number of visions that were interpreted by a heavenly shepherd. Some of the information given to Hermas is straightforward, whilst some is in the form of parables that have to be interpreted. The essential message is the choice between good and evil and the manner in which a Christian should seek to lead a life that is acceptable to God. The Shepherd of Hermas was particularly popular during the first few centuries of Christianity, but did not find a place in the emerging Bible. It is difficult to understand why this was so; the book is particularly accessible, and makes a clear distinction between right and wrong. Perhaps it was no more than personal preference that resulted in the deeply mystical, Revelation of John finding a place in the Bible, whilst the Shepherd of Hermas did not.

This brief summary attempts to illustrate the scope of the material read by early Christians. Much of the information in this chapter is taken from the work of Bart Ehrman, who has admirably chronicled the available documents in a series of books published by Oxford University Press.[386] Also published by Oxford University Press is an Apocryphal New Testament by J.K.Elliott[387] whose book augments Bart Ehrman's work and contains a number of documents not found in the former.

A salient point, and one to which I must also offer credit to Ehrman, is that the material highlighted here represents only what has survived and, as such, is probably only a fraction of a much larger body of work; a fact illustrated in the 1930's with the discovery of a previously unknown

---

[385] Ehrman B.D. The New Testament. Oxford University Press (2004) 386-406

[386] Ehrman B.D. The New Testament and other Early Christian Writings. Oxford University Press (1998); Ehrman B.D. After the New Testament. Oxford University Press (1999); Ehrman B.D. The New Testament. Oxford University Press (2004)

[387] Elliott J.D. (Ed) The Apocryphal New Testament. Oxford University Press (1993)

The Way to Christianity

work. 'The Unknown Gospel' was discovered amongst papyri obtained by the British Museum and published in 1935.[388] Only fragments remain of the original gospel, the author and date of which are wholly unknown.

Conclusion

The process by which the Christian Bible was compiled took over three hundred years and was far from straightforward. It seems clear that the largest challenge facing the compilers was that of selection from what must have been a large body of writings. In performing this they undoubtedly believed that they were inspired by God.

If it was indeed Divine intention to publish a proselytising account of Jesus' mission that would provide the foundation for the establishment of a new religion in his name, this was wholly fulfilled. As Ed Saunders eloquently puts it:

> *'The general approval of Jesus shows how well the authors of the Gospels did their job. They intended to turn to him, to admire him and to believe that he was sent from God and that following him would lead to eternal life. Seldom have hopes been more completely fulfilled.'* [389]

---

[388] Bell H.I. and Skeat T.C. Fragments of an Unknown Gospel and other early Papyri. (1935) London.

[389] Saunders E.P. The Historical Figure of Jesus. Allan Lane, Penguin Press (1993) 7-8

CHAPTER 8

EARLY PERSECUTION AND MARTYRDOM

As with a number of successful colonizing empires, the Roman Authorities' attitude to religion was one of general toleration in an apparent spirit of integrationism. In Rome and the other major cities of the Empire, large numbers of Temples to different deities could be found. Many of these Gods had come from conquered peoples, and Rome frequently supported the construction of Temples and statues to newly arrived religions. In return, all that was required was recognition of the existing Gods, and worship of the Emperor, who was increasingly seen as divine. Exceptions could be made in circumstances where this was not possible.

Prior to its first uprising, Judaism, with its exclusive adherence to a single God, was generally well regarded. Roman administrators recognised that devout Jews could not pray *to* the Emperor, instead they offered to pray *for* the Emperor, and this was readily accepted; a compromise that maintained religious harmony and avoided conflict. Yet this was not to be the case with Christianity, which, from its outset, offended Roman sensibilities.[390]

Unlike Judaism, Christianity was a new arrival in the religious world, and this of itself made it suspect amongst conservative Romans, who generally revered—and correspondingly accommodated—ancient practices. Christianity therefore, began at a disadvantage and this was to be compounded by Christian attitudes.

Whilst Christians might be prepared to follow their Jewish counterparts and pray for the Emperor, they were not prepared to accommodate Pagan Gods. Christians believed that theirs was the only

---

[390] Shelton J.A. As The Romans Did. Oxford University Press (1998) 359-404

God and this excluded all others. This exclusivity was regarded as arrogance by the Romans, and the refusal to accept Pagan Gods, as atheism.

Rome had risen from a small city-state to become the ancient world's largest Empire. Whilst the Gods were not seen as responsible for this good fortune, they had not impeded it. For Rome it remained important, both at a personal and national level, that the Gods should be appeased. Failure to do so could incur the Gods' displeasure, which could result in misfortune and perhaps even defeat in battle.

The Christian refusal to recognise the Roman Gods was not just an irritant, but a potential danger to the Empire. In meeting this threat, Rome's administration sought not so much to suppress Christianity as to recast it into a new more tolerant mould. In this they wholly failed. It soon became apparent that some Christians would rather die than make even token gestures to Paganism.

Martyrdom, which became increasingly voluntary as time went on, was a novel feature of Christianity. Suicide was certainly known in antiquity, but to elect to die for a religious belief was uncommon. Some writers have suggested that Christianity was following traditions derived from either Pagan[391] or Jewish traditions.[392] The evidence for these views is limited, and in neither case can it be supported unequivocally. Furthermore, it seems likely that the cause of elective martyrdom grew out of early Christian experience.

Death was deeply embedded in early Christianity. The first four leaders of The Way: John, Jesus, James and Simeon, met violet deaths for their beliefs, as did a number of their followers. Likewise, whilst the details of Paul's death are not known, it is probable that he also met a violent end. The mythology surrounding these executions and the possibility of personal resurrection offered by Jesus' death provided a fertile soil for martyrdom.

The first general persecution of Christians has already been described: Nero, seeking scapegoats for a disastrous fire in Rome, had executed a group of early Christians with a brutality that shocked even

---

[391] Bowersock G.W. Martyrdom and Rome. Cambridge University Press (1995) 1-23

[392] Lane Fox R. Pagans and Christians. Penguin Press. (1986) 436-437

the hardened Roman citizenry. Paul and possibly Peter, who may have been visiting Rome at the time, could have been amongst this number. This early persecution set the pattern of much that was to follow.

Roman persecution was sporadic, and rarely involved large numbers, but it had a visceral and galvanising effect on early congregations. Christians came to see themselves as a persecuted minority who must be prepared to die for their faith. In reality, had Rome concentrated its efforts into a systematic effect to eliminate early Christianity, it could easily have done so. The Roman view of Christianity is illustrated by a well-known exchange between Pliny, the Governor of Bithynia and the Roman Emperor Trajan.

Pliny in his initial appointment as a Governor had encountered Christians for the first time. In the absence of any guidelines, he: *'Asked them a second and third time (if they were Christians) with threats of punishment.'* [393] upon proving unrepentant they were sent for execution.

Trajan's response was to endorse Pliny's course of action; there was no set procedure for dealing with Christians and: *'They are not to be sought out; but if accused and convicted, they must be punished.'* [394] This correspondence occurred at some point after Pliny's appointment in 112CE.

This attitude towards Christians remained essentially unchanged until 'the great persecution,' which occurred between 303 and 312CE under the Roman Emperor Diocletian.

Ignatius

Whilst persecution of Christians was for the most part sporadic, Christian martyrs were greatly revered: none more so than Ignatius the Bishop of Antioch in Syria. When Ignatius was taken to Rome for execution in 110CE, his journey was punctuated by a stop at Smyrna, where he was able to correspond with a number of local Churches. His final letter to the Roman Christians illustrates his attitude to his fate, as he pleads with them not to intervene: Ignatius sees himself as voluntarily dying for God, and seeks to deter any intervention from well-intentioned

---

[393] Stevenson J. A New Eusebius. SPCK (1987) 18

[394] Ibid 21

Roman Christians. This rather suggests that with comparatively little effort Ignatius' life could have been spared, but that such an outcome was the last thing that the Bishop of Antioch wanted. He clearly saw his fate as a willing sacrifice for Jesus: *'I am God's wheat and I am being ground by the teeth of wild beasts to make a pure loaf for Christ.'* [395]

This willingness to self-sacrifice was a characteristic feature of many early Christian martyrs, although few expressed it with such relish as Ignatius. It seems clear that he did not see his death as an atoning sacrifice for sin; after all, Christians believed that that particular sacrifice had already been made by Jesus. Robin Fox Lane has suggested that Ignatius' sacrifice was a 'Eucharistic offering,' with his blood as wine and his body being 'ground down' to make the bread of God.[396] Whatever the validity of this approach, the enthusiasm with which Ignatius sought death cannot be doubted.

The Arena

Death in the arena—to which Ignatius looked forward—was a common feature of Roman life. Amphitheatres were found in most major Roman cities, and 'games' were frequently held to celebrate notable events, and whilst the spectacles varied in style, violent public death was an invariable constituent. Such grisly entertainment might take the form of attack by wild animals, the holding of mock battles and, commonly, fights between trained gladiators.

In the modern Western world, we are largely protected from the sight of public death by a media that removes images considered too offensive to broadcast; this was not so in antiquity. Rome was a warrior-state, which expanded its territory through conquest where battles were invariably fought 'hand to hand.' A Roman Legionnaire, using his short 'stabbing' sword, would have had no choice but to witness death at first hand: the blood, gore and desperate cries of his enemy as he was dispatched would have had none of the 'arm's length' dissociation of contemporary warfare. Battlefields were sites of slaughter, which at the end of an engagement would be blood-drenched and strewn with the

---

[395] Ehrman B.D. After the New Testament. Oxford University Press (1999) 28-30

[396] Fox Lane R. Pagans and Christians. Penguin Press (1988) 437

bodies and body parts of the numerous dead. The games were frequently family events, which were attended by whole households, including slaves and the very young.[397] As such, in part, Roman games must have played a part in inuring the young to the reality of trauma and death.

Courage in the face of death was much admired and even some defeated gladiators were spared if they had fought well. This was not so for criminals convicted of a capital offence, of which Christians formed a very small percentage. Christians met their end in a variety of ways in the arena, but they were not always popular victims. Crowds took a delight in suffering and the desperate attempts of victims to avoid their inevitable fate. Christian calmness in the face of death, which was so much admired by Christian writers, was largely met with derision from the arena crowds, and some Christians were simply killed, without ritual, for this reason.[398]

In essence, Martyrdom affords significance to the otherwise insignificant, particularly to fellow devotees. This was readily apparent in early Christianity, where martyrs were elevated to Sainthood and revered through the proclamation of Martyr days in Christian Churches.

Polycarp

One of Ignatius' letters was addressed to Polycarp, Bishop of Smyrna, who was, in turn, martyred in about 155CE. We do not have Polycarp's own account of his feelings prior to his death, but a description of his martyrdom was sent from Smyrna to the Philomelium Church and has survived.[399]

A certain Quintus, who had been a Christian, betrayed Polycarp under threat of death. Upon hearing that he was being pursued, Polycarp wisely left his Church and hid in a series of small farms until one of his slaves, under torture, revealed his whereabouts. Taken before a proconsul, Polycarp was asked to make a declaration that he was not a Christian by *'swearing by the genus of Caesar'* and saying *'away*

---

[397] Kyle D.G. Spectacles of Death. Routledge (1988) 1-10

[398] Ibid 242-253

[399] Ehrman B.D. After the New Testament. Oxford University Press (1999) 31-35

with the atheists,' which in effect meant denying his Christianity. This Polycarp refused to do and, despite his advanced years, he was executed.

The martyrdom of Polycarp was written up in a heroic manner, which echoes the death of Jesus: Prior to his arrest it was claimed that Polycarp entered a city, riding on a donkey on the 'day of a great Sabbath.' The police captain who detained the Bishop was referred to as 'Herod' and he initially tried to dissuade Polycarp from meeting his fate in the arena. When his Christianity was announced to the crowd, Gentiles as well as Jews living in Smyrna were reported to have cried out that Polycarp should be burned alive.

Initially he was tied to a stake, but at first he was unaffected by the fire which formed an 'arch' and the arena was reported to have been filled with a fragrant odour. Eventually Polycarp's body was successfully cremated, and his bones were collected and stored for veneration by subsequent generations. The description of Polycarp's death forms the first martyr-ology—a genre that was to become hugely popular with early Christians. In such accounts the deaths of Martyrs were written up in the most reverential of terms. This reverence extended to the collection and preservation of remains, where they could be gathered, which became in themselves holy objects to which miracles were attributed.[400]

Ptolemy and Lucius

The martyrdom of Ptolemy and Lucius, which probably took place in about 160CE, illustrates the dangers Christians faced from aggrieved partners in a marital dispute. A 'certain woman,' divorced her licentious husband by applying to the Emperor for a repudium, or bill of divorce. This action, which could only have been brought by a woman of some standing, effectively prohibited her husband from taking any action against her.

Prevented from further confrontation with his former wife, her ex-husband denounced her religious teacher Ptolemy instead. Ptolemy was brought before a magistrate whose sole concern was to discover whether he was a Christian. After admitting that he was, he was condemned together with a Christian named Lucius, who protested that Ptolemy

---

[400] Ibid 30-35

was: *'Not an adulterer, nor fornicator, nor murderer, nor robber, nor convicted of any crime at all, but who has only confessed that he is called by the name of Christian.'* [401]

Both Ptolemy and Lucius were 'led away,' that is taken out for execution, almost certainly in the arena. The fate of Ptolemy and Lucius graphically illustrates the vulnerability of early Christians who could be drawn into disputes with fatal consequences.

Justin Martyr

We owe the account of Ptolemy and Lucius to Justin Martyr, whose name has become synonymous with dying for a cause. Justin was an early Christian intellectual who established a Christian Academy in Rome, which was similar to the Greek schools of Philosophy, which were widespread in antiquity.

Justin published three major works that are extant. Two are philosophical discourses, defending Christians against their many detractors, whilst the third, called 'dialogue of Trypho,' is an account of a discussion between Justin—a Christian, and Trypho—a Jew. In his dialogue, Justin presents a carefully argued philosophy, which was based on Jewish holy literature and which identified Jesus as the promised Messiah. In 165CE, Justin and a group of his companions were brought before the Prefect of Rome and, when asked to describe his beliefs, Justin provided his definition of Christianity:

> *'One God existing from the beginning, maker and artificer of the whole creation, seen and unseen, and concerning our Lord Jesus Christ, the son of God who was proclaimed aforetime by the Prophets as about to come to the place of man for herald of salvation, and for master of true disciples.'* [402]

After questioning, Justin and his seven companions were tortured and beheaded.

---

[401] Stevenson J. A New Eusebius. SPCK (1987) 30-32

[402] Ibid 32

Speratus and His Companions

In 180CE a group of Christians were persecuted under Saturninus, the Proconsul of Praesens. A verbatim account of the proceedings survives, which describes a Christian named Speratus and eleven of his companions appearing before the Governor:

The Proconsul opens the proceedings by inviting the Christians to abandon their beliefs and worship the Emperor. This, in turn, the Christians refuse to do.

The following extract gives the flavour of the proceedings:

> Saturninus to Speratus: *Do you persist in remaining a Christian?*
> Speratus: *I am a Christian.*
> Saturinus: *Do you require any space for consideration?*
> Speratus: *When the right is so clear, there is nothing to consider.* [403]

At the end of the case Speratus and his followers were found guilty and were executed 'by the sword.'

The question and answer extract given above is taken from the Acts of the Sicilian Martyrs and may represent a verbatim record of what was said, given that it is known that Roman courts employed assistants to record proceedings. There are strong similarities in the records of a number of Martyr Acts, and they may represent the proceedings commonly employed in magistrate's courts throughout the Empire.[404]

Vienne and Lyons

A more general persecution broke out in Vienne and Lyons, in what is now France, in 277CE. The origin of a series of attacks seems to have arisen from a common belief that Christians indulged in incestuous orgies, during which human blood and flesh were consumed.

---

[403] Ehrman B.D. After the New Testament. Oxford University Press (1999) 36-37

[404] Bowerstock G.W. Martyrdom and Rome. Cambridge University Press (1995) 36-37

This popular misunderstanding of the realities of the weekly communal meals, where Christians exchanged the 'kiss of love' and the Eucharist, where bread and wine became the body and blood of Jesus, was widely believed.

Initially the persecutors 'debarred' known Christians from houses, baths and the forum, and then from 'any place whatsoever.' Subsequently public disorder broke out and Christians were assaulted wherever they were encountered. Many were imprisoned and tortured whilst waiting for the arrival of the Governor.

A letter written by a Christian, who managed to escape, describes the persecution: Initially suspects, under the threat of execution were asked, *'are you a Christian?'* Those who denied their faith were eventually released, whilst the remainder were subject to prolonged periods of torture, and subsequently death. After death, the victim's bodies were displayed for six days, after which they were burnt and the ashes thrown in the river Rhone to prevent the remains being used as object of veneration.[405]

The persecution of Christians in the first two centuries CE follows the pattern set out by the Emperor Trajan. Christians were not sought out, but, where they were encountered, they were given the opportunity to recant and make sacrifices to the Gods. If they persisted in their beliefs they were executed. This pattern was to change in the third century.

Third Century Rome

Rome in the third century was in crisis. Roman power and wealth was derived from the conquest of rich neighbours and the bounty of conquered Kings and Rulers had embellished Rome and rewarded its legions. However, as the Empire grew, it ran out of weak affluent countries to conquer, and Governance became more difficult as the distance to the Empire's borders increased.

With care and good management the Empire's survival need not have been imperilled, however, knowledge of what is nowadays called macroeconomics did not exist, and monetary inflation became a major problem. Rome's distant neighbours learnt to campaign in the Roman

---

[405] Ehrman B.D. After the New Testament. Oxford University Press (1999) 35-41.

manner, after many of their young men had served in the legions, and the pervasive spirit of Roman military adventure was now replaced by a defensive posture, to secure and hold the boundaries of the Empire.

Matters came to a head in the third century. The assassination of the Emperor Severtius Alexander in 235CE ushered in a period of great political and military instability. Over the next fifty-one years, twenty-six Emperors ruled over the Empire, in entirety or in part, and all but one met a violent death. Almost all had come to rule through the command of their legions, and civil war was common-place.

These Military Emperors came to replace the aristocracy, which had held power for so long, and the Roman Senate ceased to have even a nominal role after about 280CE. Many of the aristocrats retired to their vast country estates, where they were often impoverished by ruinous levels of taxation. Roman society was now polarised between the powerful military men, who were often effectively above the law, and the dispossessed, known as Humiliores.

Although military Emperors were now in the ascendancy the almost constant internal conflict, and the increasing fighting efficiency of Rome's enemies, caused problems. Rome came under attack from both the northern Germanic tribes and from the Persians, and for a time Gaul was lost. Stability was only restored with the accession of the Emperor Decius in 248CE.

During this troubled period a number of Emperors sought to restore traditional religious practices and assuage the Gods and, in so doing, oppressed oriental mystery religions, of which Christianity was one.[406]

Decius and State Persecution

The first systematic attempt to ensure adherence to ancient beliefs was made by Decius in about 250CE. Amongst a number of measures, Decius required the inhabitants of the Empire to provide sworn certificates showing that they had sacrificed to the Gods. For this purpose commissioners were appointed to every part of the Empire to oversee the operation. About fifty certificates survive, of which the following is representative:

---

[406] Lewis N. and Reinhold M. Roman Civilisation. Columbia University Press (1990) 566-567

> 'First Hand. To the commission chosen to superintend The sacrifices at the village of Alexander's Isle. From Auerelius Diogenes, son of Satabous, of the village of Alexander's Isle, aged 72 years, with a scar on the right eyebrow. I have always sacrificed to the gods, and now in your presence in accordance with the edict I have made sacrifice, and poured a libation, and partaken of the sacred victims. I request you to certify this below. Farewell I Aurelius Diogenes, have presented this petition.
> Second Hand. I, Aurelius Syrus, saw you and your son sacrificing.
> Third Hand . . . onos . . .
> First Hand. The year of the Emperor Caesar Gaius Messius, Quintus Trajanus Decius Pius Felix Augustus, Epeiph 2 (26 June, 250).' [407]

Although some Christians refused to comply and were executed, many did sacrifice, whilst others bribed the officials and some were able to use their position in the community to intimidate the commissioners. The cessation of this persecution witnessed problems for the church as, in its wake, Bishops had to decide how to readmit those who had fallen, and this led to considerable conflict. Although persecuted with some vigour, the Decius measures probably had little effect on the overall numbers of Christians.

Valerian

Of rather more effect on curtailing Christian practice, and indeed lives, were the measures taken by the Emperor Valerian. Between 257 and 270CE, Valerian issued an edict addressed to the Senate covering a number of actions. Under the edict, Christians were to be forbidden from holding meetings, or from entering Christian cemeteries, however, his approach sought to go further than merely curbing Christian gatherings. He proposed that all senior Church officials should be executed, and that aristocratic Christian Romans should lose their possessions and

---

[407] Slightly altered text from Stevenson J. A New Eusebius. SPCK (1987) 214

be killed if they failed to renounce their faith. He also proposed that similar measures were to be taken against prominent Christian women and Christian members of the Imperial household. Amongst the notable casualties of the persecution were Sixtus the Bishop of Rome, and Cyprian the Bishop of Carthage.[408]

The effect of the measures taken by Valerian was to drive Christianity underground. Some Church property was lost, and many Christian tracts burnt, but as with the persecution initiated by Decius, the adverse effect on the overall number of Christians was temporary.

Diocletian

The reign of Diocletian (285-305CE) brought to Rome a man of considerable military and administrative competence. Diocletian established a four Emperor tetrarchy, with individual Caesars responsible for different areas of the Empire. This attempt to deal efficiently with the sheer size of the Empire and to settle the question of succession was only partially successful.

In 305CE Diocletian and one other member of the tetrarchy, Maximian, retired, being the only Emperors to do so. The tetrarchy, which replaced the Diocletian administration, was short lived, lasting from 293 to 313CE and, after a period of internecine conflict eliminated most of the claimants to power, Rome was again in the hands of a single Emperor.

In 303CE, towards the end of his reign, Diocletian initiated a persecution. It is by no means clear what brought about this change of mind since he had previously tolerated Christianity, however, writing at a later date, the historian Lactantius attributed this new policy to the influence of Galerius, one of the four Caesars appointed by Diocletian.[409]

Whatever the validity of this explanation, the new persecution was embarked upon with Diocletian's characteristic efficiency and effectiveness; for the first time the increasing numbers of Christians in the Empire were, if not diminished, then at least arrested. However, although Diocletian's decree was carried out with typical vigour, it is

---

[408] Ibid 247

[409] Ibid 271

notable that the spread of Christianity may have reached the Imperial household. Both his wife and daughter were reported to have become Christians.

Initiated with the destruction of a Church in Nicomedia, the persecution was symbolically supervised by Diocletian and Maximian:

> *'When that day dawned in the eighth and seventh consulships of the two Emperors (Diocletian and Maximan), the perfect, together with the military commanders, tribunes and treasury officers came to the Church, and when the doors had been broken down ... spoil was given to all the Emperors watching from a vantage point, disputed whether it should be set on fire, the opinion of Diocletian prevailed ... and the Praetorian guard poured in from all sides in battle array, with axes and other iron implements, and in a few hours levelled that very lofty shrine to the ground. On the following day an edict was published, providing that men of that religion should be deprived of all honour and rank ... every legal action should be pressed against them ... that they should be accorded no freedom and no voice.'* [410]

Evidence of the sequestration of Church assets by the Roman authorities is shown by accounts found in recovered papyrus from Egypt and other regions of North Africa. Religious books were destroyed and Church treasures and other ephemera seized. All of this was carefully catalogued, with accounts provided to the central Roman authorities.[411]

The beginning of the end of the state persecution of Christianity came in 311CE. The Emperor Galerius, on his death bed issued an 'edict of toleration.'

> *'In view of our most gentle clemency and considering our consistent practice whereby we are wont to grant pardon to all men, we have thought fit in this case to extend immediate*

---

[410] Ibid 272

[411] Fox Lane R. Pagans and Christians. Penguin (1986) 596-601

> *indulgence, to wit; that there may be Christians once more, and they may reconstitute their places of assembly, on condition that they do nothing contrary to public order.'* [412]

The publication of the edict gave, for the first time, legal recognition to the practice of Christianity. Although, by no means completely free of persecution, Christianity now had legal status, and Christians could no longer be persecuted simply for being Christian. Galerius' 'Edict of Toleration' was followed in 313CE by the 'Edict of Milan,' a document famous in Church circles for providing a policy that recognised Christianity.

The Emperors Constantine and Licinius met in Milan in the spring of 310CE. Constantine, already pro-Christian, and Licinius, traditionally pagan, agreed a policy of religious toleration which was promulgated throughout the Empire. An extant copy of this document comes from the eastern half of the Empire, sent by Licinius, to the Governor of an eastern province:

> *'When I Constantine Augustus and I, Licinius Augustus met under happy auspices in Milan and had under discussion all matters that concerned the public advantage and security, among other measures that we saw would benefit most men we considered the first of all regulations should be drawn up to secure respect for divinity, to wit; to grant both to the Christians and to all men unrestricted right to follow the form of worship each desired, to the end that whatever divinity there be on the heavenly seat may be favourably disposed and propitious to us, and all those placed under our authority.'* [413]

Although all Governors in the Empire received a copy of the 'Edict of Milan,' their response varied, with evidence of sporadic persecutions, particularly in the Eastern Empire, until as late as the middle 320's CE.

---

[412] Stevenson J. A New Eusebius. SPCK (1987) 280

[413] Lewis. N and Rheinhold M (Eds) Roman Civilisation. Columbia University Press (1990) 572

John Larke

Numbers and Attitudes to Martyrdom

The number of Christians who died during the persecutions from Nero to Constantine is difficult to establish, with estimates ranging from a few hundred to many thousands. Perhaps the best-known appraisal is that of Edward Gibbon, who, writing in the 'Decline and Fall of the Roman Empire,' felt that the death toll in the last 'Great Persecution' numbered two thousand,[414] the majority of this number being in the Eastern Empire and North Africa.

Prior to 302/3CE there is no satisfactory estimate of the numbers who died in the sporadic and largely local persecutions. For the purposes of this book, it has been assumed that the death toll in the 'Great Persecution' was about half of the total, suggesting that in all a maximum of about four thousand Christians died, two thousand of them in the years from 65 to 303CE. Adopting this figure, which nowadays is considered to be high, gives an annual average of eight to nine deaths a year. This likely fails to reflect their incidence, which would presumably have occurred in clusters, as and when local persecutions arose.

As discussed earlier, the death of Christians at the 'Games' was not unknown and, during the reign of Augustus, there were reported to have been 65 festival days per year, whilst during Claudius' time there were 93.[415] However, the large number of festivities held in the many cities of the Empire suggests that Christian deaths in any one arena were rare. Even if the estimates given above are inaccurate, it is unlikely that the inaccuracies greatly affect the overall conclusion. Yet some Churchmen believed that the effect of these martyr deaths substantially increased the number of Christian conversions. There seems to be no way of ascertaining the validity of this argument.

Whilst witnessing 'spectacles of death' in the arena was very common for all ages, and all classes of Roman society, seeing someone die for their religious beliefs was not. As has been mentioned, the prevailing view of the apparent willingness on the part of some Christians to meet their death in public with equanimity as an article of faith seems to have been one of derision. More than one city magistrate considered

---

[414] Gibbon E. The Decline and Fall of the Roman Empire. Wordsworth (1998) 349

[415] Kyle D.G. Spectacles of Death. Routledge (1998) 77

the Christian willingness for death to be 'madness', whilst Gnostics regarded martyrdom as 'simply absurd.' Yet Christians themselves, at least in the early years, thought of it as heroic. Dying for Jesus was something that all Christians should accept and, as far as possible, be prepared for.

It is difficult to escape the conclusion that the possibility, however remote, of having to die for one's beliefs, made Christianity a 'serious' religion, in a way that was different from Pagan or Gnostic beliefs. As for recruiting more believers, we have no way of knowing; beyond a demonstration of conviction, it seems hard to imagine how witnessing Christians going passively to their death could inspire new converts.

Martyrdom and Suicide

Ignatius' last letter to the 'Romans,' in which he pleads for his fellow Christians not to interfere with his death in the Arena, includes his stated wish to be *'fodder for the wild beasts.'* Yet Ignatius fears that his Roman co-believers will prevent his desired end: '*What I fear is your generosity which may prove detrimental to me.*'[416]

Since Ignatius clearly wished to die, the question naturally arises as to the distinction between his martyrdom and suicide. The term martyrdom, which has been translated as 'bearing witness,' was not in use during the first and early second centuries, but suicide was not uncommon in the Greco/Roman world. More than one Roman died by their own hand, rather than giving their enemies the final satisfaction. Yet Ignatius was allowing others to do the killing, since the clear inference of his plea was that Roman Christians could have easily have prevented his death. As such, the distinction between Ignatius' death and suicide is not clear.

Of the various definitions of suicide, that given by Duckheim is amongst the best known:

> *'Any case of death which results directly or indirectly from any act positive or negative, accomplished by the*

---

[416] Ehrman B.D. After the New Testament. Oxford University Press (1999) 28

victim himself and in the knowledge that it would necessarily produce this result.' [417]

According to Duckheim's definition, Ignatius' death probably does count as suicide given his positive attempts to dissuade those who might have been able to prevent his demise.

Perpetua

The case of Perpetua, martyred in Carthage in 202-03CE appears to be, if not suicide, then at least a willing death. Following a period of imprisonment, during which her father pleaded with his daughter to preserve her life, Perpetua was tried and convicted. Appearing in the Arena with her slave girl by her side, she was attacked, but not killed, by a 'mad heifer.' In order to meet her end, she took *'the trembling hand of a young gladiator and guided it to her throat.'* [418]

In Perpetua's case there is little doubt that her death should be regarded as suicide. Not only had she ignored her father's pleas to save herself, in the end she even had to assist in her own execution, since she *'could not be dispatched unless she herself was willing.'* [419] The willingness of Christians to die for their beliefs was a cause of great puzzlement to the Roman authorities.

Roman Attitudes to Martyrdom

Roman attitudes to martyrdom are recorded in a number of surviving documents. Perhaps the most intellectual of all Emperors, Marcus Aurelius, contemplated with incredulity what he saw going on around him[420] and decided that Christians must be insane because of their willingness for death. This willingness was vividly illustrated by an incident before the Roman Proconsul Arius Antonius in the late 180's

---

[417] Duckheim E. Le Suicide, 3rd ed (1930) Paris.5. Translation from Bowersock G.W. Martyrdom and Rome. Cambridge University Press (1995) 62

[418] Ehrman B.D. After the New Testament. Oxford University Press (1999) 49

[419] Ibid 49

[420] Bowersock G.W. Martyrdom and Rome. Cambridge University Press (1995) 3

CE: During a judicial hearing a group of excited Christians pushed to the front of the court room, where they announced that they were Christians, and wished to be put to death. The Proconsul acceded to the request of some of them, but still more clamoured to be killed. Finally, exasperated by their attitude, the Proconsul is quoted as saying: *'you wretches if you want to die, you have cliffs to leap from and ropes to hang by.'* [421]

His remarks illustrate the earlier discussion regarding the fine line between perceptions of martyrdom and suicide; essentially the Proconsul is saying 'I will not be an agent of your own self-destruction.' Such mass martyrdoms, whilst not frequent, were not isolated events and in many instances notable Christians brought to trial would be accompanied by their followers, who would voluntarily declare their faith. Even so, attempts were made by more compassionate judges to save Christians from the fate that they appeared to so earnestly desire.

In testing Christian allegiance to Rome, many authorities suggested that all that was required was to throw a handful of incense onto a fire and to publicly acknowledge the Emperor. But it appears that some, following in the tradition of Montanus, a Christian from Asia Minor, were not to be dissuaded by even the most accommodating Magistrates: *Desire not to die in bed, in miscarriages, or soft fevers but in martyrdom to glorify him who suffered for you.'* [422] Not all Roman judges were so amenable to facilitating would-be Christian martyrs: faced with a Christian called Peregrinus, who clearly wished for death, the Roman Governor of Syria felt that the most appropriate punishment lay not in acceding to his request, but instead released him! [423]

The Decline of Martyrdom

The second and third centuries saw an increasing number of Christians electing to become martyrs. Rodney Mullen,[424] in his heroic gazetting of the Early Christian Church, has shown that few, if any, Churches were without their martyrs and that 'Martyr Days' played an

---

[421] Thomasson B. Laterculi Praesidium. Gothenburg (1984) 1 Col 232 No 162

[422] Bowersock G.W. Martyrdom and Rome. Cambridge University Press (1995) 2

[423] Ibid 61

[424] Mullen R.L. The Expansion of Christianity. Brill (2004)

increasingly important part in the yearly rituals of even the smallest congregations.

Some Church authorities were becoming concerned with the practice of voluntary death. As has been noted, the distinctions between martyrdom and suicide were becoming blurred, particularly where persecution could be so easily avoided. However, not all Christian Bishops viewed the increasing levels of martyrdom with alarm. Tertullian writing in the early part of the third century contrasted martyrdom with the punishment of '*evil doers*' who when condemned '*lament*' their fate. A Christian, on the other hand, does '*not defend himself if accused*,' indeed he glories in it. Tertullian's admiration of elective martyrdom was clearly in keeping with the sentiment of the times, as demonstrated by the sheer number of martyrs.[425] However, more perceptive voices were beginning to be heard; the great early Christian scholar Origen firmly believed that Christians should not 'compromise' when faced with genuine persecution, but he decried voluntary martyrdom.[426]

Clement, the Bishop of Alexandria also argued strongly that much martyrdom should be regarded as suicide.[427] He wanted his community, and the wider Church, to return to the original concept of martyrdom as bearing witness. For Clement people who willingly indulged in martyrdom were not true Christians, since they were murdering themselves. Furthermore, he noted, they were additionally inducing the authorities to sin by obliging them to issue death penalties. In Clements's view, willingness on the part of the martyr rendered meaningless their deaths and would not justify entry into heaven. It was an important principle that the only violent deaths that could be justified were those where there was no suggestion of complicity.

In time the Church came to see the validity of the argument of men such as Origen and Clement, but the practice of martyrdom/suicide had become well established, particularly when a notable figure was condemned. The sight of a well-known Christian facing death could inspire onlookers to share their fate, and much voluntary martyrdom took place in this way. It was problematic for Bishops to oppose these

---

[425] Tertullian Apology 1.11-13 in Stevenson J. A New Eusebius. SPCK (1987) 157

[426] Stevenson J. A New Eusebius. SPCK (1987) 198

[427] Clement Stromateis 4.4:16, 3

spontaneous and emotional actions, but increasingly they did so, and slowly the phenomenon subsided. Yet it was not until the time of Augustine of Hippo that a firm denunciation brought to an end a practice that had so perplexed the Pagan world.[428]

Christian Persecution

It has often been observed that persecution does not promote sainthood and this was clearly the case with Christianity. When adopted as the religion of the Empire, Christians became efficient persecutors and the buildings and wealth of the traditional religions of the Greco Roman world-dubbed 'Pagan' by Christianity—were taken over and converted for Christian usage. That this persecution was thorough and wide-ranging is evidenced in the destruction of Plato's Greek School of Philosophy by a group of ardent Christians. Christians also came to persecute Christians, particularly those who were believed to hold heretical views, and many who were Gnostics, including some Bishops, were subjected to prolonged and vigorous abuse (Chapter 9).

Perhaps no greater persecution was carried out than that of the Crusaders, who first arrived on the hills surrounding Jerusalem in June 1099CE. The city had a turbulent history, having been ruled for the most part by Muslims for the preceding half millennium. With some exceptions, Islam established a tolerant regime in Jerusalem, allowing Christians and Jews unfettered pursuit of their various religious practices. Many pilgrims visited the Holy city, and residences for the various groups of faithful were established in different areas.

In stark contrast to Muslim tolerance, the Crusaders fell upon the city and slaughtered its inhabitants: '*Muslims, Jews, the old, the young, men and women alike.*' Even the Christian community was expelled, in case they had become contaminated by contact with the 'Infidel.' In all some thirty thousand people died, many remaining unburied for months.[429]

It was Islam's first contact with militant western Christianity, and the long shadow of that appalling massacre remains with us to this day.

---

[428] Bowersock G.W. Martyrdom and Rome. Cambridge University Press (1995) 73

[429] Armstrong K. History of Jerusalem. Harper Collins (1997) 271-295

CHAPTER 9

GNOSTICISM

One of the most significant discoveries of ancient religious literature in the twentieth century concerned the recovery of a collection of Gnostic writings in 1945. Two brothers digging for nitrates in a naturally occurring outcrop near the village of Nag Hammadi in Egypt came across a jar whose lid was sealed with pitch. Hoping that the jar might contain something of value, one of the brothers broke it and in so doing discovered a collection of ancient papyrus codices. The books were entrusted to a local priest for safekeeping.

The antiquity of the books was only recognised by the Priest's visiting brother-in-law, who took one of them to the Department of Antiquities in Cairo where its importance was recognised. Subsequently, other books were sold in Cairo, some by a gold dealer, others by a grain merchant, and yet others by a character described as a 'one eyed bandit'. A Belgian antiquities dealer acquired some of the texts and exported them to Zurich, whilst most of the remainder were acquired by the Egyptian Antiquities Department, who were by now fully aware of the nature of the find. The books that had been transported to Zurich were subsequently returned to Egypt, and the entire collection is now housed in the Coptic Museum of Cairo.

Publication was rather haphazard, and it was not until the early 1970's that a complete facsimile edition became available. At the time of writing, translations in English, German and French, amongst other languages, are available. The edition cited throughout the present book is 'The Nag Hammadi Library' in English.[430]

---

[430] Robinson E.M. (Ed) The Nag Hammadi Library. Harper Collins San Francisco (1990)

The Way to Christianity

The books of the Nag Hammadi Library provided a literary background to some of the groups of Gnostic charismatics who developed followings during the early centuries of the first millennium. Originally written in Greek, probably in the second to third centuries, the edition found in Egypt possibly dates from the middle of the fourth century and was written in Coptic, the Egyptian language written in Greek letters. The library was almost certainly buried during a period of Church persecution of 'Heretical Texts' and there are indications that it had been compiled by a monastic order. The sealing of the lid seems to indicate that the burier intended to retrieve the material at a later date, but, as with the Dead Sea Scrolls, their retrieval was not to occur until many centuries later.

The origins of Gnosticism are obscure, but they almost certainly predate Christianity. Some writers have suggested that the Persian religion of Zoroastrianism—which portrayed good and evil as light and darkness, respectively—was a source,[431] others that lineage can be traced to Egyptian traditions portrayed in the Book of the Dead, where 'Knowledge' was needed in the 'After Death,'[432] whilst others still have suggested Gnosticism's roots in ancient Greek mystery religions. All are tenable sources of Gnosticism, as is the possibility of multiple influences, combining a fusion of these and other traditions.[433] Unfortunately much of what was known of Gnostic belief and tradition has been lost. The partial destruction of the library in Alexandria by a group of ardent Christians in 387CE, probably destroyed a great deal of Gnostic literature, and without new discoveries it is unlikely that the origins of the movement will ever be definitively known.

Unusually, Gnosticism was a religious philosophy lacking a central iconic figure, instead basing its teaching on a central, incontrovertible observation; the physical world is imperfect. Since God's status as creator of the world was accepted by Gnostics, it followed then that he must exist as an imperfect creator.

---

[431] Simon B. The Essence of the Gnostics. Arcturus (2004) 8

[432] Holroyd S. The Elements of Gnosticism. Element (1994) 9

[433] Robinson J.M. (Ed) The Nag Hammadi Library. Harper Collins, San Francisco (1990) 10

Contemporary understandings of the imperfections of our planet allow us to ascribe cause and attribute responsibility with much greater detail than was available in the past: the movement of tectonic plates produce earthquakes, volcanoes and tsunamis; the abundance of virulent pathogenic micro-organisms result in disease and death; the instability of our global climate results in drought and starvation. As a result of these and many other 'design faults,' millions die every century without distinction; the righteous and the ungodly endure suffering and dying in a world that is fundamentally unconcerned with individual existence.

Gnostic religious thought presented an optimistic answer to the traumas of the physical world, for adherents believed in the existence of separate Gods, with separate responsibilities for the earthly and the spiritual. For Gnostics, the God of the physical world was sometimes identified as YHWH, but more often referred to as the Demiurge and was apart and separate from a purely spiritual God, usually referred to as Sophia (wisdom). It was Sophia that was responsible for placing within each individual a divine spark, and the knowledge of this spiritually pure God that formed much of the basis of Gnosticism.

The term Gnosticism was derived from the Greek word for knowledge. Unlike many religions, Gnosticism eschewed a formal hierarchical structure; instead neophytes attached themselves to a noted teacher and began an internal religious journey, which could last for many years. Many Gnostics believed that, with effort, it was possible to get glimpses of the essence of the spiritually pure God, and this knowledge could have a transforming effect on an individual's religious life.

In the pursuit of inner knowledge, some Gnostics employed a practise, not far removed from some forms of meditation, utilising the repetition of a single word. However, whilst largely concerned with spiritual goals, it was the exploration by some Gnostics of an inner contemplation of sexuality that appears to have led to attacks by Christianity for supposed sexual excesses. In some cases this criticism may have had some basis, since some groups of Gnostics indulged in religious ceremonies with a strong sexual element, indeed, some Gnostics believed that true spirituality could be transiently experienced through orgasm, and conducted ceremonies around the sexual act. These groups attracted considerable criticism, but probably constituted only a very small minority.[434]

The great majority of Gnostics led a life of extreme asceticism, viewing the physical world with its many imperfections as abhorrent. Many seem to have been vegetarians and to have worn clothing made from plant, rather than animal products. Contrary to claims of sexual excess, many remained celibate—to prevent bringing children into an imperfect world—and spent their lives in deep inner contemplation. Whilst there was a prevailing belief in an adherent's potential to ascend through various levels of consciousness, or knowledge, to a higher spiritual place, paradoxically there seems to have been widespread belief that lives were preordained and that the level of knowledge that could be achieved was already determined at the start of their religious journey.

Both Christians and Heterodox Jews could also be Gnostics. They could be encountered in the priesthood, and even amongst some Christian Bishops. A number of groups considered Jesus to be a manifest expression of the spiritual God, who came to earth to provide an example of a pure life.[435]

Gnosticism was vehemently opposed by emerging Christianity,[436] with many early Christian writers and theologians condemning it from the pulpit. Whilst this may seem excessive in our own time, it was not so for the early Church; Gnosticism had a significant following, particularly in the Eastern Mediterranean, where it was probably more popular than Christianity. As it grew in size, Christianity sought to suppress its rival, a feat it was able to achieve only when it became the religion of Rome, and then by resorting to brutal, and often barbaric, methods.[437]

---

[434] Churton T. The Gnostics. Barnes and Noble (1997) 58

[435] Stevenson J. (Ed) A New Eusebius. SPCK (1987) 82

[436] Ibid 170

[437] Holroyd S. The Elements of Gnosticism. Element (1994) 22

Simon Magnus

Early Christianity's growth corresponded with the work of some notable Gnostic charismatics, one of the earliest being Simon Magnus, who was active during the reign of the Emperor Claudius. Simon, a Samaritan born in the village of Gitto, was claimed as the first Christian heretic by Irenaeus, having been baptised by the apostle Phillip.[438] Simon brought condemnation from the writer of Acts for a reported attempt to purchase the 'Holy Spirit' with silver.[439] He received no better treatment from the early Christian historians: Hippolytus accused him of *'Being adept at sorceries ... and partly also by the assistance of demons perpetrating his villainy, attempted to deify himself.'* [440]

Perhaps it was Simon's claim to godhood that drew the greatest condemnation from early Christian writers, for he clearly enjoyed some success. The church historian, Eusebius, reports Simon performing: *'Mighty acts of magic by the art of demons operating in him.'* [441] These acts were performed in Rome, where Simon was supported by the Emperor Claudius, who believed him to be *'deemed worthy of honours.'* [442] At a somewhat later date an entirely spurious Christian account of a contest between Simon and the apostle Peter is said to have taken place before the Emperor Nero. Needless to say Peter was the winner.[443]

Simon was accompanied throughout much of his adult life by a former prostitute, Helena,[444] whom he apparently viewed as the product of a series of incarnations, beginning with 'Ennoia,' [445] a name seemingly derived from his mystical beliefs. Simon felt that the most fundamental property was 'fire' which contained both a male and female element.

---

[438] Acts 8: 9-12

[439] Acts 8: 18-22

[440] Bernard S. The Essence of the Gnostics. Arcturus (2004) 82

[441] Ibid 83

[442] Ibid 83

[443] Ibid 85

[444] Holroyd S. The Elements of Gnosticism. Element (1994) 12

[445] Ibid 13

The female element was named 'silence' and from silence proceeded: *'Mind, power, thought (Ennoia), voice, name, reason and plan'*.[446] Mind and thought formed a middle level, which had six aspects: *'Heaven, earth, sun, moon, air and water'*. [447]

A somewhat idiosyncratic individual, Simon's movement survived his death and flourished in the Eastern Empire, where a number of his followers established Gnostic Meeting Houses. It was not until the rise of Christianity under Constantine, that Simon's movement was effectively suppressed.

Valentinius

Following Simon, but entirely independent of him, was Valentinius. Thought to have been born in Egypt, possibly around the turn of the first century CE, he is known to have taught in Rome during the 130's CE for a period of about five years before returning to Egypt and settling in Alexandria.[448] He wrote extensively on Gnosticism and other matters, and one of his works may have survived as the 'Gospel of Truth', recovered from Nag Hammadi. For the rest, only fragments have survived as quotations, which are to be found in the works of his Christian detractors.

Valentinius was both a Gnostic and a Christian. One noted aspect of his religious philosophy was his belief that religious enlightenment was an inner personal journey, rather than an outer formal one. In this he agreed with other schools of Gnostic thought, but not with Christianity, which was in the process of evolving a hierarchical Church structure. It seems to have been commonplace in meetings of Valentinius' followers to take it in turns to preach and administer the sacraments, a ritual which reflected the Gnostic view of the equality of personal religious experience.[449]

---

[446] Bernard S. The Essence of the Gnostics. Artutus (2004) 86-87

[447] Ibid 87

[448] Holroyd S. The Elements of Gnosticism. Element (1994) 32

[449] Ibid 33-34

This practice met with particular scorn from the early Christian theologian Tertullian: *'How frivolous, how worldly, how merely human it is, without seriousness, without authority, without discipline.'* [450]

Tertullian's scorn was perhaps understandable; had Gnosticism prevailed it would have undermined the structure of the Christian Church. However, Valentinius not only promoted a differing form of worship, he also brought together various aspects of Gnosticism and made them into a coherent, if rather variable, School of Theology.

As with all Gnostics, Valentinius believed in two influences in the world. The female spiritual influence, Sophia, was thought to pre-exist the imperfect creator of the physical world, the Demiurge. He believed that Jesus was sent to the world by Sophia to provide an illustration of a truly spiritual life. Although the concepts of two Gods and the position of Jesus were at the heart of Valentinius' Gnosticism, his views were not static, and seem to have evolved during his lifetime.

Valentinius encouraged his followers to discuss their religious experiences and communicate their views to others, as such, his aim seems to have been to encourage religious and philosophical enquiry, and to share religious experiences.[451] Other than the duality of Gods and the position of Jesus, there were few fixed points. Such an approach was anathema to Christianity, which believed that they already had a fixed interpretation of the significance of Jesus' life and death.

Carpocrates

Carpocrates, perhaps the most notorious Gnostic, taught principally in Alexandria, from 117-138CE, where he built up a sizeable local following. It was claimed that he possessed a copy of the 'secret' Gospel of Mark, given to him directly by the apostle.[452] A controversial leader, he may even have been seen as heretical by other Gnostics; his followers were said to have practised 'love feasts', which seem to have taken a radically different approach to communal worship than the Christian meal!

---

[450] Tertullian D. Praescriptione Haereticorum. 41

[451] Holroyd S. The Elements of Gnosticism. Element (1994) 32-37

[452] Ibid 91-95

> '*Men and women together. After they sated their appetites . . . the Goddess of Love enters . . . then they overturn the lamps and so extinguish the light that some of their adulterers righteousness is hidden and they intercourse where they will, with whom they will. After they have practised community of use in this love feast, they demand by daylight of whatever woman they wish, that they will be obedient to the law of Carpocrates.*' [453]

Carpocrates had clearly argued that fornication was permitted, although to what extent he was responsible for the communal 'love feast' is not clear. Aside from the more salacious aspects, Carpocrates had a distinctive theology. He believed that man was caught in a repetitive series of reincarnations, brought about by angels. The soul of a man must pass through every possible form on earth, before being able to free itself from the physical world. According to Carpocrates, Jesus was endowed with a pure spirituality that allowed him to escape the cycle of reincarnations and ascend into heaven. This opportunity could exist for all men if they could rise above the materialism of the physical world.

The popularity of Carpocrates' beliefs is difficult to establish. It was claimed that a centre in Rome was led by a woman called Marcellina. This was unusual in antiquity, where men invariably provided religious leadership, and it may indicate a more liberal view of women than the surrounding assemblies.[454]

Whatever the status of women in Carpocrates' movement, it was the sexual proclivities of his followers which earned them, and him, a scurrilous reputation—one which in time would come to taint the whole of Gnosticism.

Basileides

One of the most prolific Gnostic thinkers of his time, Basileides was reputed to have written 'four and twenty books on the Gospels'. Almost all of these writings are lost and much of his work cannot

---

[453] Simon B. The Essence of the Gnostics. Arcturus (2004) 92

[454] Ibid 93

now be reconstructed, however, it is apparent that Basileides was a particularly ascetic individual. Married people were banned from his meeting-houses as embodiments of passion, which he saw as:

> '*An unnatural accumulation which encrusted the spiritual essence, due to the latter's entanglement in the physical realm.*' [455]

Even by Gnostic standards Basileides was deeply ascetic and possessed of a powerful intellect. His view on the 'beginning' having a surprisingly modern feel:

> '*There was a time when there was nothing ... meaning ... absolutely nothing ... the seed of the cosmical was generated from non-existence ... In this was 'non-existence, God made the world out of non-existence, casting and depositing some ones seed that continued in itself a conglomeration of the germs of the world.*' [456]

Like other Gnostics, Basileides provided a complex theology to account for the presence of God and Jesus. First came the mind or logos, born of the 'unborn' father, followed by power and wisdom, which created the first heaven. In all three hundred and sixty five heavens were formed, corresponding to the days of the year, and it is from the lowest of the heavens that all things of the world were formed. The Jews were regarded as the chosen people of God, and it was to defend them that he sent his 'mind,' which was called Jesus Christ. Basileides believed that Jesus was pure spirit, and thus his place in the crucifixion was taken by Simon of Cyrene, whilst Jesus took Simon's form.

It is to one of Baseleides' detractors, Clement of Alexandria, that we owe Basileides' views on sin and suffering. He clearly regarded suffering as inevitable and positive, in that it would help to guide the sufferer towards the spiritual, rather than the physical. The few

---

[455] Ibid 77

[456] Hippolytus. Refutation of all Heresies V11.21, 1-2,4

extracts of Basileides' work that have survived show a deeply ascetic and philosophical man, whose influence on Gnosticism may have been considerable.[457]

Marcion

If the various schools of Valentinuis and Basileides presented an enquiring philosophical approach to Gnosticism, that of Marcion, born in 85CE in Pontus in what is now Turkey, was both more straightforward and popular. Born the son of a rich ship owner who became a Christian, Marcion studied in Rome, becoming a Gnostic sometime in the middle of the second century, and was probably ex-communicated from the Christian Church for his beliefs.

Marcion promulgated a form of Gnosticism known as Docetism. Docetits believed that it was impossible for Jesus to be the Son of God, and to have suffered and died at the hands of his Roman executioners. They considered Jesus to be wholly spiritual, and believed his death and suffering provoked a mass hallucination amongst those who witnessed his crucifixion. This belief was probably derived from Simon Magnus, who believed that Jesus as Son of God could not suffer at the hands of humans.

Marcion's Gnosticism was straightforward and uncomplicated. He postulated the existence of two Gods, one the 'Greater God' of the Hebrew Bible, and the second the 'Good God' of the Christian bible.[458] His theology of a 'Good God' was admirably summed up in a characteristically scathing attack by Tertullian:

> *'A better God has been discovered who never takes offence, is never angry, never inflicts punishment, who has prepared no fire in hell, no gnashing of teeth in the outer darkness! He is purely and simply good. He indeed forbids all delinquency, but only in word. He is yours if you are willing to pay homage . . . for your fear he does not want. And so satisfied are the Marcionites with such pretence, that they*

---

[457] Holroyd S. The Elements of Gnosticism. Element (1994) 41-47

[458] Simon B. The Essence of the Gnostics. Arcturus (2004) 95-99

> *have no fear of their God at all. That way it is only an evil being who will be feared, a good one will be loved.*
>
> *Foolish man, do you say that he whom you call Lord ought to be feared, whilst the very title you give him indicates a power which must itself be feared.'* [459]

Marcion rejected all Jewish teachings, including the Old Testament, and only acknowledged the Gospel attributed to Luke and Paul's letters as having any validity. Marcion dismissed Paul's view that Jesus' coming had been foretold and denied that Jesus was the promised Jewish Messiah. To substantiate his viewpoint, Marcion published a book entitled 'Antitheses,' [460] which catalogued contradictions between the 'Old' and 'New' Testaments. Consequently Marcion was denied the position of Bishop by the Church authorities in Rome and was excommunicated when he attempted to disseminate his views.

Unlike the majority of Gnostics, Marcion sought to establish a structured Church, but not one as hierarchically controlled as the Roman Church. Following Paul of Tarsus' example, he travelled extensively in the Eastern Mediterranean, but, unlike Paul, seems to have had a charismatic presence; the House Churches established by Marcion were numerous and successful.

In about 155CE Justin Martyr wrote complaining of Marcion's popularity, achieved within only a few years of leaving the Roman Church:

> *'And there is Marcion, a man of Pontus, who is even at this day alive, and teaching his disciples to believe in some other God greater than the Creator. And he, by the aid of devils, has caused many of every nation to speak blasphemies and to deny that God is maker of the Universe, and to assert that some other, being greater than he, has done greater works.'* [461]

---

[459] Tertullian. Against Marcion 1.27

[460] Flishe, Martin. Histoire De L'Eglise, ET, 525-527

[461] Martin Justin. Apology (155) 1.26. Translation from Stevenson J. A New Eusebius.
SPCK (1987) 93

Although estimates of congregations are notoriously difficult, Marcion's Churches may well have attracted larger numbers of followers than those of the Christians with which they were competing. This may have been due in large part to Marcion's uncomplicated religious ideas.

Marcionites were faced with a choice between two Gods. Following the God of Darkness—the ruler of the physical world—offered no hope of salvation, whilst following the transcendentally pure God—whose presence was illustrated by Jesus' life—offered the hope of everlasting life. These ideas were closer to Christianity than many Christians cared to admit, and the simplicity of Marcion's approach clearly had great appeal.

Whilst the Gnosticism of Valentinius, Basileides and Marcion included the figure of Jesus in their religious mythologies, there were other forms of Gnostic belief that did not.

Manichaeanism

The religion which came to be known as Manichaean possibly predates Christianity, and was based on the Persian principles of light and darkness, which, in turn, provided for the separation of the spiritual and physical.

The God of darkness had created the physical world, including man, whilst the contrasting 'supreme being' governed the pure spiritual world, which included a spiritual Adam and Eve who awaited liberation from their physical form. This led to the concept of the divine spark, knowledge of which could lead to spiritual salvation.

Manichaean religious rituals were particularly concerned with baptism and the aftermath of death.[462] Baptisms were carried out not only shortly after birth, but also at regular intervals when the believer wished to be spiritually reinvigorated. Death itself was not marked by a religious ceremony, the body being interned in an unmarked grave; however, a period of forty days of religious observance was carried out after death, as this was thought to be the time it took the spirit to ascend to the region of light.

Perhaps the greatest prophet of Manichaeism, who gave the religious philosophy its name, was Mani, born in Babylon in about 216CE. Mani

---

[462] Churton T. The Gnostics. Barnes and Noble (1997) 62

underwent visionary experiences at the age of twelve and twenty-five. The result of these visions was to convince him that he was a great prophet whose life's work was to expound his spiritual message.[463]

Initially accompanied by his father and a number of disciples, he set out on a life of almost constant missionary travels. When not travelling, Mani was based in Persia, where he enjoyed protection by the ruling dynasty for about thirty years. However, a change in ruler brought an end to toleration. Mani was arrested and spent a period of twenty-six days heavily chained in total isolation. As a result of these ordeals he died, and his period of imprisonment was regard by his followers as a *'passion prior to martyrdom'*.

Mani's followers spread his fame and teachings to many countries. Persia remained a centre of the religion, although intermittent persecution continued. Egypt became noted for a large number of converts, as did other areas of the North African coast. Italy, France and Spain had large communities of Manichaean's, and the religion eventually spread to China where Mani was declared the true successor to the Buddha.

Manichaean Gnosticism was different from the Gnosticism of Valentinius, Basileides and Marcion in a number of ways: Mani believed that Zoroaster, Buddha and Jesus were subject to the same revelation that he himself received. It was this revelation that underpinned the Manichaean belief that the influences of good and evil were inherent in the world and had existed since its creation. These influences were again represented by light and darkness.

The 'God of Darkness' was in a constant state of turmoil and wished to capture the 'God of Light', and make it subject to his control. The 'God of Light,' being spiritually pure and lacking the means of self-defence, caused the 'Mother of Light' to create the primal man who would act in defence of 'the light'. The primal man and his five sons were defeated in battle by the 'God of Darkness' who consumed their corpses, which caused the light and darkness to intermingle. In order to rescue the primal man and his five sons from their fate, the universe was created. But, in its creation, the soul remained trapped in the material

---

[463] Simon B. The Essence of the Gnostics. Arcturus (2004) 99-102

The Way to Christianity

world and the primal man was liberated from a purely physical and imperfect existence.[464]

The liberation of the primal man from the realm of darkness was important for Manichaean Gnostics because it symbolised the possibility of individual salvation and liberation from a purely physical world. Mani's religious mythology described the sun and moon as light, which had already been extracted from the realm of darkness.

The religious mythology of Manichaean Gnosticism was perhaps the most elaborate and exuberant of all. The figure of Jesus finds a place as *'messenger of the messenger,'* whilst even Adam and Eve are present as the prototype representatives of the two sexes. However, their presence is not due to divine creation, but to the actions of demons that bring into the world a self-replication species to further dilute the light in the darkness of the physical world. This exotic imagery was to find expression at a later time in the work of the English engraver, William Blake, whose opening lines in his poem 'Jerusalem' read:

> *'There is a void, outside of existence which if entered into englobes itself and becomes a womb, such was Albion's couch. A pleasant shadow of repose called Albion's lovely land.'* [465]

The 'void outside of existence,' which is Albion's lovely land, is often taken to be the spiritually pure realm of light. The poem goes on to describe a mythological structure that is deeply reminiscent of Manichaean Gnosticism. Yet, although Gnosticism was profoundly different from Christianity, there are sill descriptions of the human condition which resonate with certain aspects of Christianity:

> *'My Lord! We are full of defects and sins; we are deep in guilt because of the insatiable shameless demon of greed, we always and incessantly, in thought, word and deed, and in seeking with our eyes, in hearing with our ears, in speaking*

---

[464] Holroyd S. The Elements of Gnosticism. Element (1997) 52-61

[465] Blake W. 'Jerusalem' Quotations from Holroyd W. The Elements of Gnosticism. Element (1997) 100.

with our mouths, in grasping with our hands, and in walking with our feet, torment the light, of the five Gods.' [466]

This common view of man as irredeemably prone to sin and in need of redemption is found in many religions. In Manichaean Gnosticism it resulted in an extremely ascetic lifestyle, which could only be followed by the most devout. For Manichaeans who found the demands of such a lifestyle too exacting, confession as a means of absolution for sins was widely available.

Manichaean followers built a large number of Churches, usually with resident priests. Although this is suggestive of a hierarchical structure, there is no evidence of Bishops or other organs of authority. However, Manichaeans did develop monasteries, where a life of stark simplicity and total abstinence was rigorously followed.

Manichaean Gnosticism survived for longer than most other forms. The vigorous Christian suppression of Gnosticism, particularly in the fifth and sixth centuries, effectively eliminated Gnosticism from the Roman Empire. But Manichaeism had spread beyond the boundaries of the Empire, through India and into China, where it flourished for many centuries.[467]

Gnosticism and Christianity

Gnosticism was widespread and apparently popular in late antiquity. It provided an explanation for the world of two thousand years ago, with its acts of institutionalised violence and a structure that put the rich and powerful above the law. It also offered the possibility of personal redemption into a spiritually pure realm of light.

Christianity saw in Gnosticism a powerful competitor for converts and many early believers seem to have been both Christian and Gnostic. Many Christian Bishops vigorously derided Gnosticism, most notably Tertullian. Some engaged in debate with Gnostics, perhaps most notably Irenius, yet it was a debate that Christians did not win; at this time

---

[466] Hans J. The Gnostic Religion. Beacon Press (1963) 10

[467] Churton T. The Gnostics. Barnes and Noble (1997) 62

Christians did not have a satisfactory explanation for the rather obvious imperfections of the physical world.

Paul of Tarsus recognised the presence of 'wickedness' and 'demons' in the world. But it was not until Augustine of Hippo (354-430CE), a man permeated with profound sexual guilt, that the concept of original sin was formulated. Sin was seen as passing from one generation to the next in male semen. This then was to provide Christianity with a satisfactory explanation for God's perfectly created world being made imperfect by each succeeding generation.

However, if Christianity could not defeat Gnosticism intellectually, it had few scruples in doing so physically. When Christianity became the official religion of the Roman Empire, it accrued considerable wealth and power. One way in which it used its new influence was to suppress Gnosticism. Whereas the 'Pagan' Roman Empire had been essentially tolerant of other people's religion, the Christian Roman Empire was not. Christians had been subject to sporadic and transient persecutions, but when it came to suppressing other religious beliefs, they were organised and persistent.

During the fifth and sixth centuries vigorous pogroms were mounted against heresies, of which Gnosticism was declared to be one.[468] Individual Christian Gnostics were offered the choice of recanting their beliefs, or excommunication, whilst a number—and it may have been a large number—were simply killed. Gnostic meeting places and monasteries were destroyed or converted into Christian churches and many Gnostics were executed. Thus, as a result of considerable effort, Gnosticism was eliminated from within the boundaries of the Empire.

However, elimination of Gnosticism within the Empire was one thing; eliminating Gnostic belief itself was something else.

---

[468] Simon B. The Essence of the Gnostics. Arcturus (2004) 157-160

John Larke

The Persistence of Gnosticism

A form of Gnosticism known as Bogomilism, after 'Pope Bogomil,' arose and spread to the Balkans and beyond.[469] As with other forms of Gnosticism it was dualistic, with Satan regarded as the eldest Son of God.

The Bogomils practised an ascetic lifestyle, in contrast to many Christian clergy of the time, who had begun to lead a life of some comfort. Despite attempts to suppress it, Bogomilism spread and reappeared as Catharism in Germany, Northern Spain and particularly France, in the twelfth and thirteenth centuries. In 1179CE a papal condemnation was issued against the Cathars and a crusade initiated in which military action was taken against the many centres of Catharism, some of whom had sought refuge in fortified buildings: A castle at Monsegur, situated on a high rocky outcrop in the Languedoc region of South Western France, was besieged by a Catholic army for ten months in 1224CE. Close to starvation, the defenders were offered safe passage if they abandoned their fortress; however, on emerging, all of the surviving two hundred and twenty five Cathars were burnt at the stake.

The job of 'mopping up' the remaining Cathars throughout Southern France was left to the Inquisition, which like so many institutionalised organs of religious persecution, left meticulous records of its brutal progress.

Gnostic principles found expression in the Renaissance, particularly with the translation of ancient Pagan texts such as the Corpus Hermeticum, which incorporated strong Gnostic elements. Enlightenment scholars of the eighteenth and nineteenth centuries, as diverse as Voltaire[470] and Goethe,[471] incorporated Gnostic principles into their work, whilst the existential movement of the nineteenth and twentieth centuries also echoed Gnostic principles by regarding the imperfect physical world with disdain, and maintaining that it was only man himself who attained a higher level of being. In our own time, the widespread concepts of the duality of the conscious and subconscious mind are widely accepted as a

---

[469] Ibid 160

[470] Ibid 162

[471] Holroyd S. The Elements of Gnosticism. Element (1997) 96

valid interpretation of our actions, and are widely used in many models of counselling and psychotherapy.

Christianity's attempts to brutally suppress a movement, which it could not defeat intellectually, may ultimately have done little other than to harm its own reputation. In our own increasingly secular age, concepts of the underlying duality of human experiences have once again gained ground.

CHAPTER 10

THE GROWTH OF THE WAY AND EARLY CHRISTIANITY

There are no wholly reliable figures for the followers of The Way, or of early Christianity. The Gospel attributed to Matthew records the *'people of Jerusalem and all Judea'* going to listen to *'John the Baptist . . . along the Jordan,'* [472] but gives no estimate of their numbers. At the end of James' tenure as one of the spiritual leaders of The Way there were said to be *'many thousands of followers,'* [473] whilst after Jesus' death the apostle Simon Peter is credited with converting about *'three thousand.'* [474] On another occasion, Acts claims that *'five thousand'* [475] new followers were added to the movement by the apostle John. These numbers seem inherently implausible for conversion to The Way in its earliest days. Rather more realistically, shortly after the crucifixion a *'crowd numbering about one hundred and twenty people'* [476] who were *'believers . . . constantly devoting themselves to prayer'* [477] is cited by Acts. This number will be used to give an estimate of the growth of The Way and, for the purposes of this book, the growth of The Way will be considered separately to that of early Christianity.

---

[472] Matthew 3: 5

[473] Eisenman R. James the Brother of Jesus. Faber and Faber (1997) 196

[474] Acts 2: 41

[475] Acts 4: 4

[476] Acts 1: 15

[477] Acts 1: 14

The Way

After Jesus' death the centre of The Way was James' Synagogue in Jerusalem, which seems to have been a typical Jewish place of worship, with seventy-two Elders.[478] The movement probably spread beyond the capital as other towns and villages are reported '*to contain Jewish Christians, Ebionites or Nazarene's.*'[479] Within Jewish Palestine: Caesarea Maritime; Capernaum; Pella; Jerusalem (prior to 134CE); Nazareth and the areas of Peraea and Sharon may have been local centres of The Way.

Outside Palestine in the Roman province of Syria: Damascus, Antioch, Beroia, and the village of Khoba, just south of Damascus, may also have had Synagogues established by The Way (figure 10.1).

---

[478] Epiphanius Pan 30: 2: 8

[479] Mullen R. The Expansion of Christianity. Brill (2004) 24-39

John Larke

Figure 10.1 Probable early centres of The Way outside Jewish Palestine

The list may well be incomplete; apart from Jerusalem the two most important centres were probably Antioch and Damascus, although the evidence is so sparse that it is difficult to be sure.

If the distribution of The Way is difficult, then the numbers are even more problematic. Getting from 120 followers after Jesus' death to *'many thousands,'* at the time of James' death requires some ingenuity.

A technique used by some writers is to transpose the known growth rate of a modern day movement onto a similar one from the past. The technique is fraught with rather obvious assumptions and we should not expect great accuracy, but the exercise may be informative. The

The Way to Christianity

Way was a Jewish revivalist sect whose mission was to the poor, and, as such, had somewhat similar characteristics to nineteenth century Wesleyan Methodism.

As with The Way, Methodism arose from within an existing religion and, to some degree, both were viewed with suspicion by the 'establishment' of the existent religious authorities. Methodism eventually separated from the Anglican Church, whilst The Way declined into obscurity. The most notable feature of both movements was remarkably charismatic leaderships.

John Wesley's preaching career lasted over fifty years, and at the time of his death there were 79,000 registered Methodists; twenty-four years later there were 230,000.[480] Using these figures a simple calculation shows that Wesleyan Methodism grew at somewhat less than 70% per decade. Applying this rate of growth to James' mission gives a figure of about 600 followers at the time of his death.

There are two problems with this analogy: Firstly, John Wesley was a single preacher, whilst James was the third spiritual leader of The Way, and secondly, The Way was not founded by James but by his kinsman, John Ben Zechariah. There seems no easy way to quantify the difference between a single leader and a succession of leaders. John Wesley was clearly a remarkable preacher, who is said to have given 40,000 sermons in his lifetime, travelling great distances on horseback to do so.[481] By comparison the successive spiritual teachers of The Way seem no less impressive. Did they have the same proportionate effect on the smaller communities of Jewish Palestine? We cannot of course know.

The origins of The Way may also have had a bearing; John is reported to have attracted *'many thousands'* of Jews from Jerusalem to his mission in the desert. His popularity was so great that both the Christian bible[482] and the Jewish historian Josephus[483] cite this as the cause of his arrest and execution. Can the many thousands of John's

---

[480] Hattersley R. John Wesley a Brand from the Burning. Abacus (2002) 410

[481] Ibid 343

[482] Luke 3: 18-20

[483] Schurer.E. The History of the Jewish People in the age of Jesus Christ (1874) Revised English text Vermes. G Goodman G. Miller.F and Black. M T&T Clark(1987) 1 345

followers be added to the *'many thousand who followed James'*? It seems not; after all, many of them may have been the same people.

Early Christianity

The numbers of early Christians has been recently examined by Rodney Stark, who, using comparisons with the rate of growth for the Mormon Church,[484] has reached two basic conclusions, which were then applied to the growth of early Christianity:

> (1) Most conversion took place through personal contact with friends and relatives, and;
> (2) Church membership grew exponentially at a rate of just over 40% per decade.

The contention that early Christianity initially grew through personal contact is plausible. By his own admission, Paul of Tarsus was not a charismatic speaker; he had a poor public presence and probably converted his followers through personal contact in his business as a tent dealer (Chapter 5).

After Paul's death, the early Christian church had an indeterminate legal status, and was neither proscribed nor recognised in law. As such, Church leaders took great care with converts, and it seems likely that those who were known to church members would be more readily accepted than those who were not. In such circumstances a growth rate of less than the 70% per decade, as compared to the calculation for Wesleyan Methodists, seems entirely reasonable.

There is also support for Rodney Stark's estimate contained in references to Christians in recovered Egyptian Papyri. These provided the basis for an analysis by Roger Bagnall, who used the frequency of Christian names to illustrate the rate of growth of the early Egyptian church.[485] There is remarkably good agreement between Rodney Stark's transposed data, and that derived from the papyri. (Fig. 10.2)

---

[484] Stark R. The Rise of Christianity. Harper Collins. (1997)

[485] Bagnall R.S. Religious Conversion and Onomastic Change in Early Byzantine Egypt. Bull Am Soc Papyrologists 19. 105-124

Year	239	274	278	280	313	315
Calculated Percentage	1.4	4.2	5.0	5.4	16.2	17.4
Actual Percentage (Egypt)	0	2.4	10.5	13.5	18.0	18.0

Figure 10.2. The calculated and actual rate of Christian conversion compared.(From data originally published by Roger Bagnall)

However, there are some differences, and these may be significant: There is a very rapid increase in the papyri figures from 0 (too small to measure) in 239CE to 13.5% of the population in 281CE after which the rate of increase slows. Additionally, there is only a comparatively small increase from 280CE (13.5%) to 315CE (18%) and this may illustrate an underlying problem. Rodney Stark believes his model of exponential growth through personal contact is valid until 350CE. In my view there are reasons for doubting this.

From the middle of the third century onwards Christianity began to become accepted; in some cities House Churches evolved into purpose built structures with living accommodation for a local Bishop. There can also be little doubt that Imperial patronage dramatically promoted Christianity in the fourth century.

To these two positive effects should be added the negative effect of periods of persecution. This became particularly detrimental when efficiently organised by the State, as it did at the beginning of the fourth century. Whilst Rodney Stark's exponential growth model probably accurately reflects the earliest stages in the growth of Christianity, it may be insufficient to capture the nuances and patterns that emerged from the middle of the third century onwards.

The Social Backround of Early Christians

Who were these first Christians, and from what strata of society did they come? Wayne Meeks has carefully examined the available information[486] and has shown a fundamental difference between those who followed Jesus, and those who followed Paul:

Jesus had travelled from one small Galilean village or town to another and his parables give expression to this. His moral fables are peopled with agricultural workers and images of the countryside. Paul, on the other hand, was an urban man born and brought up in the commercial city port of Tarsus. In his business as a tent dealer he travelled from one commercial centre to another. Thus almost all his house assemblies developed in towns based on trade.

There was one further aspect to this difference: Jesus' mission was to the spiritually and materially poor and, with one or two exceptions, he drew his followers from the most impoverished strata of society. This contrasts with the majority of Paul's followers who, like Paul, were artisans and traders, manufacturing and selling the numerous goods found in ancient cities. Later Christian tomb inscriptions seem to reflect the trade-oriented nature of devotees, including a wood carver, butcher, leather worker and a boat owner.[487]

There are exceptions amongst Paul's followers from these modest trades: amongst Paul's female patrons there seem to have been women of substance—Lydia, his patron in Ephesus, dealt in 'purple dye,' a luxury item only affordable by the rich. Whilst, at the other end of the social scale, slaves were an integral part of many households.

Slaves

In some parts of the Roman world, slaves made up a third of the population. Often taken as prisoners of war, slaves came from a wide variety of backgrounds Those with administrative abilities ran households, including the numerous establishments of the Roman Emperor, and it was from one of these households that some of Paul's followers came.

Paul accepted slaves into his house assemblies, but did not wish to change their status. His advice to converted slaves was to serve their

---

[486] Meeks W.A. The First Urban Christians Yale University Press. (1983)

[487] Lane Fox R. Pagans and Christians. Penguin Press (1998) 259-308

masters *'the more'* [488] and it was rare for Christians to advocate freeing slaves. At least one Church council threatened ex-communication to anyone who tried, and the use of Church funds for freeing slaves was vigorously opposed. As Robin Lane Fox has remarked: *'Christians aimed to reform the heart not the social order.'* [489]

If slaves were not equally deserving before man, Christians did regard them as equal before God. More than one former slave rose to become a Christian Bishop, although this was sufficiently unusual for it to be remarked upon.[490] Although there seems to have been no general mission to convert slaves—few seem to have reached out to them—if they were attracted to Christianity they were readily accepted. In part this may be due to the lack of any reference to slaves attributable to Jesus, in the absence of which, Christians took their lead from Paul.

If slaves were not sought out for conversion, neither were the rich, perhaps because they were so out of reach. The gap between the rich and the rest was very great indeed.

Women

One group which seems to have been particularly attracted to Paul's teachings were women, who in Roman society, as in so many cultures, were subject to brutal discrimination. Female infanticide probably occurred at all levels of Roman society and unwanted female babies were simply left on the town rubbish dump to perish. The resulting preponderance of men was little altered by the attrition of warfare.

Should a woman survive infancy, she became in essence the property of her father and, when she came of age, could be married to whomever her father wished. Once married, she was the property of her husband who could easily divorce her at any time. Her only hope of any form of an economically independent life was through widowhood, when she might inherit her husband's property. Prior to this point she could not own anything—even her clothing was not her own. Female education

---

[488] Ibid 295

[489] Ibid 299

[490] Chadwick H. The Early Church. Penguin Press (1993) 60

was essentially non-existent, and such instruction as did take place was usually domestic.

Even a woman's role in child bearing was considered secondary. It was widely held in antiquity that the process of reproduction entailed the man planting his seed in the woman who simply acted as the growing medium for his offspring. Abortion, often carried out at the behest of men, was widely practised. Knowledge of naturally occurring herbal preparations was detailed, and midwives sometimes acted as abortionists.[491] In this environment the attractions of Christianity to women were clear-cut.

Under the Christian Church women were regarded as equal before God, although still subject to their husbands. Additionally, amongst the earliest Christian moral strictures was a ban on any form of abortion; female infanticide was regarded as indistinguishable from murder.

One of the earliest references to a female church official was to a Deacon called 'Phoebe.'[492] Although Deacons have sometimes been equated with servants, their duties correspond more closely to the modern position of 'administrative assistant,' and in this case it was Phoebe who was entrusted with the delivery of Paul's letter to the Romans.

Another feature of early Christianity, which had been credited with contributing to its growth, was the level of care that Christians extended to one another. Many ancient clubs and associations provided insurance schemes for burial expenses, but it was noted that Christians 'loved one another.' This love extended to the care of the sick, the impoverished and the elderly, and was often carried out by women. This was an unusual, although not necessarily unique feature of Christianity. More than one writer has suggested that this level of care increased the chances of survival in a world in which disease and destitution were ever-present risks.[493]

As time passed, Christianity grew in numbers, and early centres of preaching and learning began to develop. Rome was probably the first,

---

[491] Lewis N and Reinhold M. (Eds) Roman Civilisation. Columbia University Press (1990) 2. 338-371.

[492] Romans 16: 1-2

[493] Stark R. The Rise of Christianity. Princeton University Press (1996) 73-94

whilst Alexandria and Carthage also developed towards the end of the second century.[494]

The Roman Church

We know from Paul's letters that the community in Rome was not established by him.[495] It nevertheless became a large Christian centre and was well known for supporting other Churches. In about 170CE, Dionysius of Corinth praised Rome for its support:

> *'This has been your custom since the beginning to treat all Christians with unfailing kindness, and to send contributions to many churches in every city, sometimes alleviating the distress of those in need, sometimes providing for your brothers in the mines.'* [496]

This role of benevolence towards other Christians was a characteristic feature of the early Roman Church. Inevitably it was drawn into conflicts between other Churches often as an arbiter, although there were occasional exceptions. By 190CE the date of Easter had become a contentious issue. The Eastern churches celebrated Easter on the fourteenth day of the Jewish month of Nissan, whilst the Latin Church celebrated *'the day of the resurrection of our saviour'* on what was to become known as Easter Sunday. The matter was discussed at a meeting of Bishops, and after an ill-tempered debate:

> *'Victor the President of the Roman Bishops proposed that the whole of the Eastern Church should be declared heretical and all concerned should be excommunicated.'* [497]

He was dissuaded from this action by the other Bishops, amongst whom Irenaeus was said to have acted as peacemaker. Victor's

---

[494] Frend W.H.C. The Early Church. SCM Press (1982) 72-84

[495] Romans 1: 8-15

[496] Eusebius Ecclesiastical History 4, 23.

[497] Eusebius Ecclesiastical History 5, 23-24

uncharacteristic outburst may have simply arisen through irritation at an overly long 'discussion.' But the difficulty was far from over, and the date of Easter was to loom large in the later schism between the Catholic and Orthodox churches.[498]

There are few other occasions when the church in Rome acted as anything other than conciliator. However, if it largely avoided dissent, Rome did not contribute greatly to the intellectual development of the early Church. This role was filled in large measure by the church of Alexandria.

The Alexandrian Church

The church in Alexandria was, and is, the centre of Coptic Christianity. Church tradition claims that Christianity was established in Alexandria by the apostle Mark—although, as there is little evidence of Christianity prior to the second century, this seems unlikely.

The great contribution of Alexandria to Christianity began with a Catechetical School, which was the oldest of its type. Having been founded by Pontanaeus initially to teach children it rapidly developed into an adult centre of learning. The syllabus included both religion and other secular subjects such as mathematics and science. Amongst its noted scholars were Clement, Didymus and Origin, with the latter held in particularly high regard as the founder of Christian theology. Aside from its famed academics, the school also attracted many notable visitors including the Church Chronicler Jerome. Although paramount amongst early Christian learning centres, Alexandria eventually went into decline. It became an Orthodox Christian centre, with its own Patriarch, and has been invigorated somewhat in recent times.

The Church of Carthage

Carthage was the third great centre of early Christianity, forming the focus of the rapid expansion of Christianity in North Africa. It was much persecuted by the Roman authorities, resulting in its reputation as a 'Church of Martyrs' and prompting its most noted teacher, Tertullian, to write his famously ironic cry of despair against persecution:

---

[498] Chidester. D. Christianity. Penguin Press (2000) 177-182

> *'If the Tiber reaches the walls, if the Nile does not rise to the fields, if the sky does not move or if the earth does, if there is famine, if there is plague, the cry is at once, 'the Christians to the lion, what, all of them to one lion.'* [499]

Tertullian was a born debater, and infused Carthage with much of its individual character. He should, by rights, have shared the martyrdom that he so greatly extolled in others, yet he died, at a great age, in his own bed. The church in Carthage revered this great and perennially difficult old man, who had done so much to give their mission its own characteristic nature.[500]

The Second Century

Church membership grew inexorably around its three great centres. At this time still an urban movement, Christianity spread from town to town seemingly carried by the flow of trade and commerce—if there were Missionaries, we know nothing of them and the centres we know of correlate, for the most part, with the trade routes of late antiquity. There were some, perhaps many, who lapsed, but the majority seem to have remained true to their faith and spread the word amongst their friends and colleagues.

Rodney Stark's estimate for the number of Christians at the end of the second century is 217,795, or approximately 0.36% of the population of the Roman world.[501] There seems no cogent reason to doubt this figure.

Christianity was still a religion of the shadows; persecution continued, albeit in a rather random way, often at the whim of a powerful local individual (Chapter 8). Any Christian could face the prospect of martyrdom, and a small number did so with conviction and remarkable courage. A much larger number followed a more cautious line, accommodating the oppressors when it was necessary to do so, and worshipping when times were safer.

---

[499] Stevenson J. A New Eusebius. SPCK (1987) 158

[500] Frend W.H.C. The Early Church. SCM Press (1982) 80-82

[501] Stark R. The Rise of Christianity. Harper Collins (1996) 7

Although still subject to periods of persecution, Christianity was becoming more accepted, and many towns and some cities became tolerant of the new faith. A small number of civic leaders were also openly Christian, although this was the exception rather than the rule.

Rome and Its Army in the Second Century

The Roman historian Cassias lamented the changes brought about in the Empire following the death of the Emperor Marcus Aurelius in 180CE: '*our*
> *Kingdom plunges from a Kingdom of gold to one of iron and rust.*'
[502] Cassius attributed the beginnings of the decline to the Emperor Septimus Severus, who began a process of aggrandising the army:

> '*Severus . . . bestowed large donatives on the soldiers, granted them many privileges which they did not previously have: He was the first to increase their grain ration and permitted them to wear gold rings and to live with their wives in wedlock, all of which used to be considered incompatible with military discipline and with preparedness for war.*' [503]

Whilst the claims for the deterioration of the army were debatable, the concerns regarding increases in army expenditure were more than justified. Upon his death, Severus was reported to have advised his son Caracalla to: '*Live in harmony and enrich the soldiers and scorn all other,*' [504] a policy that Caracalla seems more than happy to have carried out. The practical consequences of this were twofold: Firstly, the burden of taxation started to rise, and secondly, the opportunities for personal enrichment and advancement in the army greatly increased.

In truth, the army had always been at the heart of the Roman Empire. Romans saw themselves as the warrior race and the army was an expression of that belief. Since the time of Julius Caesar the

---

[502] Lewis N. and Reinhold M. (Eds) Roman Civilisation. Columbia University Press (1990) II. 372

[503] Ibid 374

[504] Ibid 372

The Way to Christianity

civilian institutions of Rome had slowly weakened—there were of course exceptions: Augustus had carefully observed the rights of the Senate, whilst ensuring that power lay in his own hands—but from the beginning of the third century onwards rapid erosion took place. By 282CE the Senate formally ceded its few remaining powers and simply became the civic authority of Rome.[505]

Severus' obsequiousness to the army's power enhanced the career path for those with an eye to the 'main chance.' Successful soldiers rose through the ranks and increasingly came to occupy the Equestran order, with some members continuing to rise and beginning to take over the role of the established aristocracy. Some went even further: Marcus Macinus (217-218CE) became the first to rise directly from the Equestrian class to the position of Emperor.[506] These changes had greatest effect in the large towns and cities of the Empire. Civic endowments had previously been made by the local land-owning aristocracy, who provided not only the civic leadership, but also the buildings and institutions that so characterised Roman towns.

Throughout the Empire cities conformed to a common model with each boasting its own Temples, theatres, arena and forum. These buildings were sometimes the only stone structures within the city walls and were provided by the largesse of rich local families.[507] As the third century progressed, the changing social structure seems to have left a vacuum in the commission and upkeep of communal amenities.

From 270CE onwards, few plaques commemorating local civic endowments can be found. It would seem that the local aristocracy could no longer afford them, and their replacements did not wish too. The decline of the great country estates continued throughout the third century and a number were wholly impoverished. Many of the landed aristocracy had been deeply conservative supporters of traditional beliefs; as their wealth declined so did their influence and Paganism suffered.

As the third century progressed, the demands of the army became an almost unsustainable drain on the exchequer. Rome had grown rich by

---

[505] Ibid

[506] Ibid 375

[507] Ibid 272-274

defeating and expropriating its enemy's reserves, with defeat in battle invariably leading to the transfer of local riches to Rome. Even when riches were limited there were always slaves, and those not taken into slavery could be taxed. The revenue, which had previously flowed to the rulers of independent countries, now flowed to Rome. But the Empire had largely run out of rich enemies to defeat, and those that were left were often obdurate and impoverished, at least by Roman standards.

The army also faced increasing difficulties, not least because many foreign troops had served in the legions and learnt its tactics. The Empire covered a large proportion of the then known world, encompassing perhaps as many as sixty million people. The necessary size and the huge expense of the army could not be met from existing resources, and taxation continued its long-term rise. A proportion of this began to fall for the first time on the inhabitants of the Italian cities, who had previously been exempt.[508] This radical restructuring of the social order was entrenched in Roman law resulting in the delineation of two groups: an upper class increasingly composed of military men who had recourse to the law; and a lower underclass which could be exploited with impunity.

Roman Emperors

It is unsurprising that the social revolution of the third century brought disruption in its wake. This was nowhere more apparent than in the instability of the Emperors, some of whom were reduced to buying their positions:

> *'Then ensued a most disgraceful business and one unworthy of Rome. For just as if it had been in some market place or auction room, both the city and its entire Empire was auctioned off. The sellers were the ones who had slain their Emperor, and the would be buyers were Sulpicianus and Julianus, who vied to outbid each other, one from the inside and the other from outside. They gradually raised their bids up to 20,000 sesterces per soldier. Some of the soldiers would carry word to Julianus, "Sulpicianus offers so much,*

---

[508] Ibid 380-383

how much more do you bid?"... So the soldiers ... received Julianus inside and declared him Emperor.' [509]

Between 235 and 285CE there were twenty-six military Emperors and all, bar one, were assassinated. With this chaos at the centre, both internal and external threats rapidly increased, with bands of the dispossessed roaming the countryside:

'Plundering Italy under the very noses of the Emperors and a multitude of soldiers.' [510]

Externally, matters were even worse. The enemies of Rome crossed its borders and parts of Gaul (modern day France), Macedonia, Greece, Asia Minor, Egypt, Africa, Spain and even Italy were attacked. These incursions were eventually repelled with the greatest difficulty and in some cases areas previously under Roman control were simply abandoned. Dacia, on the Danube frontier, which had been Roman for 150 years, was abandoned by the Emperor Aurelian in 275CE.[511] In other instances the invaders were simply bought off. Under the Emperor Caracalla, the amount paid to the 'barbarians' outside the Empire, is thought to have been roughly equal to the expenditure on the army.

Vigorous and wide-ranging reforms introduced towards the end of the third century eventually restored order, but not before the underlying Hellenistic Roman culture was irretrievably altered.

One of the greatest changes that took place was in the formerly predominant position of Paganism. The trauma of the third century began to erode belief in the Pagan deities. Previously, the Gods of the Empire had been assuaged through widespread acts of public and private worship, and there was a widely accepted view that they had benignly acquiesced in the rise and eventual dominance of Rome. This was now brought into question;[512] whilst the Gods of the Empire were not yet abandoned, doubts began to subvert confident certainty. As uncertainty

---

[509] Ibid 373

[510] Ibid 373-379

[511] Ibid 390

[512] Goodman M. The Roman World. Routledge. (1999) 287-301

rose, so did the practice of divination and various other magical rituals, which had always been part of Roman life, but which now increased to such an extent that they began to meet with official opposition:

> *'Accordingly, neither through oracles or inscribed messages issued ostensibly under divine guidance, nor through parade of images and suchlike, is anyone to pretend to know the superhuman and discover the obscure shape of things to come.'* [513]

Alongside an increasing use of divination and other occult practices, the third century saw an increase in 'oriental' religions, of which Christianity was one.

Persecution and Paganism

Two challenges to Christianity emerged in the middle of the third century: firstly, Empire wide persecution, and secondly Pagan beliefs, particularly in the army.

Up to the middle of the third century, opposition to Christianity was usually local and spasmodic. However, a more systematic and far-reaching approach was witnessed in 249CE, when the Emperor Decius moved against the Christian leadership and a number of Bishops were executed. In a move which may have been an attempt to reassert the position of the Pagan Gods, Decius issued an Imperial decree that required a universal Temple sacrifice throughout the Empire. The measure was methodically implemented, with the issue of a certificate to each participant—although many Christians bribed the official for the appropriate document, whilst others simply lay low for a while. The death of Decius during a campaign in the lower Danube in 251CE removed the source of the persecution and Christianity regrouped, but its difficulties were not yet over.

Valerian who had been Decius' censor became Emperor in 253CE. Initially favouring Christianity, he later changed his mind and moved against the emerging religion by ordering the confiscation of its books and

---

[513] Lewis N and Reinhold M. Roman Civilisation. Columbia University Press (1990) 536

the arrest of prominent Church members. Had he persisted, Christianity could well have been seriously impeded. However, in 260CE whilst campaigning against the Persians, he was taken prisoner and executed. The death of Decius and Valerian removed potentially serious threats to Christianity and it was not until the beginning of the fourth century that Emperor-inspired persecutions were again encountered (Chapter 9).

An even greater threat than the transient persecutions of the third century came from competing religions. Worship of the Sun God was particularly widespread in the army, and echoes of this practice have come down to our own times. The Winter Solstice, when the sun was at its lowest, was celebrated on the 17th of December.[514] This festival, together with 'Sun Day' was taken over by later Christianity and reconfigured as Christian celebrations.

Throughout the third century the dominant military influence maintained worship of the Sun God as the most important deity and this influence remained well into Christian times. Great Temples to the Sun God were to be found in many cities including Rome, where a new college of Pontiffs was established, indeed, the majority of third century Emperors were adherents.

Sun worship was not unique, and several oriental mystery religions attracted large followings. The worship of the Egyptian Mother Goddess Isis had spread from the cities of the Nile to other parts of the Empire.[515] Mithras the Persian God of Light was an ascetic male religion, which envisaged the soul's persistence after death[516] (Chapter 9), whilst towards the end of March the Cybele's celebrated a death and resurrection ceremony, which was all but indistinguishable from Easter.[517]

Expansion and Difficulties

For the first time Christianity had begun to emerge from the shadows of its indeterminate status. It now competed on more or less equal terms with other beliefs.

---

[514] Shelton J.A. As The Romans Did. Oxford University Press (1998) 382-383

[515] Ibid 400-404

[516] Goodman M. The Roman World. Routledge (1998) 297-299

[517] Shelton J.A. As the Romans Did. Oxford University Press (1998) 398-399

Its offer of the possibility of personal salvation must have been particularly attractive, particularly at a time when life itself was often in doubt. Whatever the reasons, Christianity rapidly expanded, and the number of Bishops more than doubled.

Towards the end of the third century Christianity flowed into the countryside, often carried there by converts escaping from the social stress of the cities. Many of the new Bishops had congregations who worked in agriculture rather than commerce, a trend that continued as the towns began to decline and the population of the countryside increased. However, the great expansion of Christianity in the third century was not without its critics.

Churches had become efficient centres of social welfare, and in some cases the rich became associated with the emerging religion, where they could become Christian leaders, *'for the sake of a little prestige.'* [518] Alongside this ambition there were complaints of a more general worldliness: *'The Bishops were wanting in religious devotedness, the ministers in entireness of faith; there was no mercy in works, no discipline in manners.'* [519] Perhaps these and other presumed failings resulted from an overly rapid expansion during difficult, and occasionally desperate, times.

Rodney Starke's estimate of the number of Christians by the beginning of the fourth century is 6,299,832, or 10.5% of the population, assuming an Empire of 60 million. The estimate is derived from his model of exponential growth and is unrealistically precise.[520] The basic assumption of this mathematical estimate is conversion through personal contact. But with the emergence of churches and ceremonies, which were increasingly open to all, the nature of conversion was beginning to change. There are other reasons for challenging this mathematical model. It has been fairly clearly established that the number of Bishops during the third century rose to about 250-300.[521] These church leaders were augmented by a wide range of helpers, Sub-Deacons, Deacons and

---

[518] Stevenson J. A New Eusebius. SPCK (1987) 209

[519] Ibid 215

[520] Stark R. The Rise of Christianity. Harper Collins (1996) 7

[521] Williams R.L. Bishop Lists: Formation of Apostolic Succession of Bishops in Ecclesiastical Crisis. Gorgas Press (2005)

Presbyters, but not yet Priests—at least not in the sense that they were to be found in later times. Could 300 Bishops with all their attendant helpers have serviced a community of over 6 million adherents? It seems unlikely, since each Bishop would have had a congregation of almost twenty thousand. Most writers have suggested lower figures for the total number of Christians during this period.

With increased influence came increased responsibility, not only in religious circles but also in the secular world. Christians were advised to avoid civic duties, although it is apparent that some ignored this call.

> *'If Christians do avoid these responsibilities, it is not with the motive of shirking the public service of life, but they keep themselves for a more divine and necessary service in the church of God, for the sake of the salvation of men.'* [522]

The Ascetic Life

During the early fourth century, an increasingly ascetic lifestyle appealed to a number of Christians, particularly in Egypt. In 305CE a Coptic Christian called Anthony withdrew into the desert from where he called for others to follow.[523] His example is said to have impressed a fifteen-year old Christian called Hilarion, who sold his possessions, left his village, and retreated into the desert. He went to live in a small hut by the sea, where it was said that he miraculously healed both men and animals. In time, the fame of both Anthony and Hilarion spread and, despite living the life of a hermit, Hilarion travelled rather widely. At the age of 80 he died on a journey from Greece to Cyprus and was buried on the Mediterranean island.

The lives of Anthony and Hilarion were described by the church chronicler Jerome, whose purpose appears to have been to extol the virtues of an ascetic lifestyle rather than to give an accurate account of the desert hermits. In this Jerome appears to have been successful; some Christians were already leaving their towns and villages and a number became noted holy men. However, many found the isolation of a single

---

[522] Lane Fox R. Pagans and Christians. Penguin Press (1986) 416

[523] Ibid 18-20

life difficult to sustain. The answer was to come together in small groups, and the beginnings of the way of monastic life were formed. Initially, it was only men who began to congregate in this way,[524] but, at a slightly later date, groups of female Christian virgins also began to form. Such groups were well known in Antiquity. The vestal virgins of Rome were thought to aid the Empire by the maintenance of their state, and there were severe penalties for those who strayed.[525] Amongst Christians, virginity was also highly regarded; to be a 'Bride of Christ' was seen as an act of dedication to God and also had practical advantages, avoiding the considerable risks of childbirth and conferring a status that could not otherwise be attained. Living together in groups women were less susceptible to predatory male abuse and within a few years these groups were well established.

The forerunners of the monastic and convent orders were well regarded by other Christians and were supported by local believers. In time endowments were made and many communities became largely self-supporting.[526] The first use of the term 'monk' comes from a secular source: a pagan papyrus records an incident in which the owner of a straying cow was rescued from assault by 'Antoninus the Deacon and Issac the Monk.' The document dates to 324CE, implying an even earlier date for the seminal monasteries of Christianity.[527]

Eusebius

The third century saw the rise of one of the great figures of early Church history, Eusebius, who was to become the Bishop of Caesarea. Born in 260CE, as a young man Eusebius had access to Origin's library, much of which was preserved in the town, which provided him with a wide range of historical and literary sources. He was to make good use of it; whilst initially his work dealt with the dates and locations of significant Christian events, later he began a general introduction to Christianity which ran into ten volumes, four of which concerned

---

[524] Shelton J.A. As the Romans Did. Oxford University Press. (1998) 385-386

[525] Ibid

[526] Frend W.H.C. The Early Church. SCM (1965) 188-197

[527] Ibid 85

prophesies in the Hebrew Bible thought to foretell the coming of Jesus. In middle age, Eusebius survived the last great persecution against Christianity, although how he did this is not known; as a well-known and prolific author of Christian texts he would have been a natural target.[528]

In the later part of the third century he wrote a renowned 'ecclesiastical history.' However, as a Christian, Eusebius was unable to distance himself from his religion, and his contribution was not so much his objective view but his careful use of documents, and the systematic manner in which he went about his task.

His history ran to several volumes and a number of editions, and much of present day church history is based on Eusebius' earlier work. In the first part of his history he set out the timescale of Christian events and also provided the first inclusive list of Christian Bishops. In a later volume he catalogued many of the martyrdoms of the early church, a number of which he had witnessed.

Eusebius' book is not just a list of events. He describes Christianity's relationship with Judaism and also details the heresies encountered by Christianity. In all, Eusebius' book is the first great chronicle of early Christian history.[529]

It may seem remarkable that he was able to complete such a volume of work.

In composing, he probably dictated to a group of Scribes, who seem to have taken it in turn to keep up with his oratory. In all his works Eusebius is rigidly orthodox: Christianity had been founded by Jesus, and his disciples carried his message reliably to future generations. A line of authority was thus established which extended to the Bishops of Eusebius' day. During his lifetime the last great persecutions of Christianity took place, which Eusebius viewed as God's punishment for his errant people, as well as a preparation for the 'last days.'

Eusebius was one of the last major church figures to believe that the 'second coming' was imminent, although the fact that he was wrong should not detract from his accomplishments. His 'Ecclesiastical History' is rightly regarded as *'the work on which all modern accounts*

---

[528] Lane Fox R. Pagans and Christians. Penguin Press (1986) 607

[529] Ibid 627-630

of the early church must rest.' [530] And it is a measure of his importance that he is cited by virtually every major work in this field.

The beginning of the fourth century saw the last great Imperial persecution of Christians (Chapter 9). But this darkest hour was fortuitously followed by a new dawn.

In 312CE Constantine prevailed in the battle of the Milivian Bridge. The conflict had been preceded by the appearance of a 'cross' in the sky and Constantine attributed his victory to the Christian God (Chapter 12). Constantine's success reversed Christianity's misfortunes, and the influence of Imperial patronage was considerable. At this point the Roman Empire was effectively a dictatorial autocracy—the Emperor having the power of life and death over the sixty million inhabitants of the Empire—as such there was no force in law that could stand against him. Emperors came to power by the sword and, not infrequently, lost their positions by the same means.

Constantine was a successful military General who was wholly unscrupulous in his use of power. Whilst he did not make Christianity the religion of the Empire, he did make it the religion of the Emperor, and that carried great weight. Many of those seeking the Emperor's favour became at least nominally Christian, and since they were rich and powerful men they, in turn, had considerable influence. They had numerous slaves and, together with their extended households, this brought large numbers of converts. It did not end there; lesser men seeking the favour of greater men converted and brought lesser, but still considerable, numbers with them. Over time a wave of conversion spread outwards from Rome to encompass the whole Empire.

Constantine was assisted in the spread of his new religion by his mother Helena, who seems to have been particularly attached to relics. During a visit to Jerusalem she had portions of the city excavated, and felt that she had found the notable sites associated with Jesus' last week. The present day location of these sites is wholly attributable to Helena.

She was particularly interested in wooden remnants of the 'true cross.' In reality, digging anywhere in a city that had been as comprehensively destroyed as Jerusalem, would have recovered wooden fragments. Thus began a passion for collecting 'holy relics.' Eventually so much of

---

[530] Ibid 607

The Way to Christianity

the 'true cross' was recovered that a small house could have been constructed from it!

Whilst it is easy to decry Helena's naivety as an archaeologist and relic collector, her importance lay in her apparent success. She returned to Christianity its most revered holy places and, in the remnants of the 'cross,' she provided its most revered holy relics. Between them Constantine and his mother dramatically enhanced the Christian community.

Rodney Stark has given a figure of 33,882,008 for the number of Christians in the Roman Empire thirteen years after Constantine's death. Whilst it is unlikely that Christians formed the majority of people in the Empire, it is not unreasonable to assume that they formed a very substantial minority. It is likely that they were the largest group worshiping any of the individual Gods of the Empire. The distribution of Christian sites in 325CE is shown in figure 10.3.

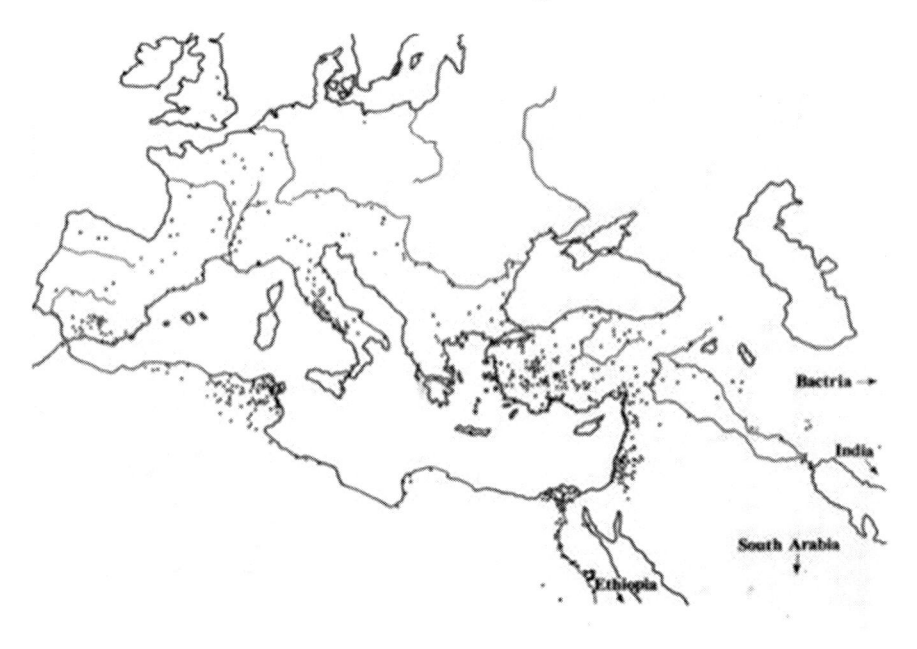

Figure 10.3 The distribution of Christian sites to 325CE. Reproduced by kind permission of Rodney Mullin.

Although one last brief period of persecution was to follow, Christianity had achieved a critical mass. It survived the fall of the Roman Empire and spread to find adherents in every region of the world.

CHAPTER 11

MAN AND GOD

Jesus

In life, Jesus Ben Joseph was a remarkably courageous and charismatic Galilean holy man (Chapter 4), who followed in the traditions of Elijah and Elisha. In common with many Galilean Jews, his appreciation of the nuances of the 'law' was less sophisticated than that of the Jerusalem Pharisees. Yet he went further than many in believing that not just the letter, but also the spirit of the law was to be upheld. As part of a family movement of prophetic holy men, he believed that he was living in the 'last days' of Judaism. Had he lived, he would have undoubtedly found a revered place in the history of the Jewish people.

Jesus Ben Joseph was above all else a Jew whose life was a living embodiment of his beliefs. Like relatively few of his contemporaries he submitted himself wholly to 'The Way of God' and his life and, more particularly, his death was an inspiration to future generations. However, these generations were not Jewish. As the message of his death and the claim for his resurrection passed from the Jewish into the Roman Hellenistic world, his image changed. Jesus the man was lost and Jesus the divine and iconic figure emerged, to take centre-stage in a new religion founded in his name (Chapter 6).

Paul of Tarsus

Paul of Tarsus was fundamental to the changing view of Jesus, although the ideas associated with him were not yet fully formed at the time of his death. Yet it is clear that his persistent advice to his followers to '*be clothed with Christ*' [531] was central to his proselytising mission. Another feature of his teachings was also of great importance: Jesus' coming had been 'foretold' in the Hebrew Bible.[532] As such, in common with the other Followers of The Way, he was also expecting the imminent arrival of the Kingdom of God, almost certainly in his own lifetime.[533]

It is now almost two thousand years since the beginnings of Christianity and God has not come, a fact that no amount of elegant revisionary semantics can resolve. For those of us descended from the sixty million inhabitants of the Roman Empire this must be a matter of some relief. Our forbear's fate would have ranged from submission to an omnipotent Jewish Kingdom of God, to being consumed in a 'fiery furnace' in one of the greatest acts of ethnic cleansing of all time.

The central prophesy of The Way was the imminent expectation of the last days, and all including Jesus and Paul subscribed to this view. Indeed Jesus seems to have gone further and felt that this process had already begun. This created difficulties for later Christians, who began to view Jesus as the 'Son of God:' *if* Jesus was wrong then God must also have been wrong, and this was clearly unacceptable. Whilst not abandoning the hope for the imminent arrival of the Kingdom of God, this aspect of the Christian faith grew less important as time went by, although it has never been abandoned and still forms a major tenet of belief across the many branches of Christianity.

God and Jesus

If Christianity was unable to explain God's non-appearance, it could, and did, attempt to resolve Jesus' relationship to God. Many modern Christians find this a difficult stage in the history of their religion, since it was sometimes conducted as fratricidal warfare. I found it exemplified in a comment by a Christian friend undertaking an introductory course in theology and philosophy, who, when confronted with some of the

---

[531] Galatians 3: 27

[532] Romans 16: 25-26

[533] Corinthians 7: 29-31

more traumatic aspects of Christian history, exclaimed: *'How could they behave like that? After all, they were Christians.'* [534]

This seems a common and understandable response, and one to which there is no easy answer. Whilst Jesus had extolled the virtue of loving your enemy, he had said nothing about loving your enemy's opinions.

Although the established church puts a benign gloss on this period when imperfect human minds struggled to discern God's perfect purpose, in reality it was anything but reverential. The disputes that pervaded the early centuries were at best vigorous, and at worst bloody. Excommunication, or at least the threat of it, was common-place, and the schism of Catholicism and Orthodoxy is held by some to have its origins in the theological disputes of these early years.[535] Dogmatic intolerance was widespread, and it is difficult to avoid the conclusion that it was often the most politically astute who won the day.

In defence of Christianity, it can be said that its problems were not unique; the early stages of Islam experienced similar traumas with schisms arising in the prophet's family after his death. Perhaps it is inevitable in the beginnings of religious movements, when the central authorities are weak, that the opportunities for disparagement are rife. However, if the journey was rough, and at times unpleasant, there were those within the Church who realised that it had to be made.

Son of God

Christianity had one central unresolved difficulty: In elevating Jesus to the status of *'Son of God,'* a deity had been created. In principle this was no different from any other Pagan God, and the situation became even worse when *'God the Father'* was added to the equation. This created a family of Gods, and the immaculate conception of Jesus found almost exact parallels in the lives of some Pagan Gods. As such, these parallels could have brought into question Christianity's unique character and the role of a single God.

---

[534] Personal Communication

[535] Chadwick H. The Early Church. Penguin Press (1990) 121-124

The Church intellectuals who were drawn to this problem were literate men who had benefited from a classical education. A good proportion of this entailed the study of Greek philosophy, which was much in vogue in late antiquity. They also studied rhetoric—the public exposition of reasoned argument. Whilst the former was to form the basis to Christian theology, the latter was to lead to energetic doctrinal disputes. Much of the ensuing debate was carried out in language that now appears arcane. Phrases such as *'hence it is clear that there was when the son was not'* were common-place.[536] Perhaps inevitably, jargon was also used to elevate the cognoscenti above the rest, and such obfuscatory expressions as *'economic trinitarianism'* are still in use. Paradoxically, the early Church intellectuals derided 'philosophy' and its influence on their work, yet the influence of Platonism and, more particularly, neo-Platonic ideas are undeniable. This makes the later destruction of Plato's School of Philosophy by a group of ardent Christians all the more disturbing.

Christianity also faced a range of criticisms from the classical world: Christians were atheists for not sacrificing to Pagan Gods; they were guilty of infanticide in baptismal ceremonies; and they indulged in sexual orgies when the kiss of friendship was exchanged. At a rather deeper level, philosophers criticised Christianity for making the unimaginably spiritual word of God, into corruptible flesh in the person of Jesus. Much of the substance of these condemnations arose through ignorance and misinterpretation as well as the result of what in modern terms might be described as poor PR.

Christianity had been persecuted from its earliest days and had grown circumspect and somewhat secretive in its dealings with the outside world. Consequently a series of 'apologies' were written to explain and defend this new religion. In these documents the ideas of early Christianity were set out. Almost all of these documents have been lost, as they were superseded by later generations of theologians who branded their predecessors work heretical. From the little that remains, and from references in other sources, a rather incomplete picture can

---

[536] Eusebius Ecclesiastical History 1. 5.

be built up. Amongst a number of early apologists probably the most important was Justin Martyr.[537]

Justin Martyr

Three of Justin's works: 'Dialogue with Trypho' and two apologies, have survived until the present day. These, and the fragments of the works of other apologists, describe Jesus as the *'logos'* of God.[538] This term can have a number of related meanings and was a concept much used in contemporary Greek philosophy. In the form used by the Apologists, it denotes the innermost mind of God, which once spoken can be a creative force, as in the creation of the world itself, or indeed in the immaculate conception of Jesus.

Hence Justin saw God as unimaginably perfect, being present everywhere and for all time, whilst Jesus, as the *logos* of God, was not a separate identity. Because Jesus arose from the innermost expression of God, he shared God's attributes, but was located in time and place in human form. This defence of Christianity and the unique role of Jesus had considerable attractions. It accounted for Jesus being *'foretold'* in Hebrew scripture, and it pre-empted the Greek philosopher's speculations on the nature of God. But it left Jesus' nature somewhat indeterminate: if Jesus was the *logos* of God did this mean that he was wholly spiritual, as some claimed, or was he simply the physical conduit of the word of God?

Justin had begun writing at some point prior to 140CE and was martyred in 163CE. A little later on in 177-178CE a churchman called Irenaeus was appointed the Bishopric of Southern Gaul.

Irenaeus

Irenaeus was a vigorous individual who was particularly active against the Gnostics who were enticing away some of his congregation; they claimed that they had secret knowledge obtained from Jesus, which gave them access to a higher level of spirituality. Irenaeus rebutted

---

[537] Stevenson J. A New Eusebius. SPCK (1987) 58-64

[538] Chadwick H. The Early Church. Penguin Press (1990) 77

these claims by publishing a list of the Popes of Rome, from Peter and Paul onwards:[539] a succession of Bishops, which was claimed to demonstrate the true inheritors of Jesus' mission. He also wrote the rule of faith which was one of the earliest statements of the central faith of the Church: *'One God . . . who made the heaven and the earth . . . one Jesus Christ, the son of God . . . the Holy Spirit.'* [540]

Irenaeus believed that the key to interpreting scripture was the bible itself, and he rejected Justin Martyr's use of the *logos*, since Irenaeus claimed that this diluted the singularity of God. This left open the relationship of Jesus to God, who Irenaeus believed were *'one and the same.'* Irenaeus developed this theme further by a literal interpretation of the Genesis claim that: *'Man (was) after the image and likeness of God.'* [541] Therefore, body, soul and spirit were present in the first perfect man created by God and it was through Adam's transgression that the spirit was lost. Jesus' presence on earth restored the spirit and restored Adam's fall from grace. Irenaeus' ideas were not wholly complete, but they formed an effective rebuttal of Gnosticism, and remain attractive, at least in part, to many modern theologians.

Tertullian

At about the time that Irenaeus was defending the Church against Gnosticism in Southern Gaul, a notable theologian began writing in Carthage, in what is now North Africa. Tertullian, held by a later Church historian to have been a lawyer, was an intolerant Church theologian, noted for his dogmatic arrogance.

Tertullian claimed that 'apostolic' churches, which had spread throughout the world, preserved the true faith handed down from the Apostles. He further asserted there was one creator, God, whose word appeared in the Hebrew Bible. The Holy Spirit brought the word to Mary, resulting in the immaculate conception of Jesus. After Jesus' ministry, he ascended into heaven and the spirit descended on those who believed. The Saints would remain in heaven and an everlasting fiery furnace

---

[539] Stevenson J.A. A new Eusebius. SPCK (1987) 114

[540] Ibid 111

[541] Ibid 120

The Way to Christianity

would consume the wicked. Tertullian believed this to be the only true *'rule of faith,'* which was handed down by Jesus. He viewed heresy as being due to 'philosophy' and provided a famous denunciation: '*What indeed has Athens (philosophy) to do with Jerusalem (Christianity).*'[542]

But, like so many other theologians, he utilised philosophical principles whilst at the same time deriding them. Tertullian was particularly scathing of innovation, which he felt was the cause of heresy. He believed that Heretics had no right to use Holy Scriptures as they were not Christian, and that only the teaching of the one true Church was valid and must be accepted. Given Tertullian's nature it seems unremarkable that he fell into a vigorous dispute with a Bishop who he sarcastically refers to as 'sovereign Pontiff,' who was probably the Bishop of Carthage. Tertullian objected to what he regarded as laxity in Church practice, particularly in granting a remission of sin for those guilty of '*fornication.*' This contradicted his own earlier published work in which he claimed that the remission of sins was available for those who truly repented of even the most serious transgressions.

Tertullian almost certainly brought about a schism in his local Church by leading a breakaway group called the Montanists. This movement was deeply pious and reactionary, condemning any lapse and maintaining very high levels of religious observance.

Tertullian was the first to use the phrase '*the trinity*' to describe the essential nature of God. Using an analogy from nature, he compared *'the Father, Son and Holy Spirit'* to a tree which has a root, a stem and fruit. This idea exploits stoic philosophical thought where God is seen as material in much the same manner as a tree is material. This is not to deny the spirituality of God, which is seen as a gas or very fine fluid, which permeates the world.[543] In contrast to stoic ideas of a material God, Platonism viewed God as entirely insubstantial and unconfined in space of time.

---

[542] Ibid 167

[543] Chadwick H. The Early Church. Penguin Press (1993) 90-93

Origen

Perhaps the best known, Neo-Platonist, early Church theologian was Origen.[544] This is hardly surprising, as a young man he is said to have attended philosophy lectures and was familiar with the work of the originator of Neo-Platonism, Platinus. Origen was a contemporary of both Tertullian and Irenaeus and was born in Alexandria in the mid-180s CE. Even as a young man he was thought to have had an unrivalled knowledge of the bible and, as a private teacher, he was employed by the Bishop of Alexandria to teach catechumens undergoing their initial formal instruction in the principles of Christianity.

Origen travelled and taught widely in the ancient world, spending time in a variety of centres, including both Jerusalem and Rome. He was ordained by the Bishop of Palestine in 231CE, and was employed as a teacher and a theologian. Amongst his many books, some of which were recovered in recent times, was '*First Principles,*' a widely read system of theology. This work was concerned with the interpretation of the book of Genesis and biblical understanding in general.

As with Tertullian, Origen subscribes to the concept of the unbroken descent of authoritative teaching from Jesus to the Apostles, and from the Apostles to the individual Churches of Christendom, but he left a wider scope for biblical interpretation than his fellow theologians.

Origen had little interest in the historical basis to Christianity, and appears to have had little knowledge of why or how the bible was written. He believed that the Apostles deliberately left the basis of their statements about Jesus unclear to give an opportunity for further spiritual interpretation, and it was interpretation that was probably Origen's greatest strength. Using a variety of ancient texts, Origen attempted to arrive at a definitive interpretation of the Septuagint, the most widely used Greek version of the Hebrew Bible. Having arrived at a satisfactory text, Origen drew on this to develop allegories, which illustrated its true spiritual meaning; in this way he was able to show that Jesus was not only '*foretold,*' as Paul of Tarsus had claimed, but was present throughout the Hebrew Bible.

As one would expect from a theologian who had studied under the Platonist philosophers, Origen's view of God followed very much the

---

[544] Ibid 100-113

Platonist model: he viewed God as pure spirit and mind, unconfined by time and space, that could not be described in any way and was quite unknowable. The only way in which He could be approached was through his word and His 'Son.' In generating the Son, the Father was, in principle, generating everything; however, Origen did not believe that the act of generation was unique, God was timeless and so was the Son, who must therefore be continuously generated.

Thus Father, Son and Spirit existed as three distinct entities, God being the most pre-eminent, followed by the Son, and then the Spirit. Both God and the Son could exist independently of scripture, but it was only through biblical knowledge that the Spirit could be revealed. It was also the Spirit that was responsible for the valid inspirational interpretation of scripture.

Origen also promulgated highly original ideas about the creation: before the creation of the world as described in Genesis, Origen believed that there was a previous existence. This anterior actuality involved the creation of pure rational spirits, which had always existed with God, however, these spirits were capable of exercising free will, and some turned from God and followed the devil. There was no apparent reason for the free spirits to follow the devil rather than God, but their choice brought into existence the entire universe.

Alongside the free spirits were archangels, who had sinned slightly, and demons, who had sinned greatly. Between the archangels and demons were some spirits who had only moderately sinned, and for them God created the world, and human bodies. This creation represented a punishment, whose effects were seen as beneficial for those souls who had transgressed. Since the spirits had varying degrees of sinfulness there were varying degrees of human experience and this was responsible for the inequalities of human life. Although Origen did not preach the transmigration of souls, as some detractors have claimed, he did believe that life was a redeeming burden whose purpose was to achieve spiritual purity. Thus, the purpose of life was to rise above the body; this contrasted greatly with early Christian hopes for the physical resurrection of the flesh, because Origen was suggesting that once spiritual purity had been achieved, the body would not be required.

Although Origen saw life as progress towards a purely spiritual objective, he nevertheless strongly emphasised the atoning sacrifice of the crucifixion. It was only through the crucifixion that the possibility of the remission of sins existed.

Whilst Origen's theology was highly speculative, it did lead to one proposition, which was seen as important for later developments: Origen's views on the creation of the body allowed for both a body and a spirit in one individual. Hence, Jesus was a uniquely pure spirit—who was both God and man combined in the same individual. Thus Jesus could be seen as a pure spirit who had never turned from God and had always resisted the devils temptation, however, in life, Jesus the man could suffer as any other human being could suffer.

Much of Origen's speculations on the nature and pre-existence of spirits was not accepted by the developing Church, but his view of Jesus as both God and man was.

Early Bishops

As Christian intellectuals refined their views of Jesus' relationship to God and the Holy Spirit, Church developments were also taking place—indeed, to a great degree, these factors were interrelated: As the theology of apostolic succession became more important, greater care began to be exercised in the appointment of Bishops. A Bishop's views on doctrinal matters had an increased bearing on his prospects for promotion within the Church.

The first Bishop to appoint another to a Bishopric in another city was probably Bishop Demetrius of Alexandria. Since Demetrius was opposed to Origen's views we can assume that his appointee was similarly minded. At this time, Alexandria was one of the great centres of Christianity, whilst Rome was not yet the centre of apostolic authority, although its importance was being increasingly emphasised; Rome could claim Paul of Tarsus as an early Christian martyr, a claim that was probably valid, and Rome also maintained that the apostles Peter, and at a later date John, had also died in the city. Both were Jewish followers of The Way rather than Christians, but in a sense this was secondary to their direct personal contact with Jesus. Peter's presence in Rome was a matter of contention between the Roman Church and later Protestants:

Peter's Synagogue was in Antioch, where there are present day claims for his tomb, as indeed there are in Jerusalem.[545]

However, Peter's presence and subsequent martyrdom in Rome is not wholly implausible. We know from one of Paul's letters that there was dissent in Rome between those Christians who had abandoned the Jewish law and the followers of The Way who had not. With Paul supporting one faction, it is possible that Peter was asked to visit Rome and counter Paul's influence. This of course is speculation, unsupported by any historical source, but some mechanism has to be invoked to account for Peter leaving his Synagogue and travelling to the eternal city. The claim for John's presence and execution in Rome is wholly unsupported and probably spurious.

Whatever the validity of Roman apostolic claims, the Bishops of the late second and early third century were particularly energetic and sought to bring about a degree of uniformity, firstly to Rome and later to other areas.

Rome and many other western Churches celebrated Easter at the time of the Jewish Passover and maintained a fast until Easter Sunday. Many eastern Churches, notably in Ephesus, broke their fast on the fourteenth day of the Jewish month of Nissan, which falls before Easter Sunday. In attempting to apply a uniform church calendar to Rome, the Bishops encountered opposition from some eastern Christian immigrants, who lived in the city and continued to observe the 14th of Nissan. This dispute, whilst seemingly trivial to modern readers, may have contributed to the origins of the great schism between Rome and the Orthodox Churches.[546]

The Roman Bishops were not only active in attempting to establish a universal Church calendar. They also acted against those who maintained that Jesus and God were one and the same entity, thus negating the need for much early Christian theology. A great deal of this defence of growing orthodoxy was attributed to the Roman Bishop and theologian, Hippolytus.

---

[545] Grant M. Saint Peter. Weidenfield and Nicolson (1994) 155-159

[546] Frend W.H.C. The Early Church. SCM (1982) Press 72-78

Hippolytus

As with many other theologians, Hippolytus was vigorously opposed to heresies.[547] He maintained that the *logos* was the inner voice of God, which brought everything into being. When Jesus was sent to earth the *logos* was revealed through him. Whilst Hippolytus does not include the Spirit as a specific entity in his writings, it is probably implied on a number of occasions.

In addition to being a competent theologian, Hippolytus was also a vigorous and combative debater. There is some evidence to suggest that his style was such that leading Roman Bishops sought to mediate between him and other authorities whom he had offended.

Perhaps Hippolytus' greatest contribution was the publication of the *'Apostolic Tradition.'* This not only supported the apostolic succession, but gave details of Church services and rituals covering ordination, baptism, the details of daily and weekly worship and liturgy. Hippolytus claimed that these patterns of Church organisation and worship went back to the earliest times, but it is more likely that they represented the custom and practice of the third century Church.[548]

As time passed, Hippolytus fell into a particularly acrimonious dispute with the Roman Bishop Callistus, who he charged with heresy and fraud,[549] but whose real crime—at least in the eyes of Hippolytus—was the erosion of Church discipline. This claim was in some ways difficult to refute: Callistus was clearly seeking to expand both his Church, and his personal authority, beyond Rome and possibly beyond Italy. Furthermore, he was prepared to admit members of other congregations to his own Church, even when they were guilty of sin, an indulgence that was extended to other Bishops, even to those who were married. He was also prepared to sanction marriage between high-born women and men of a much lower rank, which, according to Roman law, was adultery. In all of these matters Callistus was offering a forgiveness of sins, which was particularly attractive to those who came from more rigorously controlled congregations. This policy seems to have been

---

[547] Ibid 145-152

[548] Chadwick H. The Early Church. Penguin Press (1990) 261-265

[549] Stevenson J. A New Eusebius. SPCK (1987) 150-151

largely successful, and increased the authority and perhaps the influence of other Bishops in Rome.[550]

Needless to say, this was anathema to Hippolytus, who viewed Callistus as a heretic, who was conducting *'second baptisms,'* which in reality were probably no more than a laying on of hands to welcome penitents to Callistus' growing Church.

Hippolytus was to meet his end in a persecution instigated by the Emperor Maximum Thrax. Those Christians who had been aligned with the preceding Emperor, as Hippolytus had been, were arrested and sent as forced labour to mines in Sardinia, where Hippolytus reportedly died.

Fabian and Novation

After Hippolytus' death and the replacement of the Emperor Maximum Thrax, the Church enjoyed a rather brief respite from persecution. Now led by Bishop Fabian (236-50CE), the Roman Church found a capable theologian in the person of Novation,[551] whose principle work, which has survived to modern times, was *'the Trinity.'* Its principle argument relates to the Father and to the Son—although the Spirit is referred to in passing—viewed as two entities, although Novation believed that this did not imply two Gods. He viewed the Son as existing before time, although in a sense preceded by the Father, who, in agreement with neo-platonic principles, was not confined by time or space, but intimated actions through his word. These actions, particularly those found in the Hebrew Bible were *'due to the Son'* who, could appear at one time and one place. In agreement with Hippolytus, Novation's view was that this did not imply that the Son is simply a function of God; rather that he had his own existence, although this existence was not independent of the Father.[552]

---

[550] Frend W.H.C. The Early Church. SPCK (1982) 78-79

[551] Stevenson J. A New Eusebius. SPCK (1987) 230-231.

[552] Ibid 233

The Empire in Crisis.

By the middle of the third century Rome was in crisis. Economic hardship was widespread and the frontiers of the Empire came under repeated and sometimes successful attack. Army commanders competed with one another to become Emperor and factional warfare was widespread (Chapter 10). In 249CE Decius displaced his predecessor and became Emperor in his place; he sought to restore order and turned to the traditional Gods of Rome who had served so well in the past. Almost inevitably this resulted in a new wave of Christian persecution.

Unlike many previous persecutions, that initiated during the reign of Decius was centrally administered and well organised; it fell particularly heavily on the Bishops and many were executed, including Fabian of Rome. Whole congregations were required to sacrifice to Pagan Gods and obtain a statement showing that they had done so (Chapter 7). Fortunately the persecution was short-lived and relatively few died but very large numbers, including Presbyters, Deacons and even some Bishops, had fled their Churches and denied their faith. The Church now fell into a deep crisis: the majority, who had denied their faith, believed they had done so under duress, and many wished to return to their Christian communities.

Confessors

In principle, it was considered possible for an individual to be readmitted to the Church if they were truly penitent and underwent a period of further instruction and reconciliation. The difficulty lay in having sufficient senior churchmen to administer the process and to ensure that standards were maintained. To meet this challenge a group known as Confessors emerged.[553]

Confessors were those who had not renounced their faith and had survived persecution and, were to a large extent, self-appointed. Although they did not always meet with the approval of the surviving Bishops, the Confessors issued certificates to worthy individuals and readmitted them into the communion of the Church. One Bishop who objected to the confessor's actions was Cyprian, a Bishop of Carthage

---

[553] Ibid 217

who had gone into hiding during Decius' short persecution, and who was appalled by the mass desertion of Christians.[554] Cyprian was a follower of Tertullian, and assembled a group of priests who had also been in hiding; returning to his Bishopric, he condemned the Confessors and began to enact his own, more vigorous, judgements.

Cyprian's book on *'the lapsed'* became the authoritative view for dealing with the problem. In it he declared that whilst Confessors could recommend the re-admission of certain penitents, it was only the Bishops who were empowered to pass judgement. He presented his views to a Synod in Carthage in 251CE and the assembled Bishops agreed a common policy.[555] All penitents were to be individually examined by the clergy, who would lay down the terms of re-admission to the Church.

At first Cyprian's policy met with resistance, particularly from the Confessors, a number of whom had established separate Churches. However, in time, Cyprian's views gained the upper hand and Church authority was gradually restored. Resolving the situation in Rome, however, was less straightforward.

Novation and Cornelius

The death of the much-respected Fabian traumatised the Roman Church.

During Decius' persecution many—and it was probably the majority—had signed the Authority's documents and sacrificed to Pagan Gods. The resulting loss of the clergy was so great that the Church virtually ceased to function. Thus, at the end of the persecution, Novation, and a number of followers, attempted to restore order. In doing so they applied firm conditions for re-admission to those who had lapsed.[556] However, in defiance of Novation the Confessors' actions continued and a Bishop of less rigorous views called Cornelius was appointed.[557] In response, Novation's supporters proclaimed him Bishop

---

[554] Ibid 216

[555] Ibid 219

[556] Ibid 232

[557] Ibid 225

and a schism was firmly established.[558] Cornelius appealed to Dionysius of Alexander, who supported him, whilst Novation won the support of Fabius, the Bishop of Antioch.

The view of Cyprian of Carthage was crucial and, after some hesitancy, he came down on the side of Cornelius, on the grounds that he had been appointed Bishop first.[559] This was a serious setback for Novation, but he outlived Cornelius and his supporters, and the Church in Rome, continued to grow.

Rather unsurprisingly Novation's Church grew increasingly rigid in its view and refused to recognise any baptism that it had not carried out. It regarded all lapsed Christians as heretics, and treated them accordingly, and this provoked a vigorous response.[560]

Cyprian

As dissent grew, not just in Rome but also in many other centres, the need for unity and uniformity of action increased. Cyprian of Carthage, in his book on *'the unity of the Catholic Church'* denigrated all schematics and promoted a united universal Church wherein the role of Bishops was fundamental. Cyprian saw Bishops as the great unifying force in the widespread Churches of Christendom.

The system of Church management at this time was implemented in a manner which almost exactly paralleled the bureaucracy of the Roman Empire: A new Bishop should only be appointed with the agreement of three existing Bishops;[561] Once appointed a new Bishop should receive appropriate documents confirming his appointment, copies of which were to be retained in a central register; Confessors and other charismatics were to be subordinate to their Bishops, whose decisions were final and binding on all. In conducting their sacred duty Bishops also had to remain free of sin; any Bishop falling into sin could not participate in the communion of the Church, as this would be unacceptable to God.

---

[558] Ibid 230

[559] Ibid 225

[560] Ibid 232

[561] Frend W.H.C. The Early Church. SCM (1965) 142

Cyprian's views were, in time, to lead to a more coherent Church organisation, although there were initial difficulties.[562] The Confessors and other quasi-official teachers resented subordination to their Bishops and difficulties also arose with removing Bishops who had failed to live up to their spiritual calling.[563]

Cyprian, along with other Bishops, was involved in the dismissal of two Bishops. In both instances Cyprian had played a more vigorous role than Stephen, the recently appointed Bishop of Rome, who in Cyprian's eyes had a tendency to leniency—and this in time was to lead to vigorous dissent.

By the middle of the third century the Church was widespread, but not uniform.

Charges of heresy by one Church against another were not that uncommon, which created difficulties for the admission of newly arrived believers from Churches that might have been viewed as heretical. Stephen's view, that such individuals should be admitted with a *'laying on of hands,'* but no further baptism, followed a long standing Church doctrine which held that baptism was a dedication to God and signified an individual's new life as a Christian;[564] as such, baptism was an act that could not be repeated. Cyprian violently disagreed: a baptism that was conducted by heretics, or by someone not properly authorised, was no baptism at all and certainly not valid, he therefore required all new members of his congregation to undergo baptism irrespective of whether they had previously done so under the auspices of another Church.[565]

This practice was broadly accepted in the Churches of North Africa, where Cyprian's influence was strong, but it was rejected by Rome and Churches in other parts of the Empire. In an attempt to resolve this difficulty, Stephen threatened ex-communication of the Bishops of North Africa and other areas insisting on re-baptism. Perhaps understandably, this horrified Cyprian who saw Stephen's policy as an attack on the primacy of the Bishops. At a Church council in Carthage in 256CE Cyprian successfully argued for the supremacy and independence of

---

[562] Ibid 100

[563] Stevenson J. A New Eusebius. SPCK (1987) 226-228

[564] Ibid 238-239

[565] Ibid 238

the Bishops[566] and furthermore undertook not to seek to impose his own views on others, as he believed Stephen had done. Although shortly after, in 257CE, Cyprian was martyred in a persecution by the Emperor Valerian, the legacy of the dispute between Rome and the North African Churches was to encourage hostilities that in turn had an unsettling influence on some Church authorities.

The Great Persecution

At the beginning of the fourth century a *'great persecution'* of Christians took place whose origins were obscure, but whose effects were widespread—although rather uneven. As with Decius' persecution of 250CE, it was the clergy who suffered most, but, unlike 250CE, an intellectual assault was mounted against emerging Christianity and a number of anti-Christian texts were published.[567] Suppression of Christian literature was also widely carried out, and a number of Bishops were compelled to give up their books.[568]

When the persecution was over, those Bishops who had surrendered their libraries were attacked. In North Africa the ensuing dispute was particularly vigorous: One group supported Caecilian, who had usurped the Bishopric of Carthage, and gained the support of Rome; A second—led at a later stage by Donatus: the 'alternative' Bishop of Carthage—took a rigorous approach, attacking a number of fellow Bishops for handing over Church literature. This disagreement was far from gentle—with some churchmen resorting to the production of forged documents.[569] But if the situation in Carthage was factious, much worse was to follow in a doctrinal debate associated with the name of Arian.

Arian

Arian's origins are obscure: he was probably Libyan, and at some point became a Presbyter in a Church in Alexander where he fell out

---

[566] Ibid 239

[567] Ibid 269-271

[568] Ibid 273-275

[569] Ibid 302-307

The Way to Christianity

with his Bishop. Whether this was due to heresy on Arian's part or impropriety on the part of the Bishop is not clear. Almost all of Arian's writings have been lost, and most of what is claimed about, or attributed to, him was written by his enemies.

The best-known attribution that: *'there was once when he was not,'* is almost certainly invalid.[570] This statement—that God existed before his Son, and therefore, there was a time when the Son did not exist—hardly seems, on the face of it, deeply contentious, yet at this point in Christian development it was treated with great seriousness. The assertion that Arian had made this statement, although almost certainly false, was enough to condemn him.

It seems likely that Arian became a symbolically heretical figure, who was the recipient of the doctrinal disputes of others. The small amount of Arian's writings that have survived show him to be a deeply pious and rather traditional figure; in his few letters to the Bishop of Alexandra and his one poem that are extant there are a number of largely un-contentious statements:[571]

> *'Or rather there is a Trinity with glories not alike. There existences are unmixable with each other; one is more glorious than another by an infinity of glories.'* [572]

This quotation, which was hardly radical, gives a flavour of Arian's thought; yet he was declared heretical, first by the Bishop of Alexander,[573] and later by the majority of Bishops. What brought about this apparently unlikely turn of events? We cannot know with any precision since the winners, characteristically, gave their own version of events, and praised their own motivation. However it seems at least possible, that Arian was caught up in a political conflict, which was as much about power as it was about theology.

The instigators and leaders of the anti-Arian faction used him as a scapegoat to denounce everything with which they did not agree.

---

[570] Ibid 321

[571] Ibid 331

[572] Ibid 322-324

[573] Ibid 334

In doing so they created danger for his supporters, and by prevailing they won positions and influence within the Church for themselves. The mechanism of their success lay in Church councils, which were becoming an increasingly common feature of Church politics: Two of particular importance took place in 325CE.[574]

The council of Antioch was probably convened in the early Spring of 325CE. Its original purpose was not particularly clear, but it soon began to deal with:

> *'A great deal of disorder, the chief reason being the law of the Church had been in many respects slighted and despised, and the canons had in the meantime been wholly invalidated by worldly men.'* [575]

This was clearly a reference to Arianism, a point reinforced in a letter from the
President of the council:

> *'For since our brother and fellow servant the honoured and beloved Alexander, Bishop of Alexandria, had excommunicated some Presbyters, i.e., Arian and his friends for the blasphemy which they directed against our Saviour.'* [576]

Having condemned Arian, and provisionally excommunicated three dissenting Bishops, the council proceeded to issue a declaration of faith. The declaration was a somewhat wordy document, but it lay down the majority view:

> *'To believe in one God ... incomprehensible, immutable and unchangeable ... just good, maker of heaven and earth, and of all things in them ... and, in one Jesus Christ only begotten son, begotten not from that which is not, but from*

---

[574] Ibid 334-337

[575] Ibid 334-337

[576] Ibid 334-337

> *the Father, not as made, but as properly an offspring, but begotten in an ineffable, indescribable manner, because only the Father who begot and the Son who begotten know . . . For we have learned from the holy scriptures, that he alone is the sole image . . . The scriptures described him as validly and truly begotten as Son, so that we believe him to be immutable and unchangeable . . . but in a way, which passes all understanding or conception or reasoning, we confess him to have been begotten or the unbegotten Father, God the word, true light, righteousness, Jesus Christ, Lord and Saviour of all . . . This Son, God of the word, having been in flesh from Mary the Mother of God and made incarnate, having suffered and dies, rose again from the dead and was taken up into heaven and sits on the right hand of the majesty most high, and is coming to judge the living and the dead. Furthermore, as in our Saviour, the holy scriptures teach us to believe also in one spirit, one Catholic Church, the resurrection of the dead . . . and we anathematise those who way, or think, or preach that the Son of God is a creature or had come into being, or had been made and is not truly begotten, or that there was when he was not.'* [577]

The document proposed by the council was accepted by all those present, with the three exceptions already referred to. The three dissenting Bishops were proved to have the same views as Arian, and this was sufficient to provisionally excommunicate them.

However, the statement of faith as promulgated by the Bishops is, somewhat ironically, surprisingly close to a creed prepared by Arian and submitted to Bishop Alexander of Alexandria. But by now Arian had come to symbolise a token enemy, against which an array of diverse groups could coalesce and form a dominant majority. At this point Church politics had taken over, and any statement by Arian was automatically condemned, irrespective of the views it contained. The council of Antioch had issued a statement of faith, which was essentially an ad hoc arrangement that grew out of a meeting called for another

---

[577] Ibid 335

purpose. A continuation of the council reconvened at Nicaea, to which all representative Bishops were invited.[578]

The Nicaean Creed

At the beginning of the council Bishop Eusebius presented a creed that had been used in his Church and which was immediately rejected by the majority, who had presumably organised things in advance. The creed finally accepted was:

> '*We believe in one God, the Father almighty, maker of all things visible and invisible. And in one Lord Jesus Christ, the Son of God begotten of the Father, only begotten, that is, from the substance of the Father, God from God, light from light, true God from the true God, begotten not made, co-substantial with the Father, by whom all things were made; who for us men and for out salvation came down and was incarnate, was made man, suffered and rose again on the third day, ascended into heaven and is coming to judge the living and the dead. And in the Holy Spirit, and those who say, 'there was when he was not,' and 'before his generation he was not,' and 'he came from nothing,' those who present that the Son of God is of other reality, or being 'or created' or alterable or mutable, the Catholic and Apostolic Church anathematises.*' [579]

Much of this will be familiar to many Christians, although the commonly used form was only finalised at the Council of Constantinople in 381CE. The creed decried Arianism, which nevertheless persisted and continued to flourish in the East, until it was extinguished by the rise of Islam some three centuries later. The great majority of Bishops present at Nicaea accepted the creed, although with varying degrees of enthusiasm.

---

[578] Ibid 338

[579] Ibid 344

The Way to Christianity

Following the council, a series of 'canons' were produced, probably by a committee of Bishops. These documents dealt mainly with formalising Church structure and organisation.[580] It is apparent from the many councils that followed Nicaea, that some—and perhaps it was a substantial minority—had reservations about what had been decided, but a new factor had entered Christianity, one which made dissent increasingly dangerous.

The Roman Emperor Constantine, the first Christian Emperor, had been involved in Christianity since his rise to power. It was his desire for uniformity, which had galvanised a substantial faction within the Church to organise the councils that had taken place. Constantine was to have a great influence on developing Christianity, although much of his own life was conducted on wholly unchristian principles.

---

[580] Ibid 338

CHAPTER 12

CONSTANTINE

The life of the Emperor Constantine was one of bloody contradictions. He had an indelible impact on Roman society and indeed the world, but some of his basic biographical data remains elusive. The year of his birth is uncertain, with either 272-273[581] or 280-282CE being the most likely. The place of his birth is also somewhat obscure with Naissus (modern day Nish in Serbia) being the favoured candidate.[582]

Parents

Constantine's father, Constantius Chlorus, was a burly, short man of peasant origins from the Danube basin. After joining the Roman army, he had risen through the ranks to the position of Praetorian Prefect, and had an outstanding army record.[583]

Constantine's mother Helena was also of humble origins, being in all probability a barmaid, and it was unlikely, despite later Christian claims, that she was married to Constantine's father. In any event, Constantius Chlorus made a politically advantageous marriage to Flavia Maximiana Theordora, in 293CE and their union produced six further children. It seems possible that Helena remained in Constantius Chlorus' household, where she was to rise to considerable prominence when her son became Emperor.[584]

---

[581] Grant M. The Emperor Constantine. Phoenix Giant. (1998) 15-16

[582] Jones A.H.M. Constantine and the Conversion of Europe. University of Toronto Press (1962) 1

[583] Grant M. The Emperor Constantine. Phoenix Giant (1998) 16

[584] Ibid 16-17

The Court of Diocletian

As a young child Constantine was dispatched to the court of the Emperor Diocletian, who probably wished to use him as a means of guaranteeing his father's continuing loyalty. Diocletian had risen to power by the traditional Roman expedient of murdering his rivals and, once in power, divided the Empire into four, appointing Constantine's father as Caesar of the Western quadrant, where for part of the time he resided in Britain.

Diocletian appears in Christian histories as a great persecutor of their religion, and there is little doubt that this was so; events would likely not have been so traumatic if Diocletian had been a less able administrator, but he was energetic and organised, pursuing his objectives to completion and causing great Christian suffering.

Constantine's view of the persecution going on around him is not known. It has been claimed that his father was a 'closet Christian', which on the whole, seems rather unlikely. Nevertheless, he did not promote the Christian persecution as vigorously as in other parts of the Empire and this cannot have made his son's position at court any more secure. As a result, it seems probable that Constantine may have learnt the art of dissimilation at an early age.[585] As he grew, he learnt military skills, serving initially in the Emperor's bodyguard and later distinguishing himself in a campaign against the Persians.

Constantius Chlorus

When Constantine was in his early thirties, Diocletian and his co-Emperor, Maximian, who would later become Constantine's father-in-law, retired. This event was virtually unprecedented in the Empire, and gave Constantine his first glimpse of the ultimate prize. His father, Constantius Chlorus, now became co-Emperor with Galerius, who had been Caesar of the Eastern Empire. Maintaining the tradition of four rulers, decreed by Diocletian, two further Caesars were appointed, both of whom were well connected with the Emperor Galerius. Flavius Valerius Severus was a lifelong friend, whilst Miximinus II Daia, was

---

[585] Gibbon E. The Decline and Fall of the Roman Empire. Wordsworth (1998) 226

a nephew. This placed Constantine in a dangerous situation, which was made worse when he was held as a virtual prisoner by Galerius.

Escaping to join his father, who was now in poor health, Constantine made a hazardous journey across the Empire arriving in Britain in early 306CE.[586] Despite joining his son on a military campaign against the Picts (Scots), Constantius Chlorus died in York on the 25th July, 306CE. With the support of the Western legions and a German tribal leader who happened to be in Britain at the time, Constantine was declared Augustus, in the late summer of 306CE.[587] In response Maxentius, the son of Maximian, rebelled and took Rome in October 306CE. The scene was now set for a period of political instability and intrigue, which had only one, perhaps inevitable, outcome.

Civil Wars

Alliances formed and dissolved. Maximian argued with his son Maxentius and sought refuge with Constantine where, after a period of time, Maximian rebelled against him too. After putting down the uprising, Constantine's troops forced Maximian to commit suicide. This left Constantine now faced with Maxentius, who occupied Rome and the territories in North Africa, and, since both Maxentius and Constantine claimed to be the sole Emperor of the Western Empire, a civil war was inevitable. Constantine moved his army from Northern Europe across the Alps into Italy. In doing so he was militarily vulnerable, particularly in the Alpine passes, yet Maxentius did not take the opportunity to attack him.

As Constantine moved from Northern to Central Italy he avoided conflict with local populations, particularly those occupying fortified towns. This prudent action probably earned him genuine support at a later stage when he became undisputed Emperor.[588] As Constantine approached Rome he must have envisaged a long and perhaps difficult siege, against an enemy protected by the substantial walls of the capital. But, as preparations for the battle took place, Maxentius and his army

---

[586] Grant M. The Emperor Constantine. Phoenix Giant (1998) 22

[587] Ibid 23

[588] Ibid 35-36

emerged from the fortifications of Rome, and took up positions with their backs to the northern banks of the River Tiber by the Milvian Bridge.

Battle of the Milvian Bridge

Historians have long speculated on Maxentius' decision to leave the safety of Rome: Was it overconfidence based on favourable omens? Or fear of the population of Rome, who might turn against him when subjected to the deprivation of a long siege? Or was it just a tactical error, which seems so obvious in retrospect? We cannot know with any certainty because Maxentius and his generals did not survive. The battle itself was ferocious; each side knowing there was little chance of clemency from the victor. At first the armies seemed evenly matched and little progress was made, eventually, as the attrition increased, Constantine's forces managed to outflank their opponents who urgently needed to withdraw. Unfortunately Maxentius had destroyed the Milvian Bridge to prevent its use by Constantine, and relied instead on a boat bridge. This bridge became overloaded and unstable throwing many soldiers, including Maxentius, into the Tiber where they drowned. Constantine entered Rome in Triumph, displaying Maxentius' head on a lance at the front of his victorious troops.[589]

Emperor of the West

Constantine was now master of the Empire's capital and undisputed Emperor of its Western provinces. The year was probably 312CE and the date the 28th October. This date was celebrated throughout his reign with considerable splendour, and Constantine was to become increasingly addicted to ostentatious ceremonials. He was now unopposed and firmly in control of the Western Empire, but this was not the case in the East, where two men disputed the right to govern.

Constantine's future brother-in-law Linicius, who was to marry the Emperor's half-sister in 313CE, was in conflict with Maximinus Daia, the son of Galerius' sister. Constantine's interests were best served by letting these two rivals attempt to destroy each other, especially

---

[589] Ibid 38

when his own position was reinforced after he was declared the senior Emperor 'Maximus Augustus' by the Roman Senate. The two opponents now had no chance but to compete with each other before taking on Constantine for control of the entire Empire.

Resolution was not long in coming, and battle took place in Thrace in 313CE. Maximinus Daia was in much the weaker position: lacking in both men and supplies, and was rather easily beaten by Linicius, who, in typical Roman fashion, secured his position by destroying all potential rivals, including both the male and female relatives of Maximinus Daia. This slaughter brought about the deaths of a number of members of the Roman aristocracy, including the widow of the retired Emperor Diocletian. Such measures can seem barbaric in the extreme in our own time, yet it was little more than established practice, and many Emperors indulged in a blood bath on their accession to power.[590]

Constantine's position was now all that he could have hoped for, at least in the short term: With the Senate's recognition of his ascendancy, Linicius was in no position to challenge the senior Emperor whether he wanted to or not—and it seems on balance that he did not. His relationship by marriage to the Emperor's family gave Linicius a degree of security, whilst his own forceful bloodletting made his power in the east unassailable. In principle the division of the Empire between west and east was potentially stable with Constantine recognised as the premier Emperor. The appointment of Caesars to assist each Emperor meant that the structure was now similar to that of Diocletian, who had divided the Empire into a tetrarchy. The division of East and West also recognised the realities of the external threat that the vast Roman Empire faced. In the West the northern tribes, particularly those beyond the Danube, were a continuing concern, whilst in the East the Persian Empire was a traditional enemy.

Between the years 313 to 316CE the basic division of power seems to have worked well. The joint Emperors made declarations of friendship, and coins were minted in their joint names. However, in 316CE fault lines began to appear. Constantine accused a close associate of Linicius of plotting against him. The accusation was, in all probability, false, but Constantine insisted on retribution and the individual concerned was executed. When Constantine then insisted that a second individual

---

[590] Ibid 40

be killed, Linicius demurred.⁵⁹¹ Using this as an excuse, Constantine launched an attack on his co-Emperor in the early morning of the 8th October, 316CE.

Constantine was victorious, but Linicius, and a large proportion of his army, escaped. The two sides regrouped and a second battle proved as inconclusive as the first, with Linicius again withdrawing with a much-depleted force. Constantine now advanced and occupied much of Linicius' former territory including Byzantium. After protracted negotiations, conducted under considerable duress, Linicius formally accepted the Senate's designation of Constantine as the senior Emperor, and the sons of both Emperors were declared 'Caesars,' although Linicius' son was to hold the title only briefly.

The new arrangements remained in place for a number of years, but with little pretence of friendship, and matters again came to a head in 324CE. Constantine's son Crispius defeated Linicius' admiral in a naval engagement in the Hellespont. Linicius, with his position considerably weakened, had little choice but to leave the last part of Europe that he controlled and entered what is now Turkey. Assembling his entire force at Chryspous, Linicius prepared for a final decisive contest. Facing each other were armies well in excess of one hundred thousand men.

On the 18th September, 324CE battle commenced, with legionnaires killing legionnaires in unprecedented numbers. Despite having somewhat the larger force, Licinius was again defeated, leaving the bodies of tens of thousands of his men on the battlefield. Escaping from the site of carnage, the defeated Emperor withdrew to Nicomedia, were his wife Constantia persuaded him to surrender to her half-brother. Pleading for her consort's life, she agreed that her husband would renounce all hostilities, titles and positions and accept permanent exile in Thessalonica. In the spring of the following year Constantine had both Licinius and his son killed.⁵⁹²

---

[591] Ibid 40-42

[592] Ibid 48

Undisputed Emperor

Constantine was now the undisputed ruler of an Empire stretching from the Picts (Scottish) border in the West, to the furthermost reaches of the Black Sea in the East. In the South, the entire coast of Africa and Egypt lay under Roman control, whilst in the North, the Rivers Danube and Rhine formed a natural defensive line.

Constantine had previously fought a series of successful campaigns against the Goths and Visigoths tribes beyond the Danube. In the severe winter of 322-323CE, taking advantage of the river's frozen surface, the Visigoths launched a major incursion into Roman territory. Doubtless they hoped to prosper from the trauma of the conflict between Constantine and Licinius, but if so, they were disappointed. Constantine launched a massive counter-attack, which not only drove the invaders back beyond their own territory, but also resulted in the reoccupation of southern Dacia (modern day Romania) a territory abandoned by the Emperor Aurelian in 274CE. Although this territory was not held with any permanence, Constantine celebrated this victory and the phrase 'Victoria Gothica" was impressed on many of his coins.[593] Perhaps this was an understandable action by a man who had otherwise so conspicuously engaged in wars against his own people.

Having suppressed the Goths, Constantine's Empire was reasonably secure. To the West, the natural defence of the River Rhine was augmented by a fleet of narrow draft boats and a series of Roman forts, whilst a remarkable bridge was constructed by Roman military engineers. This gave access to the heartland of the Germanic tribes, should the need arise; however, it was these tribes who provided an increasing proportion of both the man-power and leadership of the Roman army.

The process of army recruitment from conquered peoples had been in place for centuries, and peace settlements between Rome and its neighbours often included the provision of auxiliaries, who were then distributed throughout the Empire. This process was greatly accelerated under Constantine and 'Barbarians' came to occupy all ranks. There was an obvious risk in such a policy: whilst the Germanic tribes were in chronic conflict with one another the situation was generally stable, but,

---

[593] Ibid 59

should they ever unite, the western Empire would become vulnerable. This was indeed the case at a later date, when the western Empire fell, or rather crumbled, into 'Barbarian' hands, a process which was undoubtedly accelerated by an army reorganisation carried out by Constantine.

Frontier defences were partitioned into two levels and along the borderlands auxiliary forces were given large numbers of farms in the hope that they would defend their new possessions and slow the progress of any invader. Further back, the regular army was garrisoned in towns that they had not formerly occupied. Their function was to provide a mobile defence in depth that could rapidly respond to incursions. Tactically this made a good deal of sense, but strategically it was deeply flawed. The auxiliary border forces were largely made up of 'barbarians' particularly those of the Germanic tribes, whose loyalty was potentially suspect. Behind these border areas, the garrisoned units of the regular army were resented by town's people unused to the excesses of large numbers of young men in uniform.[594]

At a later date the historian Zosimus was particularly scathing of the new arrangements:

> 'Constantine abolished security by removing the greater part of the soldiery from the frontiers to cities that needed no auxiliary forces . . . (he) burdened tranquil cities with the pest of the military . . . Indeed he personally planted the first seeds of our present devastated state of affairs.' [595]

Further resentment was caused by Constantine's favourable and often indulgent treatment of his troops. Army pay and conditions were generally good, and were rather frequently augmented by bonuses, often given on trivial grounds. This money had to come from somewhere and, in the absence of foreign conquest and plunder, this meant taxation.

---

[594] Ibid 71-74

[595] Zosimus Historia Nova 11, 34. cited by Grant M. The Emperor Constantine 73 Phoenix Giant. (1993)

John Larke

Taxation Under Constantine

Taxation in the Empire was already high under Diocletian, who largely taxed agricultural production. Constantine doubled the size of the army to over half a million men, and not only had to pay for the troops, but also for a new and expensive form of civilian administration, which paralleled the army structure.

Constantine was also a great and prolific builder, Constantinople, being perhaps the best known of his projects. Although rather poorly constructed it was a considerable drain on the exchequer, as were the many other towns that Constantine expanded and embellished. Previously, the balance of income and expenditure had been a challenge for Diocletian, who had been a competent administrator, and miserly by Constantine's grandiose standards. The Emperor was profligate by nature, spending considerable amounts on his own household, and was not above attempting to buy popularity with large donations to the poor. All of this had to be paid for.

Constantine sought to redress matters by introducing a poll tax. In Roman times, this tax did not yet have the odour that it was to acquire in later generations,[596] but it suffered from the fundamental flaw of all poll taxes, in that it bore most heavily on the poor. In addition, Constantine taxed members of the artisan classes, requiring payment in silver and gold. This tax, invoked every five years, was particularly oppressive and brought about the personal ruin of many tradesmen.

The means of collecting taxes were also brutal in the extreme. Many Roman authorities auctioned the tax revenue of a district to the highest bidder, with any excess above the total being regarded as profit, to be retained by the auction winner. The means of extracting tax frequently involved intimidation and violence. More than one description of the methods used by tax collectors has come down to us:

> *'It is the time when slavery is multiplied, when fathers barter away their children, not in order to enrich themselves ... but in order to hand it over to their persecutors.'* [597]

---

[596] Grant M. The Emperor Constantine. Phoenix Giant. (1993) 88

[597] Libanius Contr Florent. 427

and from an Egyptian papyrus:

> '*Pamonthius . . . was compelled by his creditors to sell all that he had . . . and when these were sold . . . those pitiless and godless men carried off all his children.*' [598]

These extreme and inhumane methods were carried out across the Empire, but were not applied by Constantine to the most senior senators, whose agricultural tax was frequently waived.

During Constantine's time not only was there an ever-increasing and evident disparity between rich and poor, but the very fabric of the commercial life of cities and much of the countryside was eroded. To make matters worse, inflation was rampant: Whilst Constantine required tax payment in silver and gold; the currency issued by the Exchequer was principally bronze washed with silver. Indeed, the demand for silver and gold for taxation purposes was so great that coins minted in these precious metals began to disappear from normal circulation. The bronze coinage that replaced them had arbitrary value, and increasingly large numbers were required to purchase even the basic necessities of life. To be fair to Constantine, monetary and fiscal policies were not even in their infancy in his day and he was by no means alone in not understanding both the cause and corrosive nature of unchecked inflation.[599]

Foreign Wars

As Constantine's reign progressed, problems with the Goths and Visigoths remained, and large payments were made to 'buy off' an ever-present threat. These payments, needless to say, only added to economic instability.

In 334CE the Persian King Sapor broke a peace treaty between Rome and the Persian Empire originally signed in 299CE. Despite an apparently friendly reception in Rome of Persian representatives, Constantine prepared for war. By 336CE his army was prepared and

---

[598] Bell H.I. Jews and Christians in Egypt (1924). 73 f.

[599] Grant M. The Emperor Constantine. Phoenix Giant. (1998) 95

ready to launch an assault, but in 337CE Constantine died and war was averted. Constantine's death was probably fortuitous, as war with Persia would have dangerously exposed the Roman armies' northern flank. As it was, the Persians seized the opportunity presented by Constantine's death to invade the Eastern Empire and a long and difficult conflict ensued.

Constantine's reign as Emperor, at least in the West, was long, and his time as undisputed Emperor was great enough to profoundly influence conditions within the Empire. The most that can be said for his period of tenure was that he maintained the Empire, but in doing so he instituted and accelerated changes that were to lead to the demise of all that he had governed, particularly in the west. As has been discussed, several factors; including the expansion of the conscription and promotion of 'Barbarians', the large numbers of auxiliary agricultural settlers in the border regions and Constantine's legendary largesse, meant that the damage to both the towns and the countryside was enormous.

It has been proposed that the Empire was simply too large to sustain and that its demise was all but inevitable, and there is much force in this argument. Once Rome had run out of rich enemies to plunder the cost of its army became unsupportable. Constantine was not alone, or even primarily responsible, for the enlargement of the army. His predecessor, Diocletian, had more than doubled the number of troops. But unlike Constantine, Diocletian, had a considerable appreciation of the realities of governance. For the most part Constantine did not—he was primarily a soldier who saw a task in front of him, and dealt with it. There is no evidence in the sources that have come down to us of any understanding of the long-term problems faced by the Empire. The changes introduced by Constantine were made along military lines and this made matters worse, by creating an impossibly expensive parallel civil administration, which largely replaced and offended its more aristocratic predecessor.[600]

Characterisation of figures in antiquity is always difficult, but Constantine's apparent legacy, at least amongst Christians, as 'Constantine the Great', might have raised eyebrows amongst observers of his rule: It is likely that Constantine was responsible for the deaths of well in excess of one hundred thousand men. His last war against Licinius was entirely unnecessary, yet it brought about the greatest

---

[600] Ibid 97-103

number of casualties. It had long been recognised that life in the Roman court was precarious, and anyone with ambitions to be Emperor ran great personal risks. This brutal logic also applied to the Emperor's family, as much and perhaps more so than anyone else. Thus the fact that this deeply flawed and brutal man was to be eternally suffixed as 'Great' can have only one possible reason.

Constantine the First Christian Emperor

At the time of Constantine's birth the number of Christians in the Empire is difficult to estimate, with figures ranging from two to ten percent (see Chapter 10), and perhaps a realistic estimate is toward the lower end of this range. Whatever the actual figure, there is general agreement that Christianity was still a minority religion. This was particularly true of the aristocratic and administrative classes, where the Gods of classical antiquity still reigned supreme, and also seems to have been true of the army, where there was a general suspicion that Christian soldiers might obey their Bishops, rather than their officers.[601] How then did Constantine, who was *par excellence* a military man, become a Christian?

There is considerable support for the view that Constantine's father Constantius Chlorus was a pagan, who viewed the panoply of classical Gods as varying expressions of one single Supreme Being. Of Constantine's mother's beliefs as a young woman, much less is known; as an older woman she became a devout and important religious figure, much addicted to the collection of relics, few of which were likely to have been genuine. However, her sincere, and strongly held beliefs, seem more likely to have been a response to her son's, rather strange brand of Christianity.

One factor not always discussed in relationship to Constantine is his upbringing in the court of Diocletian from an early age. Diocletian's persecution of Christians was the most thorough persecution of Christianity ever witnessed. However, despite Diocletian's administrative abilities and the efforts of his subordinates, Christianity was not eliminated.

---

[601] Von Harnack A. Militia Christi (19981) Fortress Press cited by Stevenson J.A. A New Eusebius (1987) SPCK 210-211

Besides martyrdom, Christian organisation was also thought to have been a major factor in Christianity's expansion and its capacity for endurance. Christian communities were invariably loyal to their Bishops, who administered a form of comprehensive social security on their behalf. Christians were cared for when sick, fed when hungry, and buried when dead. Despite later attempts by the Roman authorities to match Christian charity, no other organisation, apart possibly from Judaism, came close to Christianity in looking after its own, and this comprehensive level of care spread right across the Empire. Whilst, as a faith, Christianity might be increasingly riven by disputes, these were the exclusive preoccupation of a religious intelligentsia, and few, if any, ordinary Christians were involved; for the great majority of congregations faith and worship continued in an unchanged way.

Constantine's Faith

Whilst a junior member of Diocletian's court, Constantine would have been aware of the failure of persecution and the frustration that this caused to the Emperors. He would also have been aware of the Empire-wide nature of Christianity, which contrasted with the difficulties of unifying the Empire under Roman governance. When Constantine was a young man no single Emperor had held sway of the entire Empire for more than two generations and it was generally considered that the Empire had simply grown too large for control by any one individual.

It is impossible to say at what stage Constantine's ambition to become the single Emperor arose, but his life was to move consistently in that direction. For a man who nursed a hope of Empire-wide dominance, unity presented the greatest challenge and, with cultures as disparate as those of the sophisticated Greeks and the 'Barbaric' Germanic tribes, a religion common to all was a major attribute. In Christianity, Constantine clearly felt that he had found such a unifying force; the basis of what was taught and practised in Christ's name in Gaul was the same as that taught and practised in Egypt. If Christianity suited Constantine's purpose, he also had a strong emotional faith in his own particular interpretation of Christianity.

Constantine's belief does not appear to have been based on brotherly love and compassion for the poor, but rather on conquest—for Constantine, the Christian God was a God of victory and military

The Way to Christianity

success. As a young Emperor he recognised Mars as his personal champion, and on occasion honoured Hercules as his official patron,[602] yet Constantine's battle Gods were not his only deities. Throughout his life he gave almost as much adherence to the 'Sun God' as he did to his own view of the Christian God and it is entirely due to Constantine that 'Sun' day is the Christian day of weekly worship and that the birth of Jesus is symbolically celebrated on the day of the mid-Winter sun festival, at the time of the winter solstice.

Constantine's conversion to his own militaristic brand of Christianity appears to have been a gradual process, punctuated by visionary episodes. Amongst the most important, and the one that is invariably quoted, are the events that took place before the battle against Maxentius by the Milvern Bridge.

Prior to the battle, Constantine is reported to have seen *'before him in the sky the sign of a cross of light.'* [603] A phenomenon most likely caused by the refraction of light through fine ice crystals at high altitude. On the night before the battle, the cross again appeared to Constantine:

> *'Constantine, was directed in a dream to mark the heavenly sign of God on the shields of his soldiers, and thus to join battle.'* [604]

Constantine was known to have given great credence to the portent of dreams, and, after discussion with his officers, had some form of symbolic cross painted on his soldier's shields. The subsequent victory in this battle, coupled with Maxentius' extraordinary decision to fight outside Rome, reinforced Constantine's view of an all-powerful Christian God. It seems likely that Constantine continued to believe for the rest of his life that not only did he have God's support, but that this support would last.

---

[602] Jones A.H.M. Constantine and the Conversion of Europe. Toronto University Press (1962) 64

[603] Grant M The Emperor Constantine. Phoenix Giant. (1993) 138

[604] Stevenson J. A New Eusebius. SPCK. (1987) 283. citing Lactantius on the death of the Persecutors 44: 3-6

The practical consequence of Constantine's conversion to Christianity was the promotion of his new religion, although characteristically this was done with some caution. Remarkably Constantine was not the first to reverse the consequences of Diocletian's persecution; in 311CE one year prior to Constantine's victory at the Milvern Bridge, Galerius, previously a vigorous persecutor of Christianity, issued a Proclamation reversing Diocletian's anti-Christian Imperial Decrees, so *'that Christians may exist again, and may establish their meeting houses.'* [605]

Galerius' reversal of his previous policy was regarded by Christians as death-bed recognition of the true God. The real cause was probably more prosaic; the persecution of Christianity had not worked, and Galarius was probably simply acknowledging this. It did, however, form a useful precedent for Constantine.

When Constantine and Licinius promulgated their own edict of Milan in 313CE it was issued in the names of the joint Emperors, but the sentiment expressed is almost certainly that of Constantine:

> *'Our purpose is to grant both to the Christians and to all others, full authority to follow whatever worship each man has desired . . . it is our pleasure to abolish all conditions whatever, which were embodied in former orders directed to your office about the Christians . . . every one of those who have a common wish to follow the religion of the Christians may from this moment freely, and unconditionally proceed to observe the same without any annoyance of disquiet.'* [606]

Following the edict of Milan, Constantine wrote personally to Roman Governors throughout the Empire to ensure the full restoration of Church property:

> *'If aught of those things that belonged to the Catholic Church of the Christians in any city, or even in other places, be now in the possession, either of citizens or of any others,*

---

[605] Stevenson J. A New Eusebius (1987) SPCK 280

[606] Ibid 284-286

these thou shouldest cause to be restored forthwith to these same Churches.' [607]

Thus the most serious and best-organised persecution of Christianity was formally brought to an end. It was not the final word—after Constantine's death religious persecution was again to take place—but only relatively briefly and without the vigour known during the time of Diocletian.

Church Matters

After issuing edicts of toleration and the restoration of Church property, Constantine became increasingly involved in Church affairs. One matter of great concern was the fractured and dysfunctional nature of much Church leadership. Constantine had sought a unifying force in Christianity, and was appalled to see the antipathy of opposing camps within the Church hierarchy. It seems natural that the warring factions should appeal to the Emperor and, as the highest civilian authority, he had considerable direct influence, particularly over the Bishops.

Unfortunately, Constantine was intellectually ill equipped to deal with the competing theologies; it is clear that he often entirely failed to understand the complexities of the arguments put forward, nor the subtle distinctions which led to such disparate points of view. Because Christianity was so important to him, he failed to exercise the intolerance that so often characterised other areas of his life, which led to vacillation and inconsistency, and made him heavily reliant on his religious advisors. They, in turn, often gave the advice that they felt the Emperor wished to hear and were often divided amongst themselves; consequentially Synods and Councils became increasingly common.

Probably the most notable was the Council of Nicaea, which eventually produced the pro-forma of the Nicene Creed. This was the only unifying declaration in which Constantine could claim direct involvement, but, even here, differences of interpretation were applied to the most significant phrases. In retrospect Constantine failed to unify the Church and, because he put such effort into it, this could be said to be

---

[607] Ibid 286-287

his greatest failure. He was very much aware of his unproductive efforts and his regret remained with him for the rest of his life.

If Constantine could not unify Christianity at least he could promote it by removing the very considerable burden of taxation to which the Church was subject. Not only did congregations find that less of their collections ended up in the Roman exchequer, but Constantine also initiated a life-time's programme of Church construction.

Buildings

Small house churches existed at the beginning of the reign of Constantine, whilst larger Churches were found some in urban areas, although they were not highly embellished. Constantine set about changing this with considerable vigour. If he could not unify his new religion, then at least he could endow it with substantial and richly decorated buildings. Christian Churches increasingly became larger and more richly embellished than Pagan Temples.

The Basilicas and other structures which Constantine had built were by no means uniform in design. Across the Empire, Church architecture reflected local styles or indeed the style of any architect who managed to catch the Emperor's eye and consequently many Churches were similar in design to Pagan temples. A notable feature of Constantine's churches was the richness of decoration; windows filled with stained glass were commonplace, whilst floor mosaics and brightly painted wall decorations were much in evidence. The visual impact of these Churches has rarely been matched, at least in the west, and they were intended to be deeply inspirational, with well-known bible stories depicted in rich and vivid ways.

At a time when the great majority of people lived in simple vernacular dwellings the impact of these Church interiors must have been stunning, but it was not to last. Although maintained with considerable endowments during Constantine's lifetime, almost all fell into disrepair and disappeared entirely. There are a number of reasons for this.

The high rate of attrition can largely be attributed to poor design and construction: Constantine built so many Churches that he simply ran out of good architects and builders. Additionally, the lavish internal decorations, although undoubtedly inspiring, were a constant invitation to plunder, particularly after the fall of Rome. Over-ambitious scale was also a factor, as some Churches were simply too large for their intended congregations who could not fund the maintenance of such elaborate Structures. However, there are exceptions, the most notable of which is St. Peters in Rome.

St. Peters

St. Peters was Constantine's largest and most expensive Church,[608] yet the St. Peters we know today is not the original structure. Constantine's much repaired and modified Basilica lasted until the sixteenth century, when it was replaced by the present building. Originally its site was determined by the presence of a second century memorial stone to Simon Peter, located in a large pagan graveyard adjacent to the Vatican hill. After its selection, the site was levelled and a basilica built on the site of the memorial stone, which was enclosed by a large canopy. The building itself contained many structural elements taken from Pagan Temples, and was far from complete at the time of Constantine's death.

Family Murders

About the time Constantine took the decision to build St. Peters in 326CE he committed his most notorious crime. He had his oldest son Crispus killed and shortly afterwards executed his second wife Fausta. The enormity of this crime was so great that it was not recorded by Christian chroniclers, and the information has only come down from Roman sources.

Although Constantine's motivation for ordering the deaths of Crispus and Fausta has not survived, it is assumed amongst some Roman historians that Fausta had intrigued against Crispus, who was Constantine's only son by his first wife, in order to remove him from the line of succession.[609]

There is a considerable historical precedent for this supposition; indeed plotting seems to have been a perennial feature of the families of the Emperors, despite its often unintended consequences. If Fausta

---

[608] Ibid 196-198

[609] Grant M. The Emperor Constantine. Phoenix Giant. (1993) 110-115

had misled Constantine into thinking that his son was plotting against him, then unintended consequences did indeed occur: Shortly after Crispus' death Constantine, perhaps in a fit of remorse, had Fausta killed. Nothing more clearly demonstrates Constantine's ruthless grip on power.

Whatever his Christian belief, his position as Emperor seems to have been always foremost in his mind, and there were no lengths to which Constantine would not go to maintain his power. If Constantine's decision to construct St. Peters was an attempt to atone for his terrible crime, it can only be said that his greatest crime resulted in his largest Basilica.

Perhaps the only redeeming aspect of these appalling events was that Constantine made no attempt to disinherit Fausta's children, and appears to have remained on good terms with them for the rest of his life. This contrasts strongly with a tendency amongst some other Emperors to visit the sins of the mothers on their children.[610]

Constantine's murder of his wife and son, together with the execution of his brother-in-law and nephew, were appalling crimes. To this must be added the deaths of so many of his associates and the unprecedented carnage of his civil wars. Leadership of the Roman Empire was a perilous and dangerous occupation. There is nothing, save possibly the Sicilian Mafia, representing a comparable modern structure of command to ancient Rome. But the Roman Empire was not alone; other Empires in antiquity were run on similar lines. Augustus' much quoted remark that he would rather be 'Herod's Pig' than a member of his family reflects the murderous nature of the Jewish client King in his declining years. Yet even by contemporary standards, Constantine's behaviour was extreme and earned justified condemnation.

Helena

After the bloodletting of 326CE, Constantine's mother visited Jerusalem as his Imperial representative. Her first endeavour seems to have been to attempt to identify sites of seminal importance to Christianity. There were considerable practical difficulties in such a task.

---

[610] Ibid 109-115

The Way to Christianity

Following the first Jewish uprising against Rome, Jerusalem had been converted into a Roman military camp. After the second Jewish war, serious attempts were made to obliterate all that remained of the former Jewish capital with *'no stone left upon another'* and the Pagan city of Aelia Capitolina was built on the site. All this had happened at least two hundred years prior to Helena's visit. However, not to be dissuaded from her difficult task, Helena sought inspiration not only from local knowledge, but also in visions. Three sites in particular attracted her attention: The crucifixion; Jesus' tomb and; the place of His ascension to heaven.

Excavating a site at Golgotha, her workmen were later reported to have come upon three crosses and a plaque which had been placed on one of them inscribed with: *'this is the King of the Jews.'* Unfortunately the plaque had become detached and a sick woman was placed on each cross in turn, to see which one resulted in a miraculous cure. Having identified the *'True Cross'* she sent parts of it to Constantine together with some nails, whilst much of the remainder was placed in a silver box.[611] It is claimed that some of these remains can still be seen in the Church of the Cross in Rome.

Considerable scepticism had been expressed as to the authenticity of Helena's relics, and probably rightly so.[612] Excavation of almost any area of ancient Jerusalem would have recovered wooden fragments in a city partly constructed of timber. Added to that was the likelihood that Jesus was crucified using a cross member attached to an olive tree, which would have been inexistent in Helena's day. The claim of a plaque is almost certainly an apocryphal tradition, which grew up at a later date.

A short distance from the site of the *'True Cross'* Helena came upon a stone-cut Jewish tomb, which promptly became the site of Jesus' brief entombment. The site of Jesus' ascension to heaven on the Mount of Olives was also identified, as was his birthplace in Bethlehem.

On these sites were constructed some of the most richly embellished Churches in all of Christendom, some parts of which probably remain, although often now encased in a series of later structures. Although by

---

[611] Ibid 202-205

[612] Runciman S. Byzantine Civilisation (1933) 26. Cited by Grant M. The Emperor Constantine (1993) Phoenix 204

no means the first visitor to Jerusalem, Helena's discoveries promoted a huge increase in both pilgrimage and the collection of holy relics. So many were collected that by medieval times a considerable industry in these artefacts had developed, with Church competing against Church to claim the rarest and best.[613]

Byzantium

Despite his prowess in Church building, none of the towns and cities where Constantine's Churches stood were free of Pagan Temples. Even in Jerusalem the site of Jesus' presumed tomb originally lay under a 'Temple to Aphrodite.' Perhaps to counter the ubiquitous presence of Paganism, Constantine undertook the building of a city that would immortalise his name and be exclusively Christian.

Byzantium was an ancient and strategically important town lying on the shores of the Bosporus, the waterway linking the Black and Aegean seas. It was also close to the site of Constantine's final battle against Licinius, which may have had a great deal to do with its renaming as Constantinople.[614]

The year in which reconstruction and expansion began was probably the pivotal one of 326CE. And, as with so many of his Church buildings, quality was a serious problem. Although Constantine's architects attempted to overcome construction difficulties by using an early form of standardised prefabrication, the technique was little understood and many buildings had to be subsequently rebuilt.

Despite considerable inducements very few Romans were prepared to leave the 'Eternal City' and resettle in Constantine's new town. In this they were somewhat short sighted: Many years after Rome had been reduced to a collection of villages amongst the ruins of the former Imperial capital, Constantinople grew into the last and richest vestige of the Roman Empire. Maintaining its position as the most

---

[613] Grant M. The Emperor Constantine. Phoenix Giant. (1993) 205

[614] Jones A.H.M. Constantine and the Conversion of Europe. University Toronto Press (1962) 190-191

important European city until it finally succumbed to a Muslim assault in 1453CE.[615]

The last great military victory claimed by Constantine was against the Samarians, in 335CE. Although Constantine had minted coins with 'Samtia Conquered' on a number of occasions, the situation north of the Danube, where the majority of Samarians lived, was as unsettled as ever. Constantine had characteristically contributed to this instability by settling large numbers of Samarians along the Danube boarder as auxiliary troops. Constantine's 'victory' seems to have consisted of crossing the Danube and taking part in the on-going disputes between the various tribes. After a short campaign settlements were reached aided, no doubt, by Constantine's largesse to all and sundry.

After his last campaign Constantine appears to have given consideration to the succession after his death. His natural successor would have been the executed Crispus. Now he was left with the children of his second wife Fausta, whose oldest son, also called Constantine, was born in 316CE, a second son, Constantius, in 317CE and the youngest son, Constans, in 323CE. To these children Constantine added a step-nephew, Delmatius, to form a tetrarchy, similar to that which had been made to work by Diocletian.[616]

The proposed arrangements, however, which Constantine included in his will, were inherently flawed. Neither his children nor his step-nephew had the strength of purpose or single-minded ambition to take Constantine's place. Furthermore they lacked the sense of comradeship necessary to make a tetrarchy work. Historians have long questioned why Constantine made these arrangements, which he must have known were deeply flawed—none have found a satisfactory answer. Perhaps like so many parents he saw in his children his only hope of immortality, and simply hoped that matters would sort themselves out to secure the line of succession for his family. If this was his motivation it was to prove false, although Constantius, was to briefly rule as sole Emperor for eight years from 353 to 361CE.

In the year 337CE Constantine realised that he was dying. He moved to a state villa in Nicomedia and in a nearby village was baptised by

---

[615] The Decline and fall of the Roman Empire. Wordsworth. (1998) 996-1018

[616] Grant M. The Emperor Constantine (1993) 215-219

Bishop Eusebius of Nicomedia (not the contemporary Church historian of the same name). Normally a two-year preparation was required for baptism; however, this consideration was waived for the Roman Emperor. The question asked at baptism at this time was:

> 'Do you believe in God the Father Almighty, do you believe in Jesus Christ the Son of God who was born by the Holy Spirit from the Virgin Mary, who was crucified under Pontius Pilate and died and rose again on the third day rising from the dead and ascended to the heavens and sat down at the right had of the father, and will come to judge the living and the dead? Do you believe in the holy spirit in the holy Church?' [617]

Having replied in the affirmative, Constantine would have been fully immersed naked in running water. After the ceremony Constantine returned to the villa and died at about noon on Whit Sunday 337CE.

Thus a movement, which had begun with baptism in the River Jordan by John Ben Zechariah reached a symbolic pre-eminence with the baptism of the first Christian Emperor. The character and moral virtue of John and Constantine could not have been more different, and this disparity was reflected in the changes made to Christianity by Constantine.

The Jewish movement led by John, Jesus, James and Simon had as its central prophecy the imminent arrival of the last days of Judaism; God was coming in Judgement, to create a new perfect empire *'The Kingdom of God.'* Only those judged sufficiently righteous would be permitted to enter this new realm, where the conditions that had previously existed in heaven would now exist on earth. It was also fundamentally a movement of the poor, a sentiment admirably summed up in an extract from the letter of James:

> 'Listen my beloved brothers and sisters. Has not God chosen the poor in the world to be rich in faith and to be heirs of the Kingdom that he has promised to those who live him . . . Is it not the rich who oppress you Is it not they

---

[617] Davidson Kelly J.N. Encyclopaedia Britannica. (1971) 6: 718

who drag you into court? Is it not they who blaspheme the excellent name that was invoked over you.' [618]

Perhaps no greater contrast could be found, than in Constantine's *'battle god'* of the rich and powerful. And yet this new militaristic God bore the name of Christianity.

Constantine was wise enough not to make his Christian God the official religion of Rome. Yet he endowed Christianity with huge resources. This wealth continued to accumulate long after his death, and the fall of the Roman Empire. The legendary riches of Constantinople had their origins in their founder's largesse.

There are few military conflicts—either international or civil—since Constantine's time, where Christian combatants have not sought the aid of their God. Yet despite this tendency to call upon God as a rallying cry for conquest, elements of the humanist origins of Christianity remain. Throughout the world, and particularly in the least-developed countries, large numbers of priests live and work in the most meagre of circumstances. The mission that they carry out, together with that of the non-Governmental aid agencies, represent the only real hope in the lives of people who are much afflicted by the corruption and incompetence of their own Governments and the machinations of those foreign powers who seek to exploit them.

---

[618] James 2: 5-7

CONCLUSION

In my view the authentic origins of Christianity lie in the proselytising efforts of two quite disparate groups:

Firstly, a small Jewish revivalist sect which was exclusively concerned with the imminent arrival of the last "days of Judaism," when a wholly restored Israel would rise above its enemies and convince the world of the unique values of Judaism. This ancient hope—which almost certainly drew inspiration from the events of the Exodus, when God saved his chosen people from Egyptian slavery—achieved a particular urgency at the beginning of the first century, when Roman occupation of Judah was deeply resented by the great majority of the Jewish people. This resentment provided fertile ground for the formation of a number of liberation movements, one of which was 'The Way'

The leadership and development of The Way was so closely interwoven with the family of Jesus as to be inseparable. Jesus' cousin, John, was the first to prophesy the imminence of the 'last days' and to advocate a process of spiritual renewal and symbolic immersion in preparation for God's final judgement. After his arrest, his extraordinary cousin Jesus led a necessarily itinerant life as a charismatic holy man and prophet, preaching John's message. After Jesus' crucifixion, his devout and righteous brother James brought The Way into the body of normative Judaism and led it with wisdom and justice for almost thirty years. Of the last two leaders of The Way, Simeon and Justus, we know very little, although it is clear that they provided a continuity of leadership to a movement already in decline.

The leaders of The Way all lived at a time when to proclaim the Kingdom of Heaven, and thus imply God's replacement of the Roman Empire, was highly dangerous. Yet they were men of great courage, who did not flinch from the risks that they were taking. Their primary concern was for the poor, and they led lives of great austerity, holding what little they possessed in common. They were pacifists, and there is no evidence in the sources of violent revolutionary tactics or ambitions, yet all met deaths at the hands of worldly men for reasons of political expediency.

The second group instrumental in the genesis of Christianity was a small predominantly gentile group which, after the death of Paul of Tarsus, lost its Jewish inheritance and began to see Jesus in ways that were deeply antithetical to his original conceptualisation within Judaism, yet wholly acceptable within a pagan environment.

The language used by this group was identical to that of Paul, yet the meanings of individual words and phrases were radically different. Most notably the phrase "Son of God" which, when used in a Jewish context, was a term of respect for a deeply religious man who sought to do the will of God, and was unthinkable to be construed literally by any Jew. Yet, in a gentile pagan culture, where sons of God were almost commonplace, with every Roman Emperor claiming the title, there was no reticence in applying this term to Jesus who rapidly became the incarnate "Son of God."

This brief summary of the recovered history of very early Christianity differs markedly from the narrative described in the Christian Bible. In particular, there are two areas where these differences are particularly marked: (1) The Acts of the Apostles, probably written towards the end of the first centenary CE and; (2) The first great Church history, written by Bishop Eusebius in the early part of the fourth centenary CE.

(1)   The Acts of the Apostles

As many have pointed out the Acts of the Apostles is a misnomer: after the twelfth verse the "Apostles" are rarely mentioned. Much of the remainder of Acts becomes a eulogy to Paul, with the apostles, where they are mentioned at all, being described as dim-witted in not recognising the superiority of "the Apostle to the Gentiles" and his revolutionary new view of the 'divine' figure of Christ. Even Paul's own accounts of the transcendental events in his life are dramatically embellished by the writer of Acts; in his own description of his conversion Paul claims that he came to 'see Jesus,' and implies that this took place over a period of time. Acts on the other hand describes the well-known events taking place on the 'road to Damascus,' complete with a light from heaven and the voice of Jesus asking: why do you persecute me?

The Way to Christianity

Acts also softens the tone of the vigorous disagreements that arose, not only between Paul and his various co-workers, but also between Paul and the Jerusalem leadership of The Way, presenting instead an image of harmony, rather than the visceral disputes that Paul describes in his own letters. Yet, despite, and perhaps because of, these inconsistencies and apparent embellishments, Acts was hugely successful in achieving its aims, particularly when looked at through the lens of members of the second group discussed earlier, seeking to co-opt the achievements and direction of the first.

The purpose of Acts was to replace The Way's exclusively Jewish prophesy of the "last days" of Judaism with the beginnings of a new and predominantly gentile religion which revered the single iconic figure of Jesus. This view relied almost exclusively on the teachings of Paul of Tarsus, a man who had never met Jesus and who appears to have had little interest in his life prior to his crucifixion. In so doing Paul was elevated from a rather unimportant and increasingly heretical member of The Way to become, if not the principle figure of Christianity, then second only in importance to Jesus; a man who he revered so deeply that he advocated "putting him on" as a replacement for all that had gone before. Thus Christianity became a belief not in Jesus, but in Paul's interpretation of Jesus' life, and more particularly in the religious significance of his death.

(2)   Bishop Eusebius's Church History

Over two hundred years after Acts was written, Bishop Eusebius of Caesarea Maritime published the first great Church History. The work, probably started at some point prior to 300CE, was not completed until 315, and was only available as a final edition in late 324 or early 325. It rapidly received wide acclaim and has remained the principle source, particularly on the development of Christianity during the third and early fourth centuries, ever since.

Eusebius inherited Origen's library and quoted extensively from the works that it contained, however, the greatest influence evident in reading Eusebius' history is that of his orthodox beliefs. This led him into numerous errors, amongst which was his depiction of Jesus' brother James. Eusebius sought to accommodate James within Christianity, by derogating his role to that of the "first to be elected to the bishop's throne of the church in Jerusalem". As more than one commentator has observed: "Jews don't have bishops." Neither, for that matter, were any Christian Churches in existence during James' lifetime, and it is clear that Eusebius was transposing the conditions of his own time back onto an earlier age.

These and many other anomalies have led to an erosion of Eusebius' reputation amongst modern church historians. Yet his influence on Christian belief remains strong; his view of an authoritative line of teachings—established during the life and death of Jesus and passed on as an unbroken line of tradition, initially to the apostles and then to succeeding generations of bishops—remains at the heart of the many variegated branches of Christianity.

Perhaps the greatest harm that Eusebius did to early Christian history was to coin the oxymoron "Hebrew Christians" (Jewish Christian). Eusebius was clearly aware that Jesus was a Jew and the majority, if not all Christians, were Gentiles. In our own day this would lead to endless discussion and argument and the publication of whole libraries of books and indeed this is the case. Yet the energetic but intellectually unsophisticated Bishop Eusebius took a religiously simplistic approach. If Jesus was a Jew, then his earliest followers including his disciples must have been Jewish Christians and this was the end of the end of the matter. Eusebius ignored the fact that; for Jews, even the suggestion that any one of their coreligionists could be both human and divine was profoundly offensive; indeed it is difficult to envisage any greater blasphemy.

Whilst historically unsustainable, the phrase "Jewish Christian" has proved remarkably enduring and its usage remains largely unchallenged to the present day. Yet if the term is reversed to "Christian Jew" the inherent contradiction becomes immediately apparent.

Many Christians claim that theirs is a "historical" religion; that is to say that Christian belief is reliably and truthfully based on the events that occurred. In my view this assertion is unsustainable or at least only sustainable by selectively and judiciously editing the historical record. Such manipulations should not be thought to have been exclusively the practises of the distant past; many modern Christian historians of the early Church have followed a line of enquiry up to the point where it threatens to come into conflict with belief. Typically, it is at this point that a variety of stratagems are employed, ranging from a simple

The Way to Christianity

disavowal of a relevant fact, to an elegant exercise in semantics where the rather obvious meaning of a phrase or saying is changed to make it consistent with Christian teachings.

It is axiomatic in the recovery of the past that "the winners write the history;" an inescapable truth that is as valid for the origins of Christianity as for any other system of belief. In the battle to put forth the definitive version of events, the casualties are not just the 'truth' but also, inevitably, the reputation of those individuals and institutions on the losing side. This is nowhere more apparent than in 'historical' accounts of the life of Jesus and the beliefs of The Way. The ubiquitous and demurely draped representation of "Christ crucified," found in so many Christian churches is consistent with belief, but a historically unsustainable misrepresentation of the extraordinary Jewish holy man who prophesised the imminence of the 'last days' and so eloquently described the need for moral perfection as a prerequisite for entry into the Jewish Kingdom of God.

Index

A

Abraham 9, 10, 99, 109, 111, 119, 120, 124, 154, 161
Acts of the Apostles 123, 150, 165, 169, 290
Adam 9, 10, 27, 38, 50, 98, 128, 161, 209, 211, 246
Albert Schweitzer 5
Alexander the Great 27, 129
Alexandrian Church 226
Alvaris 16
Amos 20
Ananus 78, 85, 86, 87, 95
Apocalypse of Baruch 52
Apocryphal Acts 174
Apocryphal Apocalypses 175
Apocryphal Literature 28, 169, 173
Apostolic Succession 142, 146, 148, 234, 250, 252
Aramaic xvii, 27, 40, 62, 94, 127, 156
Arc of the Covenant 17
Arian 258, 259, 261
Assumption of Moses 44
Assyria 21, 24
Atonement 66, 75
Augustine 107, 197, 213

B

Babylon 25, 26, 37, 38, 210
Babylonian conquest 25, 31, 34, 36, 132
Bannus 63, 64
Barnabas 97, 100, 106
Basileides 205, 207, 209
Bauckham 69, 87, 89, 152, 155, 161
Bodily resurrection 39, 50
Book of Daniel 9, 29, 37, 39
Buildings 18, 56, 197, 214, 229, 280, 284
Byzantium 100, 269, 284

C

Caiaphas 78, 82, 85, 95
Canaanite 13, 16, 18, 20, 23, 35
Cataracts 72
Christ xvii, 2, 7, 45, 55, 56, 59, 62, 86, 92, 104, 109, 110, 115, 120, 122, 124, 126, 131, 136, 142, 148, 152, 181, 184, 206, 219, 236, 242, 246, 260, 261, 276, 286, 290, 293
Christian anti-Semitism 149, 150
Christian bible xviii, 3, 4, 60, 81, 84, 130, 140, 151, 158, 164, 166, 169, 172, 177, 207, 219, 290

Christianity i, xv, xvii, 2, 4, 6, 22, 41, 62, 67, 81, 83, 92, 98, 109, 111, 112, 120, 122, 124, 126, 129, 130, 133, 134, 136, 138, 141, 143, 147, 148, 150, 154, 156, 160, 166, 170, 175, 176, 178, 180, 183, 184, 187, 189, 190, 193, 195, 197, 199, 201, 203, 209, 211, 213, 216, 217, 220, 221, 223, 226, 227, 232, 233, 236, 237, 239, 242, 243, 245, 247, 250, 258, 263, 275, 277, 279, 282, 286, 287, 290, 292

Christian persecution 118, 197, 254, 265
Church matters 279
Church of Carthage 226
Church Rituals 140, 145
Church Structure 146, 203, 263
Clement of Rome 141
Common Way 100
Confessors 254, 255
Constantine 191, 192, 203, 238, 239, 263, 265, 267, 269, 271, 273, 275, 277, 279, 281, 283, 285, 287
Crucifixion xvi, 69, 77, 79, 80, 99, 103, 172, 206, 207, 216, 250, 283, 289, 291
Cyprian 189, 255, 256, 258

D

Damascus xvi, 21, 85, 96, 217, 290
Daniel 9, 29, 37, 38
David 17, 18, 24, 26, 36, 41, 43, 51, 54, 69, 89, 128, 131, 136, 145, 150, 158, 161, 173
Dead Sea Scrolls 6, 23, 30, 48, 50, 133, 199

Decius and state persecution 187
Descriptions of hell 134
Deuteronomy 24, 137
D.F. Strauss 5
Dialogue with Trypho 245
Diocletian 180, 189, 190, 265, 268, 272, 274, 275, 278, 279, 285

E

Early Bishops 250
Early Christianity xv, xvii, 2, 6, 130, 133, 135, 136, 143, 147, 148, 151, 154, 156, 170, 179, 180, 182, 202, 216, 217, 220, 224, 226, 244, 290
Early converts 103, 137
Early Prophets 19, 163
Ebionites 62, 92, 217
Ed Saunders 6, 76, 102, 118, 159, 163, 177
Egnation Way 100
Egypt 6, 13, 15, 16, 24, 27, 34, 55, 112, 121, 129, 190, 198, 199, 203, 210, 220, 221, 231, 235, 270, 273, 276
Elijah 19, 20, 41, 68, 163, 241
Emperor Constantine 263, 266, 271, 273, 277, 281, 283, 285
Emperor Hadrian 123
Emperor Nero 3, 117, 202
Emperor worship 128, 130
Enoch 40, 155
Entry into the Kingdom of Heaven 132
Essenes 30, 32, 47, 48, 51, 60, 64, 132
Eucharist 140, 143, 144, 186
Eusebius 48, 82, 84, 89, 138, 168, 180, 184, 188, 191, 196, 201, 208,

225, 227, 234, 236, 237, 244, 246, 252, 253, 257, 262, 275, 277, 286, 290, 292
Exodus 13, 14, 16, 289
Exorcism 73
Ezra 27, 53, 54

F

Fabian 253, 255
Faith xv, 1, 3, 4, 6, 9, 33, 42, 53, 70, 72, 73, 77, 85, 96, 105, 109, 110, 118, 120, 129, 154, 156, 180, 186, 189, 192, 195, 227, 234, 242, 247, 254, 260, 261, 276, 286
Faith healing 71, 72
First Christian emperor 263, 275, 286
Folk Medicine 70, 72
Followers of The Way 2, 58, 60, 62, 64, 81, 84, 89, 109, 113, 118, 125, 126, 154, 216, 242, 251

G

Galerius 189, 190, 265, 267, 278
Galilee 31, 46, 68, 76, 80, 149
Gamial 71, 85, 94
Gentiles 5, 17, 36, 40, 45, 91, 101, 103, 104, 106, 109, 110, 119, 120, 132, 147, 183, 290, 292
Geza Vermes 6, 58, 80, 127, 158
Gnosticism 170, 172, 198, 199, 201, 204, 205, 207, 209, 211, 213, 246
Gnostic Literature 170, 199
God and Jesus 206, 242
Gospel attributed to John 60, 160, 164
Gospel attributed to Mathew 66, 81

Gospel of the Hebrews 157
Gospel of Thomas 6, 82, 170, 173, 174
Growth of The Way and early Christianity 216

H

Hadrian 55, 56, 123
Hanina ben Dossa 71
Hattersley Roy 2
Hebrew xviii, 5, 9, 10, 13, 16, 19, 23, 25, 26, 28, 36, 41, 49, 54, 59, 60, 94, 109, 120, 127, 128, 136, 141, 155, 156, 157, 158, 160, 163, 166, 168, 171, 174, 207, 237, 242, 245, 248, 253, 292
Hebrew Bible 5, 9, 13, 16, 19, 23, 25, 26, 28, 36, 41, 49, 54, 59, 60, 120, 128, 141, 155, 160, 163, 171, 174, 207, 237, 242, 246, 248, 253
Hegesippus 82, 84
Hellenistic culture 28, 121
Hereditary leadership of The Way 69
Herod Antipas 68, 70, 77, 81
Herod the great 58, 68, 115
High Priesthood 85, 149
Hippolytus 202, 206, 252, 253
Holy of Holies 3, 17, 47, 52, 122, 124, 148
Holy Spirit 68, 130, 146, 165, 202, 246, 247, 250, 262, 286
Homilies and recognition of Clement 169
House of David 18, 36, 41, 54, 69, 89
Hyksos 15, 16

I

Ignatius 140, 143, 144, 148, 180, 182, 193, 194
Irenaeus 168, 202, 225, 246, 248
Isaiah 23, 24, 25, 34, 60, 132, 160

J

James xvi, 47, 64, 69, 80, 82, 83, 85, 89, 91, 93, 95, 97, 100, 104, 106, 112, 118, 120, 125, 146, 151, 152, 154, 156, 165, 166, 168, 170, 173, 174, 179, 216, 217, 219, 286, 287, 292
James the brother of Jesus 47, 166, 216
James Tunstead Burtchaell 146
Jericho xvi, 13, 85, 96
Jerusalem Temple xvi, 3, 23, 24, 26, 32, 47, 122, 154
Jesus xvi, 2, 4, 6, 8, 23, 24, 45, 47, 55, 56, 58, 60, 62, 64, 70, 72, 73, 76, 77, 80, 82, 84, 86, 89, 92, 95, 96, 98, 103, 104, 107, 110, 111, 114, 117, 118, 120, 122, 124, 126, 128, 130, 132, 134, 136, 139, 142, 144, 148, 150, 152, 154, 156, 158, 160, 162, 164, 166, 168, 170, 172, 174, 177, 179, 181, 183, 184, 186, 193, 201, 204, 205, 207, 209, 211, 216, 217, 219, 222, 223, 237, 241, 243, 245, 247, 250, 252, 260, 261, 277, 283, 286, 289, 290, 292
Jesus ben Joseph xvii, 57, 70, 137, 241
Jesus Christ 2, 7, 45, 55, 56, 59, 86, 92, 110, 115, 122, 124, 126, 131, 137, 142, 152, 184, 206, 219, 246, 260, 261, 286
Jesus' Early Life 173
Jesus' Teachings 74
Jesus the Messiah 131
Jesus to Christ 126
Jewish Christian 8, 62, 156, 217, 292
Jewish Palestine xviii, 21, 30, 34, 36, 40, 47, 68, 86, 88, 94, 106, 118, 128, 132, 217, 219
Jewish Uprising 31, 46, 52, 56, 87, 89, 93, 122, 150, 283
John ben Zechariah 47, 57, 60, 62, 69, 96, 153, 164, 219, 286
John the Baptist xvi, 62, 65, 92, 216
Josephus xvi, 32, 46, 63, 87, 96, 103, 113, 150, 152, 219
Judaism 2, 6, 9, 12, 16, 20, 22, 26, 28, 30, 32, 34, 36, 38, 41, 43, 46, 52, 54, 56, 60, 64, 65, 69, 70, 85, 89, 92, 94, 97, 98, 103, 105, 107, 111, 115, 118, 120, 122, 124, 127, 133, 135, 137, 138, 147, 149, 150, 153, 166, 178, 237, 241, 276, 286, 289, 290
Jude 84, 87, 89, 121, 151, 152, 155, 156, 161, 166, 168
Judea 18, 21, 25, 27, 32, 58, 114, 216
Justin Martyr 3, 145, 168, 184, 208, 245

K

Kingdom of Heaven 5, 40, 64, 66, 67, 70, 74, 99, 119, 127, 132, 136, 154, 167, 289
King Herod 31, 115
King Josiah 24

L

Land of Judah 21, 22
Leadership after Jesus' death 81
Letters of the Christian Bible 166
Letter to the Romans 107, 110, 114, 224
Linicius 267, 269
Logos of God 245
Lucius 183, 184

M

Maccabees 29, 36, 48, 60
Malachi 41, 68
Man and God 241
Mani 209, 211
Marcion 207, 209
Martin Luther 1
Martyrdom 175, 178, 182, 185, 192, 194, 195, 196, 210, 227, 237, 251, 276
Mary Magdalene 80
Masada 10, 32, 59
Maxentius 266, 267, 277
Maximian 189, 190, 265
Mesopotamia 34, 55
Messiah 3, 29, 37, 39, 41, 42, 44, 46, 51, 53, 54, 56, 62, 79, 80, 97, 98, 119, 127, 130, 132, 136, 149, 152, 160, 184, 208
Milvian Bridge 267
Miracles 3, 20, 37, 76, 162, 174, 183
Misogynism 107
Moses 13, 16, 19, 37, 44, 121, 141, 166

N

Nag Hammadi 6, 82, 124, 170, 199, 203
Nazarenes 61, 62, 92, 114, 121, 125
Nicaean creed 262
Nicene Creed 279
Noah 9, 10
Northern tribes xviii, 19, 20, 22, 26, 268
Novation 253, 256
Novation and Cornelius 255

O

Origen 168, 196, 248, 250, 291
Orthodox Church 83, 148, 226, 251

P

Parables 70, 76, 137, 176, 222
Passover 16, 77, 78, 113, 149, 251
Paul xvi, 3, 61, 62, 81, 85, 91, 92, 95, 96, 99, 100, 102, 104, 106, 108, 110, 112, 114, 116, 118, 120, 122, 125, 126, 131, 137, 139, 141, 142, 146, 148, 154, 156, 158, 160, 164, 166, 168, 172, 175, 176, 179, 208, 213, 220, 222, 223, 225, 241, 246, 248, 251, 291
Paul and misogynism 107
Paul of Tarsus xvi, 2, 61, 85, 92, 94, 127, 131, 139, 146, 154, 157, 166, 208, 213, 220, 241, 248, 250, 290
Paul's death 3, 117, 157, 179, 220
Paul's House Assemblies 81, 100, 102, 122, 146
Paul's letters 98, 100, 111, 157, 165, 208, 225, 251

Pella 87, 217
Perpetua 194
Persecution and Paganism 232
Persia 26, 36, 210, 274
Persian rule 27
Pharisees 30, 36, 55, 60, 63, 67, 89, 94, 112, 114, 123, 158, 173, 241
Philo 45, 46, 48, 86
Polycarp 143, 145, 183
Pontius Pilate 5, 6, 79, 286
Promised Land 11, 12, 16
Psalms of Solomon 43
Ptolemaic empire 28

Q

Qumran 6, 23, 30, 40, 47, 48, 51, 52, 62, 124, 133, 139, 155

R

Rabbinic Judaism 55, 89, 123
Ramesses II 13
Reed Sea 13, 15
Restoration of Israel 44, 54, 130, 132
Revelation of John 167, 169, 176
Richard Dawkins xv
Ritual immersion 63, 67, 139
River Jordan 10, 63, 87, 286
Rodney Stark 220, 221, 227, 239
Roman army 32, 43, 79, 264, 270
Roman Catholicism 148
Roman Church 83, 142, 208, 225, 251, 253, 255
Roman Emperors 136, 230
Roman persecution 89, 180

S

Sabbath 26, 31, 32, 60, 74, 86, 147, 158, 183
Sadducees 29, 36, 44, 55, 63, 114, 122, 149
Saint Peters 251
Samaritans 31
Sanhedrin 55, 84, 113, 122, 125, 166
Saul 17, 18, 61, 94
Scribes 30, 130, 152, 237
Second Temple Judaism 26, 70, 89, 98, 122
Secret book of John 171, 172
Seleucid Empire 28
Severus 228, 229, 265
Sheol 36
Shepherd of Hermas 167, 176
Sibylline Oracles 41, 42
Sicarii 59
Silas 106
Simon bar Kosiba 56
Simon Magnus 169, 174, 202, 207
Simon Peter 81, 83, 86, 91, 142, 155, 169, 216, 281
Slaves 107, 182, 222, 223, 230, 238
Solomon 17, 18, 26, 37, 40, 43, 168
Son of God 3, 126, 128, 130, 136, 173, 184, 207, 214, 242, 243, 246, 261, 286, 290
Sons of darkness 49, 133
Sons of light 49, 133
Sophia 200, 204
Source book 160, 163, 164
Speratus 185
Stephan 95

Synagogue 26, 30, 32, 61, 71, 74, 86, 100, 101, 102, 106, 109, 126, 146, 156, 166, 217, 251
Synoptic Gospels 6, 76, 159, 164, 167
Syria 58, 81, 141, 180, 195, 217

T

Tabernacle 16, 52
Taxation under Constantine 272
Tax collectors 66, 272
Temple Priests 30, 55
Tertullian 107, 138, 196, 204, 207, 212, 226, 227, 247, 255
The Arena 175, 181, 182, 184, 192, 194
The ascetic life 235
The Didache 138, 140
The Enlightenment 8
The Essenes 30, 32, 47, 48, 51, 60, 64, 132
The family of Jesus and James 83
The great persecution 180, 258
The Homilies and Recognitions of Clement 169
The prayer 124
The Reformation 4, 146
The Revelation of John 167, 169
The Roman army 32, 43, 79, 264, 270
The Septuagint 28, 248
The Synoptic Gospels 6, 76, 159, 164, 167
THE Way i, 1, 2, 5, 6, 8, 41, 53, 57, 58, 60, 62, 64, 69, 81, 82, 84, 86, 89, 90, 92, 95, 96, 98, 105, 106, 109, 113, 118, 120, 122, 124, 126, 135, 136, 139, 140, 148, 150, 154, 156, 166, 170, 179, 216, 217, 219, 236, 241, 251, 289, 291, 293
THE Way sources 60
Third Century Rome 186, 254
Tribes of Israel 12, 18, 20, 41, 70, 130

U

Unacceptable Works 171
Unknown Gospel 6, 177

V

Valentinius 203, 209
Valerian 188, 232, 233, 258
Virgin 3, 126, 129, 131, 132, 136, 160, 173, 236, 286

W

Weeks 16, 30, 112
Wisdom of Solomon 40, 168
W.M.L De Wette 5
Women 47, 61, 78, 107, 131, 147, 189, 197, 205, 222, 223, 236, 252

Y

Yaveh 123
YHWH 2, 5, 9, 10, 12, 16, 19, 20, 23, 24, 26, 34, 36, 92, 200

Z

Zealots 59
Zechariah xvi, 47, 57, 60, 62, 64, 69, 78, 96, 153, 164, 219, 286